Edited by Mark G. Field

Success and Crisis in National Health Systems:
A comparative approach

Routledge · New York · London

First published in 1989 by
Routledge
29 West 35th Street
New York NY 10001

Published in the UK by
Routledge
11 New Fetter Lane
London EC4P 4EE

© Routledge 1989

Printed in Great Britain by
Billing & Sons Ltd, Worcester

Library of Congress Cataloging-in-
Publication Data
Success and crisis in national health
systems : a comparative approach /
edited by Mark G. Field.
p. cm. —(Contemporary issues in
health, medicine, and social policy)
Includes bibliographies and index.
1. Medical care — Cross-cultural
studies.
2. Medical care — Comparative
method.
3. Medicine, State — Cross-cultural
studies.
4. Medicine, State — Comparative
method.
I. Field, Mark G. (Mark George)
II. Series.
[DNLM: 1. Cross-Cultural
Comparison. 2. Health Services.
3. National Health Programs.
4. State Medicine. WA 540.1 S942]
RA394.S88 1988   362.1 — dc19
DNLM/DLC
for Library of Congress
88–11332 CIP

British Library Cataloguing in
Publication Data
Success and crisis in national health
systems : a comparative approach. —
(Contemporary issues in health,
medicine, and social policy).
1. Health services
I. Field, Mark G., 1923–
II. Series
362.1

ISBN 0–415–01289–9 (Hbk)
       0–415–01290–2 (Pbk)

Contents

Contents

List of contributors

Editor

Mark G. Field is Professor of Sociology at Boston University and Fellow in the Russian Research Center at Harvard University.

Contributors

Odin W. Anderson is Professor of Sociology, University of Wisconsin–Madison and University of Chicago.

Christopher M. Davis is Lecturer in Soviet Social Policy at the Centre for Russian and East European Studies, University of Birmingham.

Jesús M. de Miguel is Professor of the Department of Sociology, Faculty of Economics, University of Barcelona.

Mauro F. Guillén is on the Ph.D. program in the Department of Sociology, Yale University.

Felix Gutzwiller is Director of the Institute of Social and Preventive Medicine of the University of Zurich.

T.D. Hunter is Chairman of the Scottish Institute of Human Relations and Chairman of the Scottish Council on Disability.

Philippe Lehmann is a sociologist and research project manager for the sociology of health and evaluation of prevention campaigns, attached to the University Institute of Social and Preventive Medicine, Lausanne.

Jean F. Martin is Canton Medical Officer, Public Health Service of the Canton of Vaud and Lecturer in Social and Preventive Medicine, University of Lausanne.

Donna E. Parmelee is Assistant Professor of Sociology in the Department of Sociology and Anthropology, Colgate University, Hamilton, New York.

Marshall W. Raffel is Professor of Health Planning and Administration at The Pennsylvania State University, University Park, Pennsylvania.

Victor G. Rodwin is Associate Professor of Public Health and Administration in the Program in Health Policy and Management, Graduate School of Public Administration, New York University, and Director of the Advanced Management Program for Clinicians at New York University.

William E. Steslicke is Associate Professor in the Department of Health Policy and Management, College of Public Health, University of South Florida, Tampa.

Introduction
Mark G. Field

The problem

Health care has emerged, toward the end of the twentieth
century, as a major social, ideological, ethical, political, and
economic issue. It has almost become a cliché to speak of the
health crisis of contemporary society, except that the crisis is
real. It is woven of an almost infinite number of strands: the
AIDS epidemic, the rise in malpractice suits in the United States,
the lack of access to care for some members of the population,
the seemingly inexorable and unstoppable escalation of costs,
the medical concerns of the growing number of the elderly, the
increased bureaucratization of hospitals and health services, the
proliferation of specialties and sub-specialties; the list is endless.
And all this is taking place at a time of unprecedented success
and technological achievements in medicine, of the "medical
miracles," the victories over previously intractable conditions,
the spectacular advances both in diagnostic techniques and
therapeutic modalities, and the vistas of genetic engineering, to
name but a few. Here again the list is long and growing, as every
day brings new conquests over pain, disease, and death. Has
perhaps the success itself led to the crisis? This paradox, this
contradiction between crisis and success, is made that much
more poignant by the fact that health and health care are

emotionally charged subjects. They touch on life, on suffering, on physical dependency, incapacitation, and ultimately on death. Just think for a moment of the agonies and the dilemmas, indeed the moral, if not legal, questioning that surrounds the decisions to "turn the machine off" or "to play God", that is deliberately choosing who is going to live and who is going to die.

It is not surprising, therefore, given the high visibility and the importance assumed by the health system today, the power and the respect enjoyed by the physician, the role and the costs of hospitals, that the whole medical enterprise should find itself scrutinized, examined, dissected, analyzed, and attacked by critics in academia, in government, in the press, and in the legislatures. Skeptical voices are increasingly questioning the worth and the utility of the health system, or specific aspects of it. Are we really getting what we are paying for, either in fees-for-service or in taxes? What about the flagrant abuses, the negligence, the callousness of some health personnel, the alienative consequences of impersonal technology in a domain where human relationships and personal support are of the essence? Others argue, statistics in hand, that the health system, costly as it is, contributes only marginally to the overall health of the population. The spectacular declines in mortality and morbidity, for example in tuberculosis, began before the BCG vaccine was introduced, and are not primarily due to medical advances. More was and could be achieved to improve the health and well-being of the population by raising conditions of living, particularly for the poor. What is really needed is more and better affordable housing for the low-income population, increased educational and job opportunities, more wholesome nutrition and exercise, less smoking and drinking. These, they say, are now more important than CT scanners or other fancy gadgets of dubious efficacy and limited reach.

Others go even further, much further indeed. For example Ivan Illich, a Catholic priest, in his *Medical Nemesis* indicts the health system wholesale. He maintains not only that the medical enterprise is unable to cope effectively with sickness, suffering, and death, but also that the physician (and particularly the hospital) may be, and often are, dangerous to our health, limbs, and life. As someone once said, a hospital is no place for a sick person: in a hospital one should be able to defend oneself. People would be better off if they stayed away from the medical system altogether. While Illich's strictures are hyperbolic, and may be dismissed as the bitter ruminations of a priesthood that has seen the care of the sick and dying slipping through its fingers, and thus has an axe to grind, they do have some validity. They also remind one of Martin Luther's theses, in the sixteenth century, when he attacked a then powerful and influential institution: the Established Church. Luther claimed that it had become bloated and corrupt; that its priests abused their monopolistic powers and did not provide access to grace and salvation, as they claimed and promised; and that man should bypass the Church and the priests and establish a direct relationship with God. And this is, more or less, the argument of Illich: man should bypass hospital and physician and re-establish his direct contact with his own health and body, since doctors in most instances cannot deliver, and worse, they often inflict iatrogenic damage. It is interesting that Illich wrote *Medical Nemesis* originally in Spanish. In that language, the term *salud* means both salvation and health!

The criticism, the skepticism, the hostility directed at the health system and medicine, in the light of dramatic advances, are relatively new. They are symptomatic, as I pointed out earlier, of the importance and of the power achieved by contemporary health care. In the nineteenth century and earlier, the physician might be held more as an object of derision and ridicule because of his pretensions and pomposity, rather than a target of attack. Health care was not seen as a major issue: it was small potatoes, indeed.

There was little the physician could do except provide solace and engage in some (hopefully harmless) rituals and manipulations. Hospitals, the descendants of hospices, were mostly places where the poor went to seek shelter and those who were sick went to die. Health care took only a very small proportion of the Gross National Product and of the active labor force. The situation radically changed toward the end of the nineteenth and the beginning of the twentieth centuries. The fusion of the therapeutic tradition with the growing availability and application of scientific knowledge led to a revolution in the treatment of the sick. It strengthened the ability of medicine to deal with illness and particularly to prolong life. Infectious diseases, the major killer until then, were brought under control. It was only after 1910 or 1912, as L.J. Henderson remarked, that a random patient with a random condition choosing a physician at random had more than one chance in two of benefiting from the encounter. But the increased power of medicine was accompanied by an inflation of costs (usually expressed as a percentage of the GNP) and by the emergence of a series of problems, dilemmas, and questions that have no easy answers. As a matter of fact, in most instances the answers, if any are to be found, must perforce lie outside the realm of science and medicine. These are often matters of judgments, of difficult choices, of ethical and religious commitments, of legal determinations. And there is every indication that research and medical progress, for example, in the area of human reproduction, will pose increasingly difficult questions and choices, legal problems and emotional issues, for example, in surrogate motherhood.

At the same time, as medicine has become more and more capable of dealing with a series of conditions that earlier could not be handled, there has been in most countries an ideological shift toward making access to medical care a right of citizenship, available to all regardless of social position, background or income. This "democratization" of health care strongly reflects the idea that health is such an important component of the human condition that it should not, any more, be considered (as it had been) a consumer good, a privilege, or even a luxury, but as a necessity and a right. (It thus has rejoined, with a time lag to be sure, education, which in earlier times was considered a privilege of rank and not a universal right.) It was possible, until the Second World War, for some to express the idea that health care was like a luxury automobile: if one could afford it, so much the better. But society did not owe everyone medical attention any more than it owed everyone a Cadillac. This view about health care has by now disappeared, except among the most die-hard conservatives and libertarians. Another reason for its disappearance was the realization that health (and healthy people) were an important component of industrial productivity and military power. But the question of moving from guarantee or promise to actual access is a different story. In most cases, it is the polity that has made a commitment to the population and proclaimed and guaranteed health care entitlement. But no government is in the position to create a health system *de novo* to fulfill this pledge. It must attempt to utilize and shape the existing system to live up to that promise. In particular, it must often deal with a difficult, independent, and recalcitrant medical profession that looks upon any government interference with hostility and skepticism. It must arrange, cajole, and sometimes use the law to control hospitals that up to that point enjoyed a fair amount of independence.

The major question I wanted to raise was whether these phenomena, these problems, these dilemmas were found in most industrial-urban societies; and if so, in what manner were they formulated and what means had been designed to cope with them. Hence the idea of a cross-national approach. I decided to ask a group of colleagues from several countries to write essays on the nature and the major issues their nations faced in this area.

The approach

Comparison is at the heart of the scientific enterprise. It permits us to examine and evaluate the features of a system by contrasting it with another one of the same general type. Comparison, therefore, adds a new perspective to an examination of the situation and the problems each society faces. And it may be instructive. If there is comparative anatomy, physiology, or religion, why not comparative health systems?

There are two types of comparative analysis, and they are not mutually exclusive. The more common is the horizontal or cross-national examination of certain phenomena across the board; we examine the same problems and issues in more than one country, and we see the differences, the similarities, and we learn of the different answers or possibilities in each. This is the center of gravity of this volume. There is, however, the other comparative dimension: the vertical or historical one. In this perspective, we look at the historical development, or the evolution of, let's say, the health system, or the mortality and morbidity trends over a period of time. This approach is more useful in explaining how things got to be that way in one society. But one can combine this kind of approach with the horizontal one, and think about the comparative evolution of health systems and of morbidity/mortality. For example, is there an orderly and fairly predictable march of events, of steps, of processes, that one can identify in each national society and its health system? Is the process of development systematic? Does it resemble the process of increased differentiation and adaptation to the milieu that one can see in the physiological realm? These are difficult questions to answer, but we know, for example, that the evolution of morbidity usually follows a certain path that is recognizable as societies become more modern, industrialized, affluent, urbanized. We talk of "diseases of civilization," or better of western diseases, and we relate them to changes in our living habits (for example, our decrease in the intake of fibers) and alterations in the environment that seem to accompany modernization and industrialization. To some degree, this affords us a certain amount of predictability: we know that as health improves, and as life expectancy lengthens, that the rate of cancer and heart disease is likely to increase with the aging of the population, and that infectious diseases recede in importance.

I deliberately limited the range of societies to those of the industrial type where the questions arise most sharply and tried to select societies that are quite different from each other in the hope of focussing on the range of variations, as well as the commonalities. I also tried to include nations whose health systems have not received wide attention, for example Switzerland, Spain, New Zealand, and Japan. The first eight essays deal with national health systems (including Scotland, which might not precisely fit into that category). The last essay, though different in its approach, illustrates the potentially didactic utility of the cross-national approach.

I have attempted to develop a typology of health systems which I present in Schema 1, and I have indicated the health systems presented in this collection of essays at the bottom of each type. The health systems in parentheses are those not formally described in the book, but mentioned in the last essay as potentially able to learn from experience the United States has had with Health Maintenance Organizations.

I asked my colleagues to be neither strictly descriptive, nor prescriptive. In most instances, of course, a certain amount of descriptive materials and statistical data were indispensable as background data for what was to follow. But what I was aiming at were the important problems and unresolved questions. I was, of course, interested in these problems not only as they affected health care, but also society, in general. And I felt that an examination of critical issues was important because they were signals that important changes and adjustments would likely take place, both in the health system and in the society.

Schema 1 A typology of health systems

Health system	Type 1 Emergent	Type 2 Pluralistic	Type 3 Insurance/ Social Security	Type 4 National Health Service	Type 5 Socialized
General definition	Health care as item of personal consumption	Health care as predominantly a consumer good or service	Health care as an insured/guaranteed consumer good or service	Health care as a state-supported consumer good or service	Health care as a state-provided public service
Position of the physician	Solo entrepreneur	Solo entrepreneur and member of variety of groups/organizations	Solo entrepreneur and member of medical organizations	Solo entrepreneur and member of medical organizations	State employee and member of medical organizations
Role of professional associations	Powerful	Very strong	Strong	Fairly strong	Weak or non-existent
Ownership of facilities	Private	Private and public	Private and public	Mostly public	Entirely public
Payments	Direct	Direct and indirect	Mostly indirect	Indirect	Entirely indirect
Role of the polity	Minimal	Residual/indirect	Central/indirect	Central/direct	Total
Types described in the book		Switzerland USA	(Canada) (France) Japan New Zealand Spain Yugoslavia	Scotland (Great Britain)	USSR

The issues

In my letter of invitation, I specified some issues. I asked my colleagues to use these as springboards for their essays. I did not expect each and every one of them to address all the issues, nor did I expect them, in any way, to limit themselves to them. They were illustrative and suggestive. Here they are:

1 The question of the evolving *mandate* of the health system: in the course of time, an increased number of conditions or problems of modern society have become medicalized, whether it be folly, deviance, gambling, obesity, juvenile delinquency, and so on. To what degree then is each health system affected by this medicalization, and what might be the implications? (For example, is medicalization simply an expression of medical imperialism, or on the contrary, is an increased number of problems being thrust upon an often reluctant medical profession such as the determination of disability? What might be the consequences in a society in which, for example, all crime, all deviance would be conceived as an expression of "illness"?)

2 The question of the increased *role of the polity* in the health care system, and the process of re-privatization: is this part of a constant dialectical process in which one orientation supersedes the other as one fails to produce what is wanted, and vice versa? (What conclusions can one make from comparing, for example, a complete staticized system of the Soviet type, to one like the United States where a great deal of private activities take place, to what goes on in Britain under Thatcherism, or even in Yugoslavia as the latter has tried to depoliticize its health system and introduce self-management?)

3 The *seductiveness of technology* and the moral imperative: as medicine learns to do more, the physician passes from the innocence of ignorance to the guilt of knowledge and of the potential. (For example, the invention of renal dialysis poses problems that did not exist before when ESRD – end stage renal disease – was a verdict of death and the physician was helpless, as he is today in facing many cancer cases. Closely allied are the questions that the use of technology has raised in the area of ethics, law, religion, morality, and so on.)

4 The question of *the mounting costs*, or opportunity costs (within and without the health system), and the problem of rationing. The issue of what proportion of the national wealth should be allowed to flow into the health system and in other sectors (and how that flow is controlled) and allocated within the health system. (How much to preventive and clinical services, and for what kinds of conditions; how much to research, basic or applied and on what areas; how much to education and training of health personnel and for what mix of such personnel.)

5 What can we say of the *growing demand* for health services? Can we determine the "need" for such services, and to what degree are both these factors the result of medicalization mentioned earlier, or the fact that an increased supply of health services increases the demand for such services? (Are both "need" and "demand" culture-bound? Is there a natural limit to demand?)

6 What can we say about the increasing *trend toward specialization* and superspecialization both among physicians and other personnel (nurses, for example), the increasing proliferation of new specialties (often spawned by new technologies), and the problem of integrating, into a viable medical product, the increasingly narrow outputs of specialists? (Is there a counter-trend discernible toward the emergence of generalists, of "specialists in generalities"? What can we learn about deskilling, the downward transfer of functions, a lengthening hierarchy of health personnel, and so on?)

7 Closely allied to the issue in no. 6 above is the increasing *depersonalization* or alienation of the patient in an increasingly technological, differentiated and bureaucratized hospital atmosphere. (What then are the implications of this trend for the legitimacy of the health system?)

8 And as a follow-up, as health care becomes increasingly expensive and bureaucratized, what can be said about the implications of the *application of managerial logic* to the nature of health care services, and particularly, to the problems of the doctor–patient relationship or therapist–patient relationship? (To what degree are the emotional needs of patients, faced with anxieties and the aleatory aspects of illness, increasingly ignored in favor of a rational, bureaucratic, and technological "fix"? And if the

emotional needs of patients are ignored by health practitioners, what alternative sources of emotional support will patients seek and with what consequences?)

9 The issue of *flexibility*: to what degree do health care systems provide the necessary flexibility, as well as rapidity of response to emergency or extraordinary circumstances? It may be relatively easy to vaccinate an entire population, but a sudden epidemic for which there is no vaccine or countermeasures readily available may pose problems of flexibility and adaptability. (Should the health care system become increasingly bureaucratized and rigid, how are "special" cases to be handled, those of life and death, where the red tape has to be cut quickly?)

10 The question of the degree of lay *control* exercised by the public in health care systems: from the feminist protest in the United States to the various public control boards in England and Australia, to the Yugoslav "self-management," to the Soviet claim that "people" are in control of their health care system.

The health system

The expression "health system" is but a shorthand word, a convention, to delineate or to differentiate or to identify the totality of formal efforts, commitments, personnel, institutions, economic resources, research efforts (both basic and applied) that a nation-state or a society earmarks or devotes to illness, premature mortality, incapacitation, prevention, rehabilitation, and other health-related problems. The word "system" is thus used in a fairly loose fashion and does not necessarily imply an organized and interrelated structure of activities, but it encompasses, as said earlier, all formal activities directed at health problems. The use of this expression thus parallels the view of society as a social system. Another possible word would be "sector." Although the delineation of the precise borders of the health system is an empirical and definitional task (what to include, what to exclude) it is possible to specify, with some degree of accuracy and consistency, what it consists of and to be reasonably assured that the definition holds across the board for different national health systems.

Philosophically, of course, one might say that practically

every aspect of societal life affects health: for example income levels, class position, the conditions of housing, nutrition, the availability of clean water and of sewers, the transportation and communications system. To this, some might add the role of families in health care, parallel medicines, medical cults, marginal practices, and so on. We might then come to a *reductio ad absurdum* by stating that the society *is* the health system. For analytical purposes, we must differentiate it from the society it serves and proceed accordingly. It should also be noted that the approach here is macroscopic, and the unit that we deal with is the nation. The nation is the largest sovereign political entity extant in the world today, with its own legal system, coinage, defense establishment, and other characteristics that make a society a nation. Perhaps the exception, as noted earlier, is the essay on the Scottish health system which is not a sovereign political entity in the full sense of the word. Our basic assumption is that any nation must, for its own survival, be concerned with the health of its population and with the health system mandated to protect that important resource. Indeed, the degree of involvement of the polity in that health care system will be (and should be) a central element in any comparative analysis, as will be an examination of the often dialectical relationships between the public (or tax-supported) medical care and the private one.

Social significance of health problems

I have spoken of health problems; this needs some definition which I shall attempt now. By health problems I mean primarily morbidity and mortality. These pose a threat to any society in that they incapacitate (partially or totally) the ability of the individual to perform his or her social functions or roles. A mother who is seriously sick is unable to take care of her child. Absenteeism caused by illness costs industries millions of dollars in lost production. And we know that the illness and the consequent incapacitation of a chief executive may soon turn into a national emergency. My approach thus is that of the much criticized functional-structural school. The departure point is that the health system, the physician, the hospital have emerged because there was a "need" for them. The health system thus performs a "function" that answers a perceived need or solves a problem. And to do so, certain types of structural arrangements have to be devised for that function to be performed. But sickness (and associated phenomena) are not necessarily seen in that "functional" perspective, particularly by those who are sick. It is an intensely personal and subjective experience, often accompanied by pain and discomfort, and an affront to one's self–image and dignity. The first series of problems (incapacitation for role performance) I would still like to call "functional," the second "expressive." Health systems are mandated to deal with both: societies are more concerned with the first one, individuals with the second one. The two constitute the "targets" of the system, and can be expressed as the five d's: death, disease, disability, discomfort, and dissatisfaction. To deal with these targets, medicine has devised a series of six modalities broadly defined as the following: diagnosis, treatment, prevention, rehabilitation, custody, and health education. Health personnel mandated to deal with morbidity (or the five d's), utilizing the above modalities (the state of the art) and provided with the necessary supports, attempt to affect, modify, eliminate the personal and societal threats posed by the five d's. In one sense, the health system may be defined as a societal mechanism that absorbs generalized inputs, resources, or supports and metabolizes them into specialized outputs or services aimed at the five d's.

What then are these "supports"? In order to function, the health system must receive from its parent society the following, at the very least:

1 Legitimacy (the degree to which what the health system and its practitioners do is considered proper and desirable, and supported by appropriate legislation);
2 Financial or economic support (the proportion of the total national wealth that goes into the health system or the per capita expenditures);
3 Personnel (the number, different types, and characteristics of those who formally work in the health system in any and all capacity, and the percentage they represent to the total active labor force);
4 Finally, the state of the art, that is the knowledge, techniques, and technologies with which health personnel attempt to cope with health problems.

As we shall see, this last "universalistic" element is easily one of the more important sources of dynamism in the evolution in health systems, and of tension with the more "particularistic" aspects of each society and its culture. In addition, this resource is different from the other three, in that it is a cultural one, and in a particular way it is infinite, it is not subject to zero sum games. The supply of manpower, or financial resources, or even of legitimacy, is never unlimited. One dollar invested in the health system is not available for investment in another sector of society, and hence the need to calculate opportunity costs. But once something has been discovered or invented, once a bit of knowledge has been added, which did not exist previously, that item can be used time and again without diminishing it by one iota. When we discover how to deal with end stage renal disease, we can apply this knowledge again and again (of course the application itself does involve limited resources in manpower and money). (See Schema 2 on page 14.)

Two approaches to the health system

I would propose two theoretical approaches, not mutually exclusive, in drawing some utility from the cross-national approach: One is the general idea of "convergence." This is a kind of soft technological determinism. It holds that industrialism is a universal force that will lead to the increased uniformity of social structures around the world under the impact of the technological imperatives of similar industrial-type production units. Ideology, culture, traditions, values will all succumb or be affected by these imperatives. For example, factories the world over are becoming similar in their structure and requirements because they use the same types of instrumentalities (advanced machinery, assembly line, discipline, hierarchy, punctuality, a time orientation, etc.). Thus, the social organization and indeed the characteriological features of the people in industrial societies will increasingly become similar. If one accepts that hypothesis, it then has some predictive value: not that all social systems will become like peas in a pod, but that the common features will increase at the expense of the differences. And the same reasoning might be applied to health systems. As the means of "medical production" become increasingly technological and

Schema 2

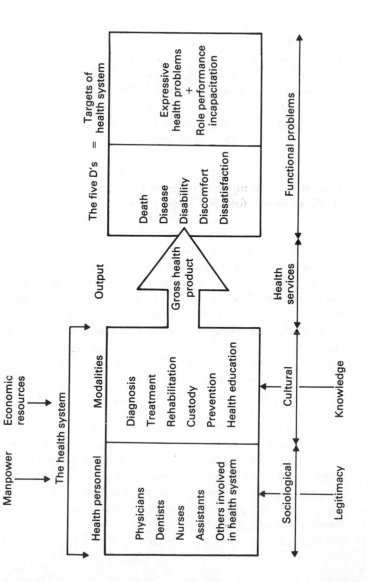

universal around the world, then the social organizations and the requirements needed to operate these means will increasingly resemble each other. In the end, hospitals because they employ the same basic technology and are under the same technologically determined injunctions (for example the need to maintain aseptic conditions in surgery) will converge toward a universal pattern. And, in fact, the increasing activities of US multinational conglomerates in England and Saudi-Arabia, for instance, are helping to bring about some of that universality. How this will affect, for example, the medical profession as a result of the increased rationalization of these organizations, their need for predictability, their desire to control costs, their interests in having physicians on fixed salaries, and so on, is still a moot point.

The other theoretical approach is that the health system and the practice of medicine are affected by two major factors and the tension between them: one is the technological, that is the "universalistic" nature of medicine as an applied science, with its imperatives and injunctions as mentioned earlier that hold true in all settings, for example, the ever-present possibility of infection. The other factor is that of cultural or national diversity, that is of "particularism": the universalistic nature of the medical arts is adopted *and* adapted in a variety of ways depending upon the nature and the type of culture of the recipient society, its traditions, its ideology, class relations, political and administrative structure and its economic resources. Thus a French hospital may look superficially like an American or British hospital. But French culture and habits do not stop at the hospital door: they penetrate and affect every aspect of that hospital's setting, even perhaps to the bottle of red wine at the bedside. It is then this dialectic between the universalistic and the particularistic aspects of different national health systems (or even national health subsystems) that provides that variety that one can observe around the world, even in advanced industrial-urban societies. The question whether the health systems of such societies increasingly converge toward one single pattern, as the convergence hypothesis would lead us to assume, is still debatable. Thus though the resemblances are often striking, so are the areas of divergence. To use an oenological analogy, medicine in its universalistic aspects resembles a generic grape or varietal, let's say Gamay, Chenin Blanc, or Cabernet Sauvignon. But the wine that will be produced from the *same plant* in different vineyards around the world, or even within the same country, or on each side of a hill, will depend on the nature of the soil, ambient temperature, the amount of sunshine, the amount of rainfall, acts of God (the sudden rain squall that ruins a crop), the amount of knowledge, motivation, resources, the patience and devotion of the wine grower, and so on.

Toward the end of these introductory notes, I shall return to these theoretical questions, and attempt, in the light of my review of the major issues raised by my contributors, to assess which theoretical position best fits the case.

The essays

Let us now turn to the essays in this book and briefly make some general remarks, then focus on some more specific issues.

What is striking first is the degree to which each health system is described as a product of its specific society, culture, and history. It is fascinating, for example, in reading the essay by Hunter on the Scottish health service to see how sharp the differences appear to be between Scotland and what goes on south of the Tweed. The British emphasize the management and organization of health services in a rational and economical way. In Scotland, according to Hunter, the emphasis is not so much on doing things right as on doing the right thing (seen in the perspective of Scottish democratic humanism). This implies, for example, a great emphasis on the public good and the community, integrated and holistic health and allied services, a distaste toward the private practice of medicine and specialization, and an acceptance of group practice and sensitive help to the population.

In the case of Yugoslavia, as Parmelee's essay so aptly demonstrates, the very nature of the health system, its basic organizational structure, has reflected the political and ideological vicissitudes of that country after the Second World War: a reliance and imitation, at first of the Soviet centralized and bureaucratic model, and then with the break from Moscow, a more democratic, more decentralized, less state-dependent medical care type of organization. Parmelee shows incisively that such a policy has its price in terms, for example, of a pursuit of national goals, and the realization of a degree of equity between the different regions of the nation. The same is true, as

Davis reports, of the Soviet health care system, a product of Soviet society rather than the expression of common medical knowledge and techniques. In the United States, as remarks Anderson, the business entrepreneurial ideology is nowadays shaping a health delivery system that is duly influenced by that entrepreneurial spirit.

In each one of the cases examined by the contributors, the national setting, history, ideology, traditions, culture, basic philosophical approaches are thus said to have affected and to affect the nature of the health system. If this has been so true, in the past, there is good reason to assume it will continue to be so in the near future.

In addition to the realization that the health system is a product of the society it inhabits more than simply the embodiment of the contemporary state of the art in medicine and public health, many of the authors do emphasize that health levels themselves (not only in Spain, as de Miguel and Guillén state) are the results not primarily of the workings of the health system, but of general conditions, for example, regional and class differences, and is perhaps most visibly evident in areas that are sensitive both to general conditions and standards of living *and* to the provision of medical care, particularly in infant mortality. Thus, the rise in that index in the last twenty years or so in the Soviet Union may be tied both to a decline in the standard of living (probably due to the large investments in the defense establishment) and also in a gradual degradation of the medical services.

Generally speaking my colleagues chose to emphasize only some of the general issues I had mentioned. This is perhaps indicative of their relative importance. Among them was the relevance, and indeed the increasing, if not dominating, role that the polity plays regarding the health system in practically every country. The issue of the management of that system also loomed large in several of the essays though with some interesting variations. One might thus contrast the situation in Switzerland which is decentralized and in which there is no national health ministry or its equivalent and the vastly different case of the Soviet Union which is highly centralized and managed. And yet, the Swiss decentralized pluralism has led to the creation of a highly effective health care system, the one in the Soviet Union of a rather ineffective and highly bureaucratized one. It just seems that a highly centralized management, particularly a large national health system, in which certain national goals are mandated, carries the problem of the creation of an extensive bureaucracy to carry its plans and the programs. These bureaucracies often do become concerned with their own existence and operations perhaps even more than with the goals they are trying to implement. Managerial efficiency, the means rather than the ends, receive exaggerated emphasis at the expense of the service, as Hunter makes the point in his comparison of the Scottish and British health services.

Of equal interest is the issue of power and control; there are often many constituencies involved in the health system: the polity with its agenda, the professions, the public (and the taxpayers), and those who are the recipients of health services. Attempts to "democratize" the system by introducing some degree of lay control over professional practices have been made, but usually have not met with great success as the case of Yugoslavia demonstrates. At the same time, efforts to place health facilities and personnel under some kind of local or community controls often create or perpetuate inequalities between different regions, and thus run contrary to national policies.

The impact of technology is seen by several of the authors as a most significant aspect in contemporary health systems. Technology, of course, is part of that universalistic state of the art mentioned earlier. The consequences of the introduction of technology have not yet been traced thoroughly, but at least the following elements, as issues, should be noted:

1 In most instances, medical technology is both labor *and* capital intensive. Contrary to technology in industry, it does not substitute capital for labor (thus saving costs) but it tends to be additive, thus increasing costs.
2 Once ı technology has been devised and proven to be effective (whether diagnostically or therapeutically) it exerts a powerful influence for its adoption, often regardless of costs since it deals with human life and suffering. The physician, unable, let's say, up to a certain point in helping patients with a specific condition passes, as seen earlier, from the innocence of ignorance or impotence to the guilt of the possible: once dialysis is invented, for example, life now can be prolonged. Thus pressures for the purchase of that technology will be extreme. In many instances, the purchase of expensive technology for the few

is at the expense of simpler treatment modalities for the many.

3 As pointed out, particularly in the paper by Raffel on New Zealand, the existence of high-level technology makes it often frustrating for physicians, who have been trained to use it, to practice in a country or a setting where it is not available because of costs. Thus New Zealand is losing trained specialists to Australia or the United States because these physicians are frustrated.

4 It should be pointed out, as the case of the Soviet Union makes it clear, that technology is not an independent, autonomous force that affects health systems: countries can deliberately decide not to introduce available medical technology.

5 Medical technology often tends to be alienative in that it depersonalizes treatment.

Cost containment is an issue that affects, without exception, all health systems. As health systems have become more and more expensive, and as the demand for health care has increased, so have the costs. But in seeking to contain these costs, countries very often become more concerned with the financial aspects, than with the very services the health system is expected to provide. This concern of means over ends (parallel to some extent with that of bureaucratization) has led to a variety of devices and arrangements for the financing of health services. Several effects are discernible: one is that in most instances, the manner in which the financing of the health services is organized *does* have an effect on the way in which services are offered to people. In a system in which a fee-for-service system exists, the temptation will be for health personnel to provide more services than needed as there will be a relationship between volume of services and personal incomes. On the other hand, where the payment is in the form of a salary or capitation fee, the temptation will be to provide fewer services. The second consequence is the following: in most societies, the aim is to provide access to health services so that those who need those services will be able to have them or to afford them. But the almost insoluble problem is to devise a system whereby overuse, abuse, or unnecessary use will be curbed without constituting a barrier for the service that is really needed or necessary. The cost containment dilemma raises another related one: the question of opportunity costs both at the societal level *and* within the health system. Every society, in the final analysis, makes a choice or "decides" how much of its national wealth it will invest or commit to the health system and what it must give up as a result of that choice and second, when that portion of that wealth has been committed or allocated to the health system, the choice has to be made on where the money will go, and the mix of services it will support: clinical services, public health, education or personnel, research (basic and applied), and so on. In a country like the Soviet Union, as Davis shows, these allocations to a large extent are the results of the decisions made by a small group of persons at the apex of the health bureaucracy's pyramid, and enforced through budget allocations. In decentralized systems, for example Switzerland or the United States, these "decisions" are the result of myriads of personal and institutional choices that are not, except in the broader sense, controlled or controllable by a central authority. But the major issue here is that of decisions and choices since resources in personnel and finances are never unlimited.

The issue of rationing then has entered into the agenda of health systems. As Anderson points out in his description of the American health system, the use of DRGs (Diagnostic Related Groups) has meant that some patients have been complaining that they have been released from the hospital prematurely as a result of efforts at cost containment.

Increasingly the world over, as we have seen, access to health care is considered as a right, rather than a privilege (or charity) as it was in the past. The issue of access, sponsored by or guaranteed by the polity, immediately brings in the question of equitability in that access. Usually the inference is that such access must be the same for all, particularly when it is tax supported. In fact, this is a chimera, an illusory goal as Anderson points out. Every society, particularly industrial society, is stratified. And generally speaking, access to care does tend to follow that stratification pattern. Even in Britain, care is often unequal, and those who have the money can opt out and purchase private health insurance or amenity beds. In addition, as de Miguel and Guillén point out in their essay on the Spanish health system, those who are in the higher socio-economic classes do benefit more from a system even if it is available, in principle, equitably to all. Anderson predicts that if the United States were to establish an arrangement for universal health insurance or service, some 40 per cent of the population would buy private health insurance so as to get better, or at least more pleasant health care. Even the Soviet Union, as Davis indicates, has a stratified health care system with the interesting feature that the care for the elites (the equivalent of private health care in most other countries) is also socialized, that is it is 'free' and paid for by the state as a perquisite of rank.

I have only touched on the major issues and dilemmas raised by the authors in their contributions. The paper by Rodwin, as I indicated earlier, is a bit different: it deals with some of the major problems faced by Canada, France, and Britain, and suggests that the one distinctive contribution to health care made by the United States, the concept of the Health Maintenance Organization, may represent a partial solution to their problems.

Which approach fits best?

It remains to re-examine the two theoretical approaches we proposed earlier, that of convergence and that of a combination of universalistic and particularistic factors, that define the nature and the evolution of health systems.

The convergence hypothesis may turn, in the final analysis, to be correct. Not really a convergence but a resemblance due to the facts that health systems will (just like societies) increasingly share common elements. But for the time being, the weight of the evidence seems to be that cultural factors (in the broad sense of the word) are just as important (if not more) than the structural similarities engendered by the use of the same or universal means of medical production. Thus in conclusion we can state that each health system evolves as a result of the combination, and sometimes the dialectical contradictions between the universalistic aspects of the state of the art, the knowledge, the technology that are valid and can be applied anywhere around the world, and the particularistic aspects of each society and culture. And it is the particularism of different cultures that continues to produce that variety and diversity in health systems we see around the world. This feature thus puts some limits on the degree to which organizational features, and even medical technology, can be transferred or applied from one society to another. The World Health Organization learned this lesson the hard way when it tried simply to extend medical knowledge, practices, and techniques to countries that were

hav
Structuurl
through

culturally unable to accept them because of what they meant in terms of their consequences for their traditions, their culture, their ways of life, and their native practitioners. This emphasizes the basic duality of medicine, health care, and therapy in general: not only is it a set of knowledge, techniques, the state of the art, if you please; it is also a practice that is embedded in the society, a way of relating to people, a manner of organizing the way in which practitioners practice their art and their science. And this is why I believe, strongly, that studying the health system and medicine does provide an "insight" into social processes. The study of health systems, particularly when one does it in a historical and comparative perspective, resembles peeling an endless onion: as soon as one issue is uncovered, examined, and analyzed in terms of its consequences and implications, another one emerges just as intricate and just as fascinating, and so on. And one cries in the process. But just as often the tears are those of joy, the sheer pleasure of discovery.

Acknowledgements

Finally, I want to express my personal gratitude and admiration for the work and the contributions made by the authors of this book. Each and every one of them has tried to follow my original specifications and written an essay that is original, and rich in ideas and suggestions. Their patience and forbearance at the inordinately long process of putting a book like this together, and their understanding of the need for such a patience, is in the best tradition of academia. But I would be remiss in my task as an editor if I did not pay tribute to my colleague John B. McKinlay whose idea it was to undertake such a book. His enthusiasm and his enormous expertise in all things sociological and medical have been an inspiration. And finally, my editor at Routledge, Gill Davies, deserves a special halo for her understanding and steadfast assistance.

References

Henderson, L.J. (1935) "The patient and physician as a social system", *New England Journal of Medicine*, 212: 819–23.
Illich, I. (1976) *Medical Nemesis*, New York: Pantheon.

Part One
Pluralistic health systems

One

The Swiss health system:
the paradox of ungovernability
and efficacy

*Philippe Lehmann, Felix Gutzwiller,
and Jean F. Martin*

Introduction

The predominant opinion that users, professionals, policy-
makers, and observers have of the health care system in
Switzerland is that it works well. They seem convinced that it
provides care of quality for probably all categories of diseases
and patients, from birth to death, for the poor (almost) as for the
rich, in a not too different manner in all regions of the country.

This could probably be confirmed (if the data were available)
by a systematic study of the outcomes of the health care system.
It is customary to associate this opinion with the mortality
indicators for the Swiss population, which are quite favourable
in comparison with other countries. It should be however
remembered that mortality, as well as other health indicators,
are affected not only by the health care system, but also by
social, political, and particularly economic conditions.

Furthermore, the health care system in Switzerland receives
approval from most quarters, not only for its results, but also for
its structure and functioning; it is seen as "natural" and the
differing solutions adopted in other countries seem "inappropriate" or even "pernicious" in comparison.

If one steps back a little and considers Switzerland in a
comparison of health systems, the first point to emerge is the

extremely complicated and diversified nature of its special case (*Sonderfall Schweiz*). One cannot but be surprised that a puzzle of so many pieces, guided by so many different rules, and directed by so many competing committees, governments, and enterprises, under so many varied influences, is capable of obtaining such results.

No one is able to describe clearly and concisely who governs the health system in Switzerland and how: this is certainly due to the fact that this system is neither governed nor even governable "as a system" and that the will to steer it is generally lacking. Facts concerning hospital and technology planning, health personnel, cost containment, and sickness insurance reform all confirm this statement.

Moreover, one could certainly ask whether, through being ungoverned, the care system in Switzerland is not behind with respect to the possibility of obtaining better results in terms of health outcomes, considering the amount of resources and means available on the economic, scientific, and technological levels.

The aim of this contribution is to present this paradox of a health system which is not governed and is ungovernable, yet which produces results which are commonly judged to be among the best in the world. These two aspects will be successively developed by investigating their social, political, and medical explanations, and by drawing attention to some of the system failings. In several respects, the Swiss case illustrates rather well the discussion about the convergence of epistemological and technological models of medicine on the one hand and the particularities of the organization, system of values, and political structure of a country on the other.

Rather than systematically documenting all characteristics of the Swiss health care system, we will instead illustrate them with some specific examples and debate the perspectives and challenges at the end of the 1980s.

Is the Swiss health care system governed? Is it governable?

The question of manageability

"Is Switzerland governable?" was asked by one of the former members of the Federal government in the title of his quite successful book (Chevallaz and Dubois 1984). Apart from problems raised by the federal structure formed by twenty-six cantons (only three of which have more than 500,000 inhabitants), the linguistic, cultural, and religious diversity of the population (6.4 million) and the frequent use of direct democracy procedures, the major question on this subject is that of the unwieldiness and limits of the so-called democracy of concordance.

This notion means that before any important decision is taken in Switzerland, consensus has usually to be obtained among the twenty-six cantons, six main political parties, lobbies of professional and economic bodies, representatives of the farmers, mountain regions, large and small towns, and so on, plus the "experts" who populate the universities and administrations. Besides, the competence to make decisions is distributed between several federal and cantonal authorities.

When aiming at satisfying all interests, it is not easy to draw up clear, innovative policy projects; Switzerland always prefers incrementalism. The best Swiss authors in political science devoted an entire volume of the *Annuaire suisse de science politique* for 1983 to this question of governability, showing the limits and constraints of the system. Governability is the degree to which state decision procedures are adapted to problems as they occur. Thus it is a functional problem. However, questions need also to be asked as to the evaluation of the range of problems submitted to the state and the services expected from it. An interpretation therefore depends on the ideological premises of the actors and observers, which vary according to whether they are interventionist or conservative.

Although more or less "unsteerable," Switzerland does not exist in a state of anarchy – far from it. It is, if anything, a paragon of order and stability.

Raising the question of the manageability or governability of the Swiss health system opens up an even greater range of issues; it is a question not only of the state as a political institution, but also of a global system in which the technological and sociological models of the health professions, the attitudes and behavior of the population, the types of state intervention and regulations, and more or less socialized financing structures intervene.

The aims of a health system are also multiple. Even if the search for ways of preserving the population's health by fighting disease predominates, the economic functions of the health care sector (production, market, employment) should not be neglected.

The characteristics of the (implicit) Swiss health policies can be summarized as follows:

1 The delegation of care and decisions about it to professionals and medical establishments;
2 The reimbursement of medical costs by various schemes;
3 The entrusting of some tasks of medical and health policy to the state.

Questioning the governability of the system implies the idea that the better (not necessarily the more) a system is governed, the better the services it offers in response to needs; a study of the Swiss situation might challenge this hypothesis.

The weakest health ministry

It should first be mentioned that Switzerland has no such thing as one identifiable national health ministry and that the conglomerate of institutions that act as such probably represent, on a national level, the weakest health ministry of all developed countries (including other federal states).

The responsibilities for health policy, nationally, are distributed between several administrations: mainly the Federal Offices of Public Health (OFSP) and Social Insurances (OFAS), both attached to the Department (Ministry) of the Interior, and services involved in health that depend on other departments (ministries): medical service of the Federal Office of Trade and Industry (OFIAMT), the medical services for the workers in post and telecommunications, the federal railways, and the army, and so on.

Each office is in charge of a list of specific tasks which are delegated explicitly by articles of the Federal Constitution.[1] Thus no office is entrusted with defining globally the objectives of a health policy for Switzerland. Even the federal government could not, without a fundamental change in the constitution, decide on an overall health policy outside the specific domains designated by the above mentioned constitutional clauses.

The provinces of the Confederation are

- sickness insurance   (legislation and supervision)
- disability insurance   (federal public fund)
- accident insurance   (public fund)
- protection of the environment   (legislation)
- epidemics   (surveillance)
- control of foodstuffs   (legislation)
- toxics and radiation   (surveillance)
- work safety   (legislation and supervision)
- examinations for physicians, dentists,
  veterinary surgeons, and pharmacists   (legislation)
- medical service of the army
- promoting scientific and medical research
- statistics (few are collected)
- international relations
- development aid to the Third World.

More than 80 per cent of the Confederation's budget for health is spent on funding sickness, accident, disability, and military insurances. On the whole, the Confederation spends four times less in the health field than the cantons together.

The competence at the national level is limited first by the federalist legal organization of delegating tasks to the Confederation (principle of "general sovereignty" of the cantons). It is very restricted in health domains and the federal offices respect a strict conception of this "subsidiary" principle. Second, the Federal government is currently involved in restraining trends towards centralization by reorganizing the allocation of tasks between the Confederation and the cantons to the advantage of the latter (Chancellerie fédérale suisse 1984). Finally, the fact that no institution is really in favor of an overall health policy explains the relative weakness of the Confederation in this matter.

The fact that there is no growth in federal centralization is finally part of a general rhetoric of "less State," supported by the "bourgeois" political majority, that has dominated the Swiss political system since the beginning of the economic crisis in 1974 (Rey 1983). "Less State," here, means both a reduction in the financial participation of the state in social insurances (7 billion Sfr less in ten years, cf. Gilliand 1986: 51–64), a refusal to reinforce legislation and planning (LAMM) and renunciation to new legislation (law on prevention).

The cantons' sovereignty

Do cantons, which in principle are sovereign with respect to health care organization (contingent on what has been delegated to the Confederation), have more power to guide the system?

The health action of the cantons mainly concerns the management of general and psychiatric hospitals: almost all the cantons have direct control of the main hospital centers (twenty-nine cantonal hospitals, 31 per cent of acute beds – see Table 1.1) and participate in the financing and planning of other non-profit hospitals (which depend on districts, communes, or foundations: 199 hospitals, 62 per cent of beds). Psychiatric hospitals that belong to the cantons represent 76 per cent of beds in this sector (*Annuaire statistique de la Suisse* 1981: 514). Expenditure for hospitalization represents almost three-quarters of expenditure on health by the cantons (Gygi and Frei 1984).

Table 1.1 *Short-stay hospitals (except psychiatry) according to their legal form (status in 1975)*

Owners	No of hospitals		No of beds	
	N	%	N	%
Confederation	2	0.7	131	0.3
Cantons	29	10.7	12,635	30.6
Districts, municipalities, public foundations	79	29.0	12,016	29.1
Private non-profit foundations and associations	120	44.1	13,693	33.1
Private (for profit) companies	42	15.4	2,837	6.9
Total	272	100%	41,312	100%

Canton contributions cover from 30 to 90 per cent of non-profit hospitals' operating deficits, and these subsidies have increased remarkably in the last two decades. The major goal of canton governments' regulations has been to avoid that the financial burdens on the cantons grow too markedly. Exactly how these governments are attempting to accomplish it is not known.

It is probably safe to presume that at least 25 different concepts are operating. Perhaps even the term "concept" is misleading in this context as it connotes a degree of organization, coherence, and foresight that may be true of some cantons, but certainly does not characterize them all.

(Gebert 1978: 110)

The other health sectors in which the cantons are active concern the following

- health and hygiene policy
- medical schools (five in the country)
- paramedical training schools
- nursing homes (surveillance and subsidies)
- home nursing care and social welfare
- primary and secondary prevention (especially school medical services).

In contrast, they have nothing or little to say about ambulatory medical care or private clinics.

The means the cantons have to manage their health systems are very modest: only seven cantons' health departments have more than ten managerial staff (Güntert and Hofer 1983: 22). It should be remembered, however, that nine of the twenty-six cantons have fewer than 100,000 inhabitants. During the past ten years, some cantons have developed comprehensive management and planning of the health tasks which are under their political responsibility. This trend has not been without problems, considering the relations of prestige and power between the medical profession and the planners. Moreover, the principle of freedom of enterprise, which concerns physicians setting up in practice, the opening of private clinics, as well as the acquisition of technological equipment, can only allow limited action. In other cantons, medical planning remains at the level of programming hospital construction and nursing homes (Wienke 1985; 1986).

A top organization, the Conference of Directors (Ministers) of Cantonal Health Departments (CDS), brings together periodically the health ministers of the twenty-six cantons. In his study, published in 1978, A.J. Gebert observed that "in its almost 60-year history, this organization has . . . contributed very little toward a comprehensive health policy based on cantonal authority. Rather, the CDS has only facilitated solutions to strictly technical problems" (Gebert 1978: 106). Furthermore, he deplored its weakness in proposing adequate solutions for planning, for example for certain very specialized care units which concern the whole of Switzerland. He explained that "these ministers do not consider the national boundaries of their country, but act only on the basis of their own cantons or regions" (Gebert 1978: 109). An analysis of the CDS over the last ten years would not show major change; it still has only a very limited staff (two members on the managerial staff and one secretary).

The different key roles of the private sector

The health care system in Switzerland is thus characterized by the essential and predominant place of the private sector. This notion should however be clarified and relativized.

By private sector is generally meant companies ruled by market economy, oriented toward profit and totally independent of the state. This definition can never be applied completely to institutions in the health domain as there are many different types of private structures. First, many of them are non-profit institutions (regional hospitals, nursing homes, mutual aid, and social welfare, etc.) which function mainly thanks to public subsidies and are integrated in public planning. Second, the sickness funds must have a mutualistic and non-profit character; they are subject to state surveillance and receive considerable subsidies from the Confederation. Third, practicing physicians have to respect the tariffs for medical acts that are established by agreement between their associations, the sickness funds, and public authorities. Fourth, even for private clinics and pharmaceutical manufacturers, income from socialized funding (sickness funds and subsidies from the public authorities) represents an essential part of their resources.

With these reservations, the principle of economic liberalism, which is one of the foundations of the social order in Switzerland, remains an economic as well as ideological reference of the health care system. It is the result of a very ancient historical evolution in which doctors' independence was never threatened and in which charitable or public interest institutions always had an important role. This tradition has not been perturbed (unlike in neighboring countries) by war, economic crises, or changes in the political regime.

The strength of the private sector is threefold:

1 Legal, because the freedom of trade and industry is laid down in the constitution and social order of Switzerland.
2 Economic, not only because the income level of the Swiss population enables them to acquire health care services, but also because the financing of health care is largely socialized and supported by direct and indirect subsidies (and therefore largely guaranteed).
3 Ideological, because Switzerland is founded on a liberal political culture; in the health sector this notion is even stronger, as freedom of enterprise and of therapeutic decisions by the care providers are merged in the same notion of independence.

The nature and role of the private sector has a fundamental effect on the ungovernability of the health care system: any new regulation is usually seen as an intolerable constraint which would be damaging for both patients and the country's prosperity. Furthermore, the diversity and multiplicity of private enterprise (more than 10,000 medical practices, 400 sickness funds, hundreds of hospitals and local or regional institutions) would not readily allow concertation and decision-making. This multiplicity and the tradition of contractual negotiation and muddling-through rather than planning hinder the establishment of a global conception of the health system and of mechanisms of adaptation.

Diversity and multiplicity of solutions

The political and economic restrictions to the governability of the Swiss health care system are augmented even more by the diversity of solutions in each canton, the smallness of collectivities, and the multiplicity of institutions involved.

The cantons' sovereignty with respect to their political organization as well as implementation in the domains for which they are competent allows each of them to adopt different forms of management of the hospital sector, home care, social welfare, and prevention. The financing structures, planning conceptions, and the degree to which services are actually developed diverge strongly, due to historical and economic circumstances, the relations between different political forces within each canton, the extent of the problems, and so on. Differences are increased even more by the fact that Switzerland does not have a unique urban hierarchy and that each canton, whatever its size, constitutes quite a distinct geographic and socio-economic entity.

The same diversity is to be found in the social insurance sector. Besides the three national public funds – disability, accident, and military insurances – there are more than 400 sickness funds serving between 500 and 500,000 insured people. Their number has been steadily decreasing, as up until 1964 there were more than 1,000. The trend towards concentration which has benefited the five "big funds" until now seems to be slowing down. The smallest funds often have a high proportion of aged and low-income people insured with them, that is "bad risks" who do not interest the other companies.

An extreme example of mosaic-type management appears in the fixing of care tariffs: these are determined by individual conventions negotiated between each cantonal sickness fund federation and the representatives of the health professions and medical institutions, under the surveillance of the cantonal authorities. Different tariffs are fixed for care covered by the national social insurances.

The impact of abundance

The absence of rules and models for the overall orientation of the health care system had few consequences when medicine was based mainly on the family doctor and local hospital; the evolution of medicine since the 1940s occurred in an environment of general and prolonged economic prosperity which enabled each canton, hospital, or doctor to acquire new material and technologies, increase their staff, and prescribe care which was reimbursed more and more frequently by the sickness funds. After the Second World War (during the period 1946–50), care was covered for 60 per cent of the population, this figure increasing to 73 per cent in 1960, 82 per cent in 1965, and reaching 97–8 per cent since 1980 (*Annuaire statistique de la Suisse*).

This growth has created major difficulties as to the feasibility of funding in the future. It also creates problems for the habits which have been acquired during at least forty years: those responsible for expenditure, for both infrastructure and treatment, have never been educated to calculate the cost of their acts since their financing was guaranteed; neither have they learnt to measure the relation between the quantity of care, its cost, and the benefit obtained with respect to health.

On the contrary, both politicians and physicians are conscious that Switzerland has the necessary resources to offer itself more than sufficient medical and hospital equipment in all regions. This is also explained by the undeniable attraction technology and the "concrete" have for professionals and other decision-makers.

The economic situation of public collectivities has changed since the mid-1970s, leading to budgetary limitations, including in health budgets. Since this period, it has also been realized that Switzerland is over-equipped in sophisticated and costly installations. This is the case especially for acute hospital beds, whereas nursing homes, home care, and lodging for the elderly are relatively lacking. Sensitization to the "health costs explosion," which has mobilized the energies of governments and social insurances, has caused the emergence of threats of "rationing" which occasionally give the impression that the health of the population is being endangered (Kleiber 1986). In fact, and not only in the health sector, structural changes in the economy cause politicians and planners to confront problems of distributing resources which no longer allow growth in all sectors.

The Swiss health services: unplanned, but effective

This chapter first argues that Switzerland enjoys a favourable health situation supported by a functioning health system, in spite of the absence of any real planning process. Economic prosperity has resulted in good health status indicators, and abundance and technological advances have led to high consumption of care and consumer satisfaction with services. It will be shown that this result is obtained at relatively high cost, with rather clear inefficiencies on the supply side (examples: physicians, hospitals, and medical technology). With the resources Switzerland has, it would certainly be possible to improve health outcomes.

Health outcomes: in the top league, yet inequalities remain

This country enjoys a health status, at least as measured by some of the crude indicators available today, that puts it among the top nations in the health league. A considerable reduction in infant mortality during this century and a low overall mortality rate have resulted in a life expectancy at birth that is now almost 73 years for males and 80 for females (see Table 1.2).

Table 1.2   *Switzerland: selected demographic and health data*

	Total	Female	Male
Population (in 1,000) (1.1.83)	6,423.1	3,294.3	3,128.8
over 65 years	890.8	534	356.8
	(13.9%)	(16.2%)	(11.4%)
Infant mortality			
(per 1,000 live births)			
1949–52		27.1	35.0
1979–82		7.1	9.2
Mortality rate			
(per 1,000 inhabitants)			
1949–52	10.1	9.7	10.9
1979–82	9.3	8.7	9.9
Life expectancy at birth 1950		72.6	67.7
1980		79.3	72.6
Life expectancy at age 65 1950		14.6	12.7
1980		18.3	14.4

However, there are still some major inequalities (Lehmann *et al.* 1987). Clear regional differences remain, for example in neonatal mortality (Ackermann *et al.* 1985), coronary heart disease death-rates (Wietlisbach and Gutzwiller 1984) as well as in the incidence and death-rates for certain types of cancer (Tuyns and Paccaud 1984; Tuyns *et al.* 1985).

The first mortality data according to socio-professional categories have recently become available (Minder *et al.* 1986) showing a life expectancy difference of about six years between lower and higher socio-economic categories among males, that is of the same order of magnitude as the difference between the sexes. The same mortality trends have also been observed for chronic illnesses in the under-50s (Lehmann *et al.* 1986; Bucher 1985; Haour-Knipe 1984). In addition, for certain risk factors such as smoking or overweight, there is a clear gradient according to social class.

Thus, even though the health situation of Switzerland is favorable, there remains a large potential for improvements, which depend not only on medical and health progress, but also – as in the past – on progress in social policy.

Subjective health indicators: use of health services and consumer satisfaction are both high

Table 1.3 gives an overview of the health status of the Swiss population as obtained, within the framework of the first Swiss health survey in 1981–3, by interviewing a national random sample of the resident population (4,255 interviews, participation rate 72.9 per cent) (Somipops Collaborative Group 1985; Gutzwiller *et al.* 1988).

Table 1.3 *Subjective health status of the Swiss population 1981/82 (4,255 interviews)*

		%
Subjective health	excellent	20.8
	good	63.5
	not particularly good	14.4
	bad	1.3
Physical health	impairment of well-being (previous 4 weeks)	82.4
	impairment of activity (previous 4 weeks)	13.7
	chronic impairment(s)	26.0
Mental health	impairment of psychic well-being (previous 4 weeks)	23.9

Although almost 85 per cent of those interviewed rated their own subjective health status as good or very good, 82 per cent indicated at the same time some impairment to their well-being during the weeks preceding the interview, and 13.7 per cent reported a reduction in their usual level of activity due to impaired health. For almost all indicators of subjective morbidity, and across all age groups, women scored higher, thus worse than men (Zemp *et al.* 1985). Finally, the health survey also defined some further socially disadvantaged groups: as an example, the rate of chronic impairments mentioned by workers with a low educational level was double the rate for highly educated professionals (Bucher 1985).

The same health survey indicated a high level in the use of

services; 80 per cent of the population, within a given year, have contact with a physician, with an average of six consultations per person per year. Women not only have a higher consultation and hospitalization rate, in part due to their reproductive history, but also consume more medications and have a higher rate of use of preventive services (see Table 1.4).

Table 1.4   *Use of health services, Switzerland 1981/83*

	Female	Male	Total
	%	%	%
Use of ambulatory services			
physician consultation(s) (12 months)	85.9	73.4	80.0
family physician consultation(s) (12 months)	68.2	63.6	66.0
visit to pharmacy (4 weeks)	31.4	24.2	28.4
Use of hospital services (12 months)	13.0	8.5	11.0
Medications – analgesics (7 days)	18.8	10.6	15.0
Use of preventive services (12 months)			
blood pressure measurement	76.6	67.1	72.2
PAP smear	41.7		

A sub-sample (n=443, 20–65 years old) was further investigated during the health survey and allows some inference (see Table 1.5) to be drawn about the degree of customers' satisfaction with their physicians (Buchmann *et al.* 1985).

Table 1.5   *Consumer satisfaction with physicians*

Very satisfied	29%
Satisfied	44%
No opinion	20%
Not satisfied	4%
Very dissatisfied	3%

Increase in costs: unchecked?

During the last decade, the debate on health policy has centered far more on increased costs, without producing any effective solution on cost containment, than on the health status of the population.

As a fact, costs for health services in Switzerland have grown faster over the last thirty years than the Gross National Product (GNP): whereas in 1960, 3.3 per cent of GNP went into health

services, in 1980 this figure was up to 7 per cent – an increase by
a factor of two in the fraction of GNP and by a factor of ten in
absolute numbers in twenty years (Table 1.6). Thus an ever-
increasing portion of the limited resources of society are invested
in health services. Currently total health care costs are an
estimated 18 billion Sfr or 7.8 per cent of GNP (1986).

Table 1.6   *Health services costs in Switzerland, 1950–82*

	in million Sfr	in % GNP
1950	560	2.8
1960	1,225	3.3
1970	4,404	5.0
1980	12,284	7.0
1982	14,577	7.1
1986 (estimated)	18,000	7.8

Source: Gygi and Frei 1982; 1985

In order to finance these expenditures, a whole series of
mechanisms are used. In fact the system has become so complex
that a clear view of the financial channels is not easily obtainable.
Basically 31 per cent of this expenditure is being paid for directly
by the consumer and private sources, 30 per cent by the different
social insurance carriers, and 39 per cent by communal,
cantonal, and federal taxes.

Although the problem of costs and deficits has generated
several approaches toward a solution to this problem, none of
them has provided the means to control the current evolution.

Since 1969 revision of the Federal legislation governing
sickness insurance has been demanded in order to extend the
coverage of services and balance socialized funding (Rapport de
la commission fédérale d'experts 1972). All the projects and
models presented since that date have failed, either during the
usual consultation process, or in parliament, or through referen-
dums in 1974 and 1987. The need to control costs and better
distribution of federal subsidies have been the main objectives
since 1981 (Conseil fédéral 1981), but also without success. Even
when it seemed that there is agreement on the minimum which
should be upwardly revised on an emergency basis, the parlia-
mentarians have not been able to come to an agreement (Bridel
1985; Häfliger 1983; 1986). Faced with the prospect of an
unchanging system that is hybrid (half social insurance, half
private insurance), costly, socially flawed, and state subsidized

according to out-of-date principles, several propositions have been made. Two popular initiatives have been handed in, one by the sickness funds and the other by the trade unions and socialist party, which demand that financing of the sickness insurance by the state and/or employers be increased. Other quarters suggest experimenting with a system similar to the Health Maintenance Organization in the United States and introducing more competition between the systems of health care reimbursement (Hauser 1984; Sommer 1987).

Simultaneously, the Federal government decided in 1976 to devote 6 million SFr to a ten-year national research program on the "Economy and effectiveness of the Swiss health system" (NRP8), the conclusions of which were published in 1986 (Sommer and Gutzwiller 1986). The research dealt with numerous aspects of the health care system; in particular, it showed that the financial mechanisms applied in the health domain at the moment are contrary to economical health care and favor behaviors which lead to costs increasing out of proportion. This is equally valid for consumers, hospital managers, the medical profession, and sickness funds.

Under the pressure of increasing expenditure, the various financing bodies seem to have one overriding concern: instead of re-examining priorities, resource allocation, and coordination of services, their concern is to increase their income, or at least not let expenditure increase even more. Accordingly, at the federal level, subsidies to sickness funds were, in 1978, frozen at the level of the 1976 subsidies. In 1981 they were further reduced by 5 per cent. At the same time, many cantons decided to increase the part of hospital costs to be paid by sickness insurances in order to reduce their part in covering hospital deficits.

Nevertheless, between 1966 and 1983, there was an annual average increase in costs per insured person of 11 per cent – much higher than the consumer price index (CPI) (4.5 per cent) or wages (6.8 per cent). Particularly great during that same period was the increase in the cost of hospital services. If the cost to the health insurances is indexed at 100 for 1966, in 1983 the index was at 874 for hospital services, 502 for ambulatory physician services, and 489 for medications (CPI: 213; wages: 308).

A part of this increase was passed on to the consumer whose (per capita) health insurance premiums have gone up steadily. In a system of this kind, controlling expenditure does not improve the cost/benefit ratio, and is generally a simple effort at transferring costs.

Moreover none of the current propositions for the reform of financing health services envisage reorienting financing in a way more judicious for the health of the population.

Increasing physician density: potential or threat?

Between 1960 and 1984 the number of physicians grew by 135 per cent to 18,124. The population, however, grew by only 18 per cent during the same period. Thus in 1984 Switzerland had one of the highest physician densities in the world: 355 inhabitants per active physician, and 729 per physician in private practice. The "big boom" still seems to be in front of us: currently there are 7,192 resident physicians in postgraduate training; in addition, every year over 800 new physicians obtain a license. Based on the students already in the educational system, the prognosis shown in Table 1.7 has been made.

Table 1.7 *Physician density 1960–2030*

Year	Inhabitants per active physician	Inhabitants per physician in private practice
1960	708	1,093
1970	700	1,138
1980	421	852
1984	355	729
Prognosis		
1990	320	520
2000	280	420
2010	250	360
2020	220	320
2030	200	290

Sources: Gilliand and Eichenberger 1981; Statistique 1984 des membres de la Fédération des médecins suisses 1986

The future will thus bring a further increase in the physician density with all its potential, but also dangers. These problems are well illustrated by a recent study made as part of the National Research Programme 8 (NRP8), "Economy and effectiveness of the Swiss health system." Based on a detailed analysis of data from the central body of the Swiss federation of sickness funds, this study showed the impact of an increasing physician density on the country over a six-year period (see Table 1.8).

Table 1.8 *Impact of a changing physician density, Switzerland*

	1982	± % since 1976
Inhabitants per practicing physician	769	−17
Annual number per 100 inhabitants		
home visits	19	+11
office visits	423	+52
Annual costs per inhabitant reimbursed by health insurance		
ambulatory physician care	208 SFr	+79
prescribed drugs	46 SFr	+64
total ambulatory care	254 SFr	+76

Source: Schmid 1985

Nobody has ever planned to double the number of physicians, or to increase the volume of services by 52 per cent. However, it has happened that way, and will probably happen again until some as yet undefined limit has been reached at some time in the future.

The increase in the number of physicians has not at this point been accompanied by a lowering in the quality of training, which however concentrates mainly on the fundamental and clinical sciences and does not prepare future physicians sufficiently for primary health care or community health. Almost all physicians, including family practitioners, follow five to eight years' postgraduate training and afterwards they remain in contact with the hospital and university structures.

One of the major issues of the future will be the extent to which an oversupply of physicians will lead to an overuse of certain procedures and therapies, and thus create new health hazards.

Hospital beds: too many?

Switzerland has one of the highest densities of hospital beds in the world: 12.7 beds per 1,000 population. As regards acute care, it has a capacity that is about 50 per cent higher (6–7 beds per 1,000 population) than countries with quite varied types of health services, as for example the United States, Canada, Britain, or Belgium. Swiss hospitals constitute a very decentralized network and taken as a whole have more than sufficient technical equipment. The average length of stay in acute care hospitals is 14.3 days (1980), twice the one in US hospitals (1979:

7.6 days). Besides some differences in the age structure of the populations, recent analyses have shown that this is in part due to long-term patients hospitalized in (expensive) acute care beds, although such hospitalization may lead to a loss of autonomy for chronically ill patients. In some regions of the country, the hospital physicians in charge estimated, as part of a bed census, that up to 25 per cent of patients on a given day did not need an acute care bed, but rather some other facility or assistance (Sommer *et al.* 1983). Thus an estimate of the "true" average length of stay for acute care hospitals is 10–12 days (Huguenin *et al.* 1986). In addition, the (over)supply of hospital beds has led to sub-optimal occupancy rates, particularly in certain geographic areas and services such as obstetrics/gynaecology and pediatrics.

Further estimates seem to indicate an overcapacity of about 12,000 acute care beds in Switzerland. The fact that the cantonal hospital planning concepts mention only a few hundred as over-capacity sheds light on the effectiveness of such planning documents.

The excess amount of resources invested in hospitals could be used more profitably in other health sectors, such as occupational health and health education, for which legislation and initiatives are insufficient.

Medical technology: planning after the fact?

During the last few years, the term "medical technology" has been used in many different ways. It is taken here as including all the "equipment, drugs, procedures and combinations of them used in health services for prevention, diagnosis and treatment of illness and for rehabilitation" (Chrzanowski and Gutzwiller 1986).

No country can bear economically the introduction and uncontrolled use of all new technologies. For most countries, it is imperative that priorities be set and a choice made. The way these choices are made, explicitly or implicitly, or are not made at all, are revealing for the way Swiss health services are organized.

In addition, a society has to answer ethical and social questions concerning the introduction of new technologies. Is the high cost of a new technology an argument against its introduction with public funds if the new method is of benefit to only a few patients? Should expensive technology, destined for small groups of patients, be installed if it means a reduction in resources for prevention, basic health care, or other social services? Who is authorized to decide these issues (Martin 1987a)? It is clear that many of these questions remain unanswered, while the health care system actually adopts technologies: a good case in point is the dramatic development in reproductive techniques (test tube babies, freezing of human embryos, etc.) (Gutzwiller 1985; Martin 1987b).

The need for a systematic approach to the problems of health care led, more than ten years ago, to the creation of two non-governmental institutions: the Swiss Hospital and Public Health Institute (SKI) and the Association of Swiss Hospitals (VESKA), both based in the city of Aarau. The Conference of Directors (Ministers) of Cantonal Health Departments calls on the SKI to study specific problems, among them new medical technologies, and to prepare recommendations.

During the last few years, the SKI prepared reports about computerized tomography (CAT), various expensive new diagnostic and therapeutic technologies, coronary artery bypass graft surgery, the treatment of urinary lithiasis using shock waves, and recently also magnetic resonance imaging (MRI) (SKI 1980; 1984).

In the case of both CAT and MRI, the need for determined numbers of diagnostic units was established but, in reality, those numbers were already surpassed at the time the reports were published. In other words, even though the cantons commissioned these reports, they circumvented the conclusions in many instances: the pressure of local interest groups, the competition among physicians and among hospitals often exerted greater influence.

Conclusion: outlook uncertain

Besides the factors that have already been discussed (demand for services, costs, physician density, hospitals, and technology), an additional major issue in shaping the future of the Swiss health care structure is the demographic development. According to indications from the Federal Statistical Office (*Annuaire statistique de la Suisse* 1985), there will be a slight growth in the population to 6.8 million until the year 2025. However, the proportion of inhabitants aged 65–79 will grow by 52 per cent and the proportion aged 80 and over by as much as 217 per cent, up to 351,000 persons. This will have a marked impact on the morbidity and care structure within Switzerland. Today, from age 60 and over onwards, there is a doubling of the number of days of care in geriatric institutions for every five-year age group.

In view of what has been argued here, namely that the Swiss health services perform relatively well, however at a high cost with clear signs of inefficiency, the prognosis as to the future is uncertain. Doubtless, however, costs will grow further owing to:

1 Demographic changes resulting in an ever-older population.
2 The high degree of utilization of services (already now).
3 The further-increasing physician density.
4 The technology revolution in health care that has only started and is not controlled.
5 The increased demand and expectations of a public partly stimulated by growing mass media attention.
6 The very structure of the Swiss health services, in which all (financial) incentives push towards expansion.

(Sommer and Gutzwiller 1986)

In order to face these challenges, the health policies in Switzerland require thorough reorientation: away from a concern with mere cost control and towards attaining clearly specified health goals in the context of an organized system. However, until now no signs of a major change have been apparent.

If ever this does occur, it remains to be seen to what extent changes in the health care system will improve the overall health of the Swiss population.

Note

1 Art. 24quinquies, 33, 69, and 69bis of the Constitution Fédérale de la Suisse for the OFSP; 34bis and 34quater for the OFAS; art. 34 and 34ter for the OFIAMT.

References

Ackermann-Liebrich, V., Romanens, M., Bisig, B., and Paccaud, F. (1985) *Geburtsgewicht und Säuglingssterblichkeit in der Schweiz 1979/81*, Bern: Bundesamt für Statistik, Beiträge zur Schweizerischen Statistik no 126.

Annuaire statistique de la Suisse (1981) Bern: Office fédéral de la statistique.

Annuaire suisse de science politique (1983) *Gouvernabilité*, Bern: Verlag Paul Haupt.

Bridel, D. (1985) "Les méandres de la politique sociale concernant l'assurance maladie," *Les Cahiers médico-sociaux* 29, 1: 21–30.

Bucher, H. (1985) *Gesundheit und soziale Ungleichheit in der Schweizer Bevölkerung*, Basel: Dissertation.

Buchmann, M., Karrer, D., and Meier, R. (1985) *Der Umgang mit Gesundheit und Krankheit im Alltag*, Bern/Stuttgart: Paul Haupt.

Chancellerie fédérale suisse (1984) *Les grandes lignes de la politique gouvernementale 1983–1987*, Bern: Chancellerie fédérale suisse.

Chevallaz, A. and Dubois, P. (1984) *La Suisse est-elle gouvernable?*, Lausanne: Editions de l'Aire.

Chrzanowski, R. and Gutzwiller, F. (1986) "The assessment of medical technologies. Examples from Switzerland," *Health Policy* 6: 45–55.

Conseil fédéral (1981) *Message sur la révision partielle de l'assurance-maladie*, Bern: Feuille Fédérale II: 1069ss.

Gebert, A.J. (1978) "Cooperative federalism or muddling through: the Swiss case," in C. Altenstetter (ed.) *Changing National–Subnational Relations in Health: Opportunities and Constraints*, Bethesda: Geographic Health Studies.

Gilliand, P. (1986) *Les défis de la santé. Les coûts et l'assurance*, Lausanne: Editions Réalités sociales.

Gilliand, P. and Eichenberger, P. (1981). "Démographie médicale en Suisse. Perspectives et projections à long terme," *Bulletin des médecins suisses* 62, 38: 2,743–55.

Güntert, B. and Hofer, M. (1983) *Die Institutionen des schweizerischen Gesundheitswesens*, vol. 20, Aarau: Schriftenreihe des SKI.

Gutzwiller, F. (1985) "Editorial. Technology assessment: Answers to all questions?" *International Journal of Health Care Technology* 1: 779–80.

Gutzwiller, F., Leu, R.E., Schulz, H.-R., and Zemp, E. (1988 in press) *Eine Schweizerische Gesundheitsbefragung (SOMIPOPS). Methoden zur Definition und Erfassung von Gesundheits- und Versorgungsindikatoren*, Bern/Toronto: Hans Huber.

Gygi, P. and Frei, A. (1976–84) *Das Schweizerische Gesundheitswesen*, Bern: Hans Huber; Basel: G. Krebs.

Häfliger, K. (1983) *Die Teilrevision der Krankenversicherung*, vol. 23, Aarau: Schriftenreihe des SKI.

—— (1986) *Die Teilrevision der Krankenversicherung*, vol. 35, 2nd edition, Aarau: Schriftenreihe des SKI.

Haour-Knipe, M. (1984) *The Health Burden of Social Inequalities in*

The Swiss health system

Switzerland, WHO Meeting on the Health Burden of Social Inequities, Copenhagen.
Hauser, H. (1984) *Mehr Wettbewerb in der Krankenversicherung. Voraussetzungen einer wettbewerblichen Reform der scheweizerischen Krankenversicherung*, vol. 8, Horgen: Schriftenreihe der SGGP.
Huguenin, M., Paccaud, F., and Gutzwiller, F. (1986) *Recensement des patients dans les hôpitaux, cliniques, établissements spécialisés et homes valaisans*, Lausanne: Institut Universitaire de médecine sociale et préventive.
Kleiber, C. (1986) "Faudra-t-il rationner les soins ou quelques réflexions à propos de la maîtrise des coûts," in P. Gilliand (ed.) *Les Défis de la santé. Les coûts et l'assurance*, Lausanne: Editions Réalités sociales.
Lehmann, Ph., Mamboury, C., and Minder, Ch.E. (1987) *Swiss Country Report on Social Inequality in Health*, WHO Meeting of Principal Investigators on Inequities in Health, Lisbon.
Lehmann, Ph., Martin, J., and Gutzwiller, F. (1986) "Inégalités sociales face à la santé et à la maladie: un sujet qui mérite études et réflexion en Suisse aussi," *Médecine et Hygiène* 44: 1,921–8.
Martin, J. (1987a) "Vers un rationnement des traitements onéreux? Acuité actuelle d'une problématique permanente," in J. Martin, *Pour la santé publique*, Lausanne: Editions Réalités sociales.
—— (1987b) "Procréation artificielle et santé publique," in J. Martin, *Pour la santé publique*, Lausanne: Editions Réalités sociales.
Minder, Ch.E., Beer, V., and Rehmann, R. (1986) "Sterblichkeitsunterschiede nach sozio-ökonomischen Gruppen in der Schweiz 1980: 15- bis 74 jährige Männer", *Médecine sociale et préventive* 31: 216–19.
Rapport de la commission fédérale d'experts chargée d'examiner un noveau régime d'assurance-maladie (1972), Berne: Chancellerie fédérale.
Rey, J. N. (1983) *Trop d'état?*, Lausanne: Editions Réalités sociales.
Schmid, H. (1985) *Datenanalyse in der Krankenversicherung, NFP8*, vol. 29, pts I–II, Aarau: Schriftenreihe des SKI.
SKI (1980) *Empfehlungen über den Bedarf und Betrieb der Scanner (CAT) in der Schweiz*, Bericht SKI-Arbeitsgruppe, Aarau: SKI.
—— (1984) *Entwicklung, Bedarf und Betrieb von Magnetic Resonance Imaging (MRI) und Magnetic Resonance Spectroscopy (MRS) Anlagen in der Schweiz*, Aarau: SKI.
Somipops Collaborative Group (Gutzwiller, F., Leu, R.E., Schulz, H.-R., Schroeter, R., and Zemp, E.) (1985) "The Swiss Health Survey (SOMIPOPS): An example of a data collection effort from various sources," *Sozial- und Präventivmedizin* 30: 76–9.
Sommer, J.H. (1987) *Das Malaise im Gesundheitswesen. Diagnose und Therapievorschläge*, Zurich: Orell Fussli.
Sommer, J.H. and Gutzwiller, F. (1986) *Wirtschaftlichkeit und Wirksamkeit im Schweizerischen Gesundheitswesen*, Bern/Stuttgart/Toronto: Hans Huber.
Sommer, J.H., Leu, R.E., Schaub, Th., Gutzwiller, F., Borner, S., and Frery, R.L. (1983) *Strukturanalyse des Gesundheitswesens von Basel-Stadt*, vol. 20, Diessenhofen: Verlag Ruegger, Basler Sozialökonomische Studien.

Statistique 1984 des membres de la Fédération des médecins suisses (1986) *Bulletin des médecins suisses* 67, 5: 176–86.

Tuyns, A. and Paccaud, F. (1984) *Geografische Verteilung der Krebssterblichkeit in der Schweiz*, Bern: Bundesamt für Statistik, Beiträge zur schweizerischen Statistik no. 119.

Tuyns, A., Levi, F., Raymond, L., Baumann, R.P., Enderlin, F., Schüler, G., and Torhorst, J. (1985) "Incidence des cancers en Suisse (1979–1981)," *Bulletin des médecins suisses* 66, 42: 1,900–6.

Wienke, U. (1985) *Gesundheits- und Krankenhausplanung in der Schweiz, Stand 1984*, vol. 28, Aarau: Schriftenreihe des SKI.

—— (1986) *Braucht die Schweiz eine Krankenhausplanung?*, vol. 32, Aarau: Schriftenreihe des SKI.

Wietlisbach, V. and Gutzwiller, F. (1984) "Mortalité cardio-vasculaire en Suisse: 1970 à 1986," *Médecine et Hygiène* 42: 430–4.

Zemp, E., Leu, R.E., Gutzwiller, F., and Doppmann, R.J. (1985) *Frauen und Gesundheit*, Bern: Eidg. Frauenkommission. Frauenfragen 8(3).

Two

Issues in the health services of the United States

Odin W. Anderson

I

Preamble

When the issues in the health services are examined across developed countries one is struck more by their similarities regardless of sources of funding, ownership, and organizational characteristics than by their differences. The differences are a matter of degree but vary enough along a continuum which can be explained by the historical, economic, political and social contexts from which the health services evolved. The continuing major difference between the United States and other developed countries is that all other countries now have some form of universal health insurance so that all people are assured rather complete personal health services with little or no cost at time of service. Another important difference is that universal health insurance is financed quite equitably so that the well-off are taxed more than the not so well-off in the population.

The health service in the United States is of interest because it lies at the extreme end of a continuum of what I call market plus to market minus, the United States being market plus. All developed countries in the liberal democratic orbit have a mixture of public–private ownership, sources of funding, range of services offered, and degrees of concepts of equality of cost sharing, distribution of facilities and access along this continuum. In the liberal–democratic orbit the health service in Britain represents the market minus extreme in the continuum with its highly structured system, mainly one source of funding, one entry point, the general practitioner, and complete range of professionally recognized health services and goods. If the socialist countries are included, the USSR is furthest out on the continuum from the United States.

What are the issues which are common to all developed countries? They can be listed in no particular rank order as financial, distributional, access, quality, equity, and organizational. All agree in principle on equality of access regardless of income, age, and residence; however, equality of access is difficult to define and they do vary considerably in their attainment of utopian objectives. No one claims to have attained these objectives, but all have hopes for improvements in some undefined future.

I will deal with each of these issues for the United States and try to show how they are products of the particular historical context in which its health services emerged and policies were formulated.

The historical socio-political crucible

After the Civil War in 1865 the American economy took off on a tremendous period of expansion of basic industries – from food production to steel and transportation – in a political philosophical environment of limited government. Government was for the purpose of maintaining law and order, and to control the currency, educate the public through high school, run the post office, and defend the country from foreign enemies. The political process was representative government, open and periodic elections, pressure group politics, and sovereignty of the people through elections. For those who could not cope with making a living because of unemployment or sickness, the young because of loss of parents, and the old because of inability to work and no savings, the local governments and private charity provided a subsistence level of living after passing a rigid means test. Medical care was among the items of subsistence.

Personal health services were regarded as a personal problem rather than a public one. During this period, however, communicable disease control, clean water, clean food, and sewage disposal were increasingly regarded as public problems because households could not manage these individually, thus the rise of public health departments.

At the same time that the United States was going through this tremendous economic and industrial development the personal health services – general hospitals, physicians, nurses, and pharmacies – also took off in response to antisepsis and anesthesiology, which made surgery relatively free from post-operative infections and relatively painless. Medicine tied itself to the rising interest in science and more and more specific disease entities were diagnosed with specific therapies.

Medical care therefore became costly. Hospitals were transformed from store houses for the indigent sick to institutions housing medical technology for everyone. The physicians were in fair abundance and those who were surgeons sought admission privileges for their private patients and in turn the physicians provided free care to the indigent sick. Later, general physicians also began to use the hospitals.

As stated earlier, personal health services were regarded as a personal problem (except for the very poor) and the public treasury was not thought of as a source of funding for the working population who were relatively self-sufficient. Still, there was some ambivalence in that personal health services were not regarded as an ordinary consumer good either like clothing, furniture, wagons, and horses. Physicians and hospitals should not be regarded as pure profit-making entities and services, but should serve all people who sought their services. Undoubtedly this objective was breached frequently but, nevertheless, the basic value was there. The method of accommodation to this ambivalence was the creation of the chartering of hospitals as non-profit service institutions governed by citizens' boards in community after community. They were exempt from taxes, had no stock-holders, and were obliged to provide some free care in order to earn their tax exempt status.

The capital to build the hospitals came from private philanthropists who were the new millionaires created by the enormous economic and industrial development before the First World War starting in 1914 in Europe. For example in 1860 there were 41 millionaires and in 1870, ten years later, there were 545! In addition there were countless local community fund drives to capitalize hospitals and make up the annual deficits for respectable deficits were the norm rather than embarrassing surpluses. By 1930 there were 6,700 hospitals, the overwhelming majority private non-profit hospitals. Fifty years earlier there were only 178 hospitals.

The rapid economic and industrial expansion mentioned perforce resulted in a fast-growing segment of consumers with discretionary income such as the world had never seen before – a mass consumer and mass production economy. This mass consumer economy was apparently able to support the daily operation of the hospitals and physicians with hardly any support from the public treasury. Other countries, except possibly Canada and Australia, have been unable to capitalize and sustain a personal health service of the magnitude of that of the United States. In fact the private non-profit sector in this country became the main-stream delivery system rather than an adjunct of the public system as in other countries. When government in the United States was mandated through legislation to cover the elderly (Medicare: 1965) and the poor (Medicaid: 1965) it had to buy services from the private non-profit system by bargaining. A seeming anomaly, however, is the health services system for war veterans presumably for service-connected disabilities funded and administered by the Federal Government through the Veterans Administration. This program, however, accounts for only 5 per cent of health services expenditure in the United States.

As personal health services became more expensive and costly episodes of illness increased, private insurance companies emerged to sell health insurance to employed groups beginning in the late 1930s. Eventually labor unions used health insurance as a bargaining chip for fringe benefits and in time the great majority of private health insurance was paid for by employers in lieu of wages. Even here there was ambivalence about profit companies because by volume about one-half of the health insurance is provided by non-profit companies. Non-profit companies claimed to be more community oriented than profit ones.

Concurrently with the growth in voluntary health insurance there was proposed legislation in the Congress from 1937 to 1952 for some type of national universal health insurance, but the Congress seemed never to consider universal health insurance seriously. As voluntary health insurance grew – covering 75 per cent of the population in 1965 – the issue of universal health insurance receded, exposing the remaining inadequately insured or uninsured, mainly the elderly, the poor, and the self-employed. Thus government insurance entered by the back door for elderly and poor people.

As has been mentioned the hospitals are owned largely by non-profit boards of directors as custodians. The physicians are free-standing private practitioners still mainly paid on a fee-for-service basis although there is a shift to salary or shared income in private group practices. Physicians and hospitals in the United States reflect the entrepreneurial culture of American business. Over time a high proportion of physicians in private practice organized their own groups to facilitate division of labor in specialization and joint ownership of medical technology and utilization of supporting personnel.

As can be inferred from the foregoing the US health services delivery system and its funding are very pluralistic. The private and public sectors are exceedingly intertwined through funding sources for daily operation and capital. These characteristics, of course, feed directly into the current problems and issues which I will now deal with categorically.

II

Introduction to major issues

Chronologically over the last one hundred years since the emergence of science-oriented medicine, issues have emerged more or less in the following order. At the beginning of the modern period (latter part of the nineteenth century) the major issue was the improvement in the quality of the physician through increasingly scientifically based medical education. The hospital became the physicians' workshop and rapidly reflected the improved training of the physician. Next was an issue of supply of hospital beds and admission privileges of physicians. A concurrent issue was the distribution of hospitals and physicians for relative ease of access. However, the economy and the population were expanding and moving so rapidly that distribution did not become an issue until the health services system came to full maturity by the 1930s.

Perhaps curiously I have not yet mentioned financial issues. It seems that funding for both capital expansion and day-to-day operation was sufficiently available from the sources mentioned so that supply was meeting effective demand, say, up to the 1930s. In the late 1930s effective demand without insurance became an issue for the broad middle income groups because of the rising costs of diagnosis and treatment. In that sense access became an issue, that is access without families becoming bankrupt. During the last ten years the financial issue is now the major one transcending all others.

By any sense of reasonable standards of equity, this issue was not given high priority by the body politic or the Congress and State Legislatures until the 1960s as expressed in the Medicare Act for the elderly and the Medicaid Act for the poor. Implicit, I believe, was the concept of equity or justice to provide for those who had little, a basic minimum as expressed in the two acts mentioned rather than completely fair shares of the existing supply as is quite explicit in the British National Health Service. In other countries it seems there has been an attempt to move from equity to equality, the latter a utopian objective, which other countries are reconsidering as a practical goal. The United States has never been politically willing to meet the equity issue head-on by universal health insurance.

Interestingly the issue of the organizational structure of the health services delivery system came relatively late (and also elsewhere). The free-standing hospital and the independent physician were accepted as a given first by the public, who paid directly for services as used, and later by industry and government. The payment mechanisms were grafted to the contemporary structure of the delivery system with little or no attempts to control volume or cost. Now, the organizational issue is a paramount one along with the financial one.

I will elaborate on these issues in the order in which they were mentioned as related chronologically to the development of the US health services.

Quality issues

The issue of quality is being raised again after having been taken more or less for granted from the 1930s to the 1970s. In the US context the issue is being raised again because the big buyers of services – the employers, insurance companies, and the government – riding hard on the continuing rising costs are now insisting that they get quality for price like buying an automobile or a television set. There are allegations of an excessive number of orders for laboratory tests or recommendations for "unnecessary" surgery or "unnecessary" hospital admissions and length of stay. The third party buyers of services, including the government, are also sensitive to allegations on the part of patients that they are being denied "necessary" services because of an obsessive concern, in their minds, of buyers with costs. Already there are Medicare patients who complain to their political representatives in Congress that they are being discharged from the hospital before they are well enough to leave in order to save money. The US funding and reimbursement system to providers enables the collection of records relating use to payments. Use is not buried in the general budget of a hospital or a physician's practice, for example, but clearly accounted for, an example of customary cost accounting in business. Employers seem to assume that quality control methods which are common to manufacturing industries could be applied to personal health services as well. The personal health services are responding in organized services like group practice prepayment plans by setting up methods to monitor physicians' practice to flush out the "outliers" those who appear to fall outside of usual practice patterns. The Federal Government in 1983 instituted what is known as Diagnostic Related Groups (DRGs) for controlling hospital costs for Medicare patients, to be described later.

These methods, and there are more, are still quite unthinkable in other countries with global budgets for hospital and physician services. The actors sort themselves out, as it were, within the global budget and make their own decisions within it. The physician's decisions are not intruded on directly. American business management methods are being applied in personal health services to an extent still unimaginable in other countries where professional prerogatives are so far a given. The American style is not conducive to overall social planning with clear structural boundaries and global budget caps. Its style is rather one of moving directly into the decision-making centers and now even for physicians.

Access issues

As alluded to briefly access issues did not surface until the late

1930s when it was felt by the broad, self-sufficient middle
income groups that episodes of illnesses had become so costly
that only the rich through their own resources and the poor
through government and philanthropy could get adequate care
without becoming bankrupt. Access to health services then
became regarded as a problem of insuring risks against large
medical bills which could be actuarially determined. The
response was the rapid growth of private health insurance
agencies, both non-profit and profit companies to meet this
apparent need, and potential demand like fire and life insurance.

The idea of legislating a government program of universal
health insurance was under political consideration from 1937 to
1952 during Democratic administrations, ending when the first
Republican president since 1932 was elected, General Eisenhower (of the Second World War). The Congress always
appeared ambivalent about universal health insurance and was so
split on the issue that the numerous bills proposed never reached
the floor for a vote. The ambivalence was based on the concept
of compulsory taxation for a personal responsibility and the
justifiable fear that health insurance would press hard on other
priorities of the Federal Government such as highways, social
security pensions, and the military. The policy was to keep
expenditures for personal health services in the private sector
balance sheet as much as possible. On the other hand, however,
elementary and high school education for every child was, and
is, regarded as a right, paid for by taxes, and attendance made
compulsory beginning during the latter nineteenth century. The
American value was to enable everybody to have an equal start
in life by education, but not necessarily equal results in the
income and job hierarchy. It took a long time to regard personal
health services as a public problem and this view continues in
various subtler forms.

In addition to the desire of the general public for some kind of
insurance to protect themselves from costly medical contingencies, hospitals were in dire economic circumstances during the
depression of the 1930s and could benefit from a steady income
from insurance payments. Interestingly enough, however,
health insurance for hospital services was not accepted readily by
hospitals and not even initiated by them but proposed by a
young leadership not directly connected with the hospitals.
Quite soon, nevertheless, the American Hospital Association

endorsed the concept after experience showed that non-profit hospital insurance was a viable concept for hospitals.

It can then be said that from the 1930s to the Medicare and Medicaid Acts passed by the Congress in 1965 access was regarded as a broad middle-income problem. Private health insurance, or rather the usual designation, voluntary health insurance, was regarded as an adequate solution to access, that is avoiding bankruptcy. The term "voluntary" was congenial to the American value of self-reliance through insurance without government compulsion. Still, given the ability of human nature to accommodate to contradictions, when the enrollment in health insurance as a fringe benefit was eventually made a condition of employment the issue of compulsion was not raised. Basically the foregoing actions were regarded as equitable in the American context until public consciousness somehow was raised to the realization that elderly and poor people were not sharing adequately in the expanding health services enterprise, and that voluntary health insurance was inherently incapable of covering the elderly, the poor, and the uninsured through marketing to employed groups because these sectors of the population were outside of the labor market and could not practically be included.

In so far as voluntary health insurance and Medicare were designed to protect households from acute short-term illnesses the problem of long-term illness and its financing has remained a severe problem. Voluntary health insurance and Medicare in an *ad hoc* fashion threw this problem to Medicaid which became responsible eventually for financing around 50 per cent or more of nursing home care, the balance coming from private sources of the patients who had the means. If the latter patients lived long enough they would eventually deplete their resources so that they were then eligible for Medicaid through the federal-state program. This is called the "spend-down" concept and is demeaning to people who have been self-sustaining all their lives.

Congress has recently enacted (1988) after long debate a so-called "catastrophic" addition to the Medicare Act which will soften the financial impact of very expensive and relatively long-drawn out costs of convalescing from acute illness. The costs of long term chronic illness leading to long stays in nursing homes e.g. to replace the means test through Medicaid are also under consideration, but was too big a leap for Congress to make at this time. It is pertinent, also, to observe that this "catastrophic" measure is completely financed within the Medicare population, an income transfer within the elderly age group. It is believed that there are now a large enough proportion of "affluent" elderly to help support the less affluent ones estimated at 40 per cent of the elderly. Thus there is no burden on the public budget.

Distributional issues

The US health services enterprise developed rapidly without let or hindrance funded mainly from the private sector. Up to the Medicare and Medicaid Acts funding from various levels of government – federal, state, local – amounted to less than 21 per cent (which included the Veteran's Administration). The number of hospital beds, physicians, nurses, dentists, pharmacists, and supporting personnel kept pace with the growth of the population. Naturally these facilities and personnel were not distributed more or less equally in relation to population clusters. There had been no overall planning, inherently impossible in the American context. The dynamo of the health services delivery system, the general hospital, was regarded as the most inequitably distributed for reasonable ease of access and for attracting physicians as well, particularly for rural areas. The agricultural lobby in the Congress was strong. The issue of distribution became politically viable right after the end of the Second World War in 1945.

During the depression in the 1930s and the war in the 1940s hospitals were neglected as to maintenance, improvements, and distribution. The early philanthropic sources of capital funding were drying up and capital had to come from other sources such as community fund drives, as a part of per diem charges, and loans. (The minority of government-owned hospitals were, of course, funded by taxation.)

The American answer, congenial to its private–public sector interrelationships, was a federal subsidy to hospital building or renovation for start-up costs to which local communities would match a certain per cent of the total cost. The legislative vehicle was the Hospital Survey and Construction Act of 1946 popularly known as Hill–Burton in honor of its sponsors. The result was a shot in the arm for hospital expansion in the United States with emphasis on rural areas to attract physicians. The major purpose was to buttress the voluntary hospitals. The Federal Government through general revenue contributed around 25 per cent of the total cost and the states and communities the balance. The Federal legislative strategy was to make a one-time contribution and then pull out so as not to be accused of interfering with local autonomy in the operation of the hospitals. The Act had multipartisan support from all relevant political pressure groups – labor, the American Hospital Association, American Public Health Association, and the American Medical Association. These pressure groups could agree on supply but not on universal health insurance to facilitate access. This Act was in effect for over twenty-five years. It accomplished its legislative purpose according to all observers, an unusual political achievement. Some retrospective critics felt that the Act stimulated the building of too many *small* hospitals in rural areas which could not equip or staff themselves for adequate hospital care as more and more technology emerged. As of 1946, however, and for quite a few years thereafter the original intent was carried out as of the state of the art at that time. Currently many relatively small rural hospitals are in jeopardy because of low-occupancy rates, low technology, and pressures for low rates from government and insurance companies. The larger hospitals are the magnets for referrals today, but still rural areas are reluctant to give up their hospitals.

During the three decades after the Second World War there were federal initiatives to increase the supply of personnel as well – physicians, dentists, nurses, pharmacists, and laboratory technicians by a variety of means – loans, scholarships, subsidies to educational institutions. There was a political consensus that there would be a shortage of personnel as well as hospital beds. The hope was that an increase in physicians, for example, would induce some of them at least to practice in rural areas. A particular method to induce graduating medical students to practice for a period in under-served areas and who had received loans for their costs of training was to write off a portion of their loans for each year in such practice. A large minority, incidentally, paid off their loans early and shortened their obligated service period. "Indenturing" physicians has not been successful by any reasonable standard. There is an economic assumption that an increase in the supply of physicians would force physicians to set up practice in the small cities and rural areas.

There is some evidence for this improved distribution, but inner cities and poor rural areas cannot inherently be well served without rather generous public subsidy, even then, high turn-over can be expected.

During this same long period there were attempts by the Federal Government through the Public Health Service to subsidize voluntary community hospital councils in order to get hospitals to work together in evolving a rational distribution of hospital beds and high medical technology. All of the major cities had such a council made up of hospital, medical, and citizen and consumer representatives. These councils were not particularly successful in terms of the objective of avoiding duplications but they did get communities to review their total hospital facilities.

Another federal government initiative was to hasten the distribution and application of new medical procedures for heart disease, cancer, and stroke by giving grants to medical schools to relate them systematically to practicing physicians in their areas. The methods of doing so were continuing education, consultations from medical schools, and possibly also some kind of affiliations with the medical school. This was known as the Regional Medical Program. All the foregoing was superseded by the Health Resources and Planning Act of 1974 but more of this under financial issues.

It should be evident from the foregoing that the many free-standing pressure group interests floating on an essentially private non-governmental delivery system and valued as such in the American historical context led to the seeming welter of measures to improve distribution. Effective distribution requires, it would seem, a large degree of mandated direction and financial incentives. Mandated direction is not conducive to the American political ethos hence the body politic settles for a comparatively low common denominator of a concept of equality and justice to which I now turn.

Equity issues

It would seem that the equity issue came to a head with the passage of the Medicare and Medicaid Acts of 1965. President Lyndon B. Johnson became president in 1963 following President Kennedy's assassination. The next five years opened a flood-gate of social welfare type legislation. Johnson declared "war on poverty." The employed segment of the population was in the main covered by voluntary health insurance. The poor had a wide variety of state programs with some subsidy from the federal government. They came to be regarded as largely inadequate. The elderly were in the main not in the labor force and the standard employer–employee health insurance could not or would not raise premiums to continue coverage for the increasing number of retired workers.

Universal health insurance for the elderly became a viable political issue with eventual bi-partisan support and that of the broad middle income groups as well. The euphoria of the "war on poverty" also included the poor, thus Medicaid. Medicare was conceived as a federally financed and administered program. Medicaid was conceived as a federal-state jointly financed program, but administered by the states. The states were given the option to participate or not, but all but Arizona came in because of the temptation of federal subsidy if the state complied with certain standards of range of services. The American Medical Association vigorously opposed Medicare because many elderly could not be classified as poor. The Association more or less went along with hospital services as long as physicians' services were not included. The Association supported Medicaid for the poor. By a brilliant political move the Congress then made physicians' insurance voluntary for the elderly but hospital insurance compulsory, thus retaining the voluntary character of American health insurance. As it turned out close to 95 per cent of the elderly applied for physicians' insurance, paying a large part of the cost directly. Medicare is financed by payroll deduction on the working population by both employer and employee. For Medicaid, the financing comes from federal and state general revenue, the states received subsidies on an average of 50 per cent of expenditures for a rather comprehensive range of benefits as mandated by the subsidy. By and large state programs for the poor were upgraded. These two programs, the poor and the elderly, and the 80 per cent or so of the population covered by voluntary health insurance muted the political issue drive of universal health insurance. Only around 10 per cent of the population for a variety of reasons remained without insurance. They were not a political force in an interested group political process. The poor through Medicaid rode the wave of greater equity despite their lack of political clout. The country was prosperous and general revenue was quite adequate. The poor and the elderly were to be integrated into the main stream of the American delivery system of free choice of physicians and hospitals. It was thereby hoped that there would be a one class system.

The euphoria of equality was short-lived as the general inflation of the economy affected the health services economy as well. The inflation in the health services economy was exceeding that of the general economy exacerbated by increased use by the elderly and the poor. It should be noted that the increased use by the elderly and poor was intended, but when the price tag for greater equity came in, the Federal and State governments were shocked. By the late 1970s methods to slow costs began to be applied and more and more financial controls were established. A fiscal policy replaced an equity policy, although the relevant decision makers disagree that equity has been jeopardized. They feel that there is so much fat in the health services delivery system that by squeezing out this fat a more efficient and equitable system will emerge. I now turn to financial issues and their management.

Financial issues

Only a few years after the enactment of the Medicare and Medicaid Acts the country began to enter a period of attempts at cost containment, not necessarily an absolute expenditure reduction but a slowing of the pace of increase which was the most realistic alternative possible. A few suggested that the expenditures for health services be tied to the rise in the GNP and no higher. This latter alternative was clearly unrealistic. The health services were then entering a period of as much direct management and control as possible – the "as possible" a very nebulous concept. Up to the early 1970s the unexpressed general policy had been "more"; now it was less expenditure at less volume but good quality and also care for the elderly, the chronically ill, and the under-served. Highest priority, however, was given to the acutely ill under Medicare for which this act was designed and became untouchable politically.

Attempts to control expenditure took several forms indicative of the complexity of the problem since no one method seemed to be sufficient; in fact they might be contradictory. Some controls were directed at the supply of hospital beds in order to stop their increase and gradually decrease them. There was a consensus that there was an oversupply of beds thus increasing the overall social costs of hospital-based services. Occupancy rates were falling as well. State after state passed so-called "certificate of need" laws to regulate the supply of hospital beds. Similarly state after state passed "rate review" laws to regulate the charges that hospitals made for their services, in other words price control. There were no similar controls on physician charges, although by the early 1980s the Federal Government simply froze the physicians' fees for Medicare and the states, in effect, did the same for Medicaid. Further, beginning in the early 1980s the Federal Government established around 467 Diagnostic Related Groups (DRGs) of diagnoses that were more or less similar in use of resources in order to set average length of stay standards and average cost per case. In effect, then, there were 467 budget caps rather than a negotiated cost plus retrospective global budget for each hospital for Medicare patients. If hospital costs exceeded the average national costs they or the patients had to pay the excess; if the cost was less hospitals could keep the surplus. Fiscal controls on the patients were also increased by charges at time of service to discourage "unnecessary" use. It is unlikely that the DRG method of cost containment will become permanent. It is a very complex and cumbersome method. At most it may be simplified. Hospitals are learning how to cost account by diagnosis. Possibly, as in Canada, there may be global budgeting for hospitals allowing a fair degree of internal budget allocation discretion. It is also likely that both physicians and hospital administrators will be using the quality imperative as a tactic to loosen the DRG method. There are already anecdotes in testimony before Congressional Committees of "premature" discharge of elderly patients.

The foregoing relates to the programs and populations mandated for services through the government sector from payroll taxes and general revenue. The private sector represented by business and industry which was contributing around 80 per cent of the costs of voluntary health insurance through labor – management fringe-benefit contracts was also aroused by the pressures on their payrolls and profit margins. Business and industry began to set up so-called coalitions for cost containment as bargaining agencies with the providers. It will be recalled in the private sector there are many buyers negotiating independently of each other – literally thousands throughout the nation – and coalitions might be helpful in driving hard bargains with providers to reduce their charges.

Still, regulation of supply and price, and freezing fees did not seem to keep the expenditures from rising either. There was an inherent cost expansion dynamism in personal health services transcending all attempts at whatever was regarded as "affordable," a term that now had wide use but not specified. One is assumed to know what "affordable" means.

Affordable implicitly got to mean what would be the market price where the classical concepts of supply and demand would cross. Whatever the consumers (and third party) thought they would be willing to pay if the health services would be provided by groups of physicians competing on price, quality, and convenience, an efficient delivery system would emerge according to classical market principles.

Thus in the early 1970s the concept of employers offering competitive options to their employees began to spread. Employers would offer several options from the main-stream system plus insurance to group practice prepayment. The employers would offer a flat percentage contribution of the premiums above which employees would pay out-of-pocket for more or less expensive health insurance plans depending on their preferences. The Federal Government also began to ask for bids from group practice prepayment plans (eventually being called Health Maintenance Organizations, HMOs) in order to reduce costs. (This is still in an experimental and developing stage.)

The much-touted advantage of the HMO type of health services delivery method is that there is a known group of physicians, a known supply of hospital beds under contract, a known population to be served, a known range of services guaranteed, and a known annual budget all under one management responsible for the whole enterprise and voluntary enrollment. The physicians, the dominant resource allocaters, are under risk as well as the management and thus have an incentive to prescribe services that are truly necessary rather than only questionably necessary or marginal. They compete with other health services plans for patients.

Currently roughly 12 per cent of the population of the country is enrolled in HMOs and the competitive option concept, but in local areas such as Minneapolis – St Paul there are penetrations up to 50 per cent of the health services market. Hospital use is falling, physicians are scrambling for participation in the HMOs or be left out, and expenditures were rising less rapidly but are accelerating again. (The foregoing is a brief and stark description of a competitive option concept and its current application which could fill a book.)

So, out of the pervasive entrepreneurial and competitive culture the United States is the only country which is trying out this concept in the health services, an enterprise usually regarded as not appropriate for the market place. American pragmatism seems, however, to want to try everything, and all at once. The existing combination of regulation of supply and prices and competition may, however, vitiate the possibility of really testing out the competitive option approach.

Organizational issues

Organizational issues became important as expenditures for personal health services rose rapidly. They thus are concurrent, and some allusion has already been made to them in the previous section. Still, organizational issues, that is how to deliver health services in order to carry out their health care mission efficiently and conveniently, have a long history in the development of the US health services.

It will be recalled that the dominant health services delivery pattern became the autonomous hospital charging on a per diem and per service basis and the autonomous physician charging fee-for-each service and obtaining hospital admission privileges. Until the 1930s this system functioned without health insurance, that is third party payor. When voluntary health insurance did emerge and later the enormous governmental programs of Medicare and Medicaid, this going system was taken as a given, the third party agencies simply paid the charges more or less as submitted.

Early on, however, mainly in the 1930s when voluntary health insurance was grafted on to this mainstream system, organizational innovations appeared in the form of physician group practice prepayment described earlier as HMOs. The group practice prepayment concept with salaried physicians was organized by consumer groups as cooperatives in various parts of the country, and later also by community boards such as the

Health Insurance Plan of Greater New York in 1946 and by industry backing such as Kaiser Permanente on the West Coast during the Second World War for the shipbuilding industry. Counter moves were made by county medical societies in the states of Washington and Oregon but physicians retained their own practices and were paid (and still are) fee-for-service with monitoring of physicians' profile characteristic of HMOs. The fee-for-service types are now called Independent Practice Associations (IPAs).

These organizations were an issue within the medical profession, the mainstream profession attacking them vigorously and on occasion venomously. They grew very slowly, however, not entirely due to medical opposition but also due to public indifference. Interestingly, *private* group practices organized and owned by physicians themselves without prepayment and charging fees grew quite rapidly among specialists. There was some hostility from the solo-fee-for-service practitioners (the great majority of physicians until after the Second World War) but this had no effect. After all private group practice was still private practice under medical control.

When costs became an issue both for the employers and government in the early 1970s the group practice prepayment type of delivery caught the attention of the big buyers of services as a means of controlling costs by competition between groups of physicians as described. For example in the early 1970s, the Nixon administration did not want to embrace universal health insurance as a method of controlling costs, fearing it was not possible anyway, and accepted the concept of competition, a concept congenial to the political position of that administration. In fact, an agency was set up to sponsor and stimulate the growth of HMOs through low-interest loans. This agency was supported with various degrees of enthusiasm right through the Carter administration and into the Reagan administration. It became attenuated as the years went on in that the HMO concept took off anyway as private lending agencies saw their growth possibilities. There are now over 600 HMOs of various types covering around 12 per cent of the population as cited earlier.

At the present time the organizational issue is no longer an issue. In fact the mainstream health services delivery system is on the defensive as more and more physicians join HMOs in order to maintain and protect their practice turfs. The US health services delivery system is restructuring itself into corporate arrangements which would take a book to describe. We are in an extremely dynamic era and it is difficult to predict what the system will look like after it reaches some kind of an equilibrium, as all systems must in due course, even temporarily. What is of interest in cross-national comparisons of health services delivery systems is that the US system has evolved with little government-directed planning and regulation. The changes have taken place by fiscal measures from both private and government buyers. In this sense it can be said the system has been reactive, but it would seem as the system began to react a momentum of change was set in motion so that it now appears to be more proactive than reactive. It is pertinent to observe that countries with universal health insurance and which therefore have been monopoly buyers of health services for at least two generations have had the effect of freezing the health services delivery system as of the time that universal health insurance was enacted. Accustomed bureaucratic patterns are not easy to change.

Overview

Given the review of the foregoing major issues present in all health services delivery systems of developed countries what appears to be distinctive in the United States? The primary one is the continued presence of the uninsured segment of the population estimated at over 10 per cent of the population plus the relative inadequacy of the insurance for another portion of the population (difficult to estimate depending on the criteria used). This condition is peculiar to the United States today, but not peculiar to the evolution of universal health insurance in all currently developed countries. All countries have started with segments of the population for inclusion under health insurance, usually the low-income employed segment and the unemployed poor being served by public welfare. Gradually other countries included the self-employed, and the farmers, segments normally difficult to cover operationally because of methods of tax collection and geography. In time all countries covered the entire population in some way or other assuring more or less equal services for all as far as payment was concerned. The distribution of services, another element of equity, remains a problem everywhere particularly in rural and remote areas.

The aversion to a single universal health insurance system in the United States has then led to an extremely incremental approach, comparatively, starting with the elderly and another system for the poor, or particular diseases like kidney disease for dialysis or transplants. The heart of the concept of coverage has been employed groups through labor–management fringe-benefit negotiations. Other segments of the population are approached as special problems around this core. Current concerns getting more public attention are the uninsured and those with long-term illnesses. Again, these segments are handled as special problems to be solved by special programs and financial arrangements without affecting the public treasury but to be done through employers, out-of-pocket expenses for insurance from individuals, and so on. The public treasury is politically untouchable. In the United States the issue is to contain the expansion of the public sector by relying on the private sector. Elsewhere it seems the issue is to contain the possible expansion of the private sector, and its assumed inequities, and maintain the status quo of the public sector and its assumed equity.

In its incremental way the United States is groping toward universal coverage without an overall universal governmental health insurance system made up of segments of the population with literally separate budgets, sources of finance, and programs, a layer cake, as it were, reflecting the occupational and social structure of US society. Currently cost containment is to be a combination of regulation of supply and price, competitive options facilitated by employers, and selected budget caps like the DRGs. Other countries are relying, so far, mainly on global budget caps.

The United States is trying to assure universality and equity without overall planning as is being attempted more and more in other countries. The Health Resources Planning Act of 1974 – signed into law by a Republican president, Gerald Ford, to set up a framework to contain supply and cost – is being dismantled. Planning attempts and methods in other countries can also fill a book, but so far they have not been overwhelmingly successful in their objectives. The usual complaints of the technocrats trying to make and apply plans is that politics get in the way. Indeed, what is planning but essentially a political process? Planning in the United States has become planning by separate giant medical complexes sparring for markets and turf with other complexes similar to business and industry. The volume and quality of health high-tech facilities equipment and personnel in the United States are the envy of the world, but we are not envied for our sense of equity in making them accessible. We may be trading off equity for innovation in delivery and cost and responding to a broad segment of the population with discretionary income. I have predicted that were the United States to embark on a truly universal health insurance system like the European countries and Canada, 40 per cent of the population would opt out for a private system to assure convenience of access and amenities which government in the United States and elsewhere seem incapable of providing for upper income groups wanting more than the standard but possibly medically adequate convenience and service. All countries are beginning to ponder the concept of a basic minimum of health services to be available to everyone, because a professionally prescribed standard for everyone is not regarded as "affordable" through taxation. The value question then arises: If all cannot have it should no one have it? In other countries the issue of "privatization," that is encouraging or at least tolerating the growth of private health insurance to take the pressure off the competing priorities placed on the public treasury, is emerging as a political issue.

References

Abernethy, D.S. and Pearson, D.A. (1979) *Regulating Hospital Costs: The Development of Public Policy*, Ann Arbor, Mich: AUPHA Press.

Aday, L.A., Fleming, G.V., and Andersen, R. (1984) *Access to Medical Care in the U.S.: Who Has It, Who Doesn't*, Chicago, Ill: Pluribus Press, University of Chicago, Center for Health Administration Studies, no. 32.

Anderson, O.W. (1972) *Health Care: Can There Be Equity? The United States, Sweden, and England*, New York: Wiley.

—— (1975) *Blue Cross Since 1929: Accountability and the Public Trust*, Cambridge, Mass: Ballinger.

—— (1985) *Health Services in the United States; A Growth Enterprise Since 1875*, Ann Arbor, Mich: Heath Administration Press.

Anderson, O.W. and Gevitz, N. (1983) "The general hospital: a social and historical perspective," in D. Mechanic (ed.) *Handbook of Health, Health Care, and the Health Professions*, New York: Free Press.

Anderson, O.W. and Shields, M.C. (1982) "Quality measure and control in physician decision making: state of the art," *Health Services Research* 17: 125–55.

Anderson, O.W., Herold, T.E., Butler, B.W., Kohrman, C.H., and Morrison, E.M. (1985) *HMO Development: Patterns and Prospects: A Comparative Analysis of HMOs*, Chicago, Ill: Pluribus Press, University of Chicago, Center for Health Administration Studies, no. 33

Brown, L.D. (1983) *Politics and Health Care Organizations: HMOs as Federal Policy*, Washington, DC: Brookings Institution.

Campion, F.D. (1984) *The AMA and U.S. Health Policy Since 1940*, Chicago, Ill: Chicago Reviews Press.

Corwin, E.H.L. (1946) *The American Hospital*, New York: Commonwealth Fund.

Dahl, R.A. and Lindblom, C.E. (1976) *Politics, Economics and Welfare; Planning and Politics–Economics Systems Resolved into Basic Social Processes*, Chicago, Ill: University Press.

Enthoven, A.C. (1980) *Health Plan: The Only Practical Solution to the Soaring Cost of Medical Care*, Reading, Minn: Addison-Wesley.

Falkson, J.L. (1980) *HMOs and the Politics of Health System Reform*, Chicago, Ill: American Hospital Association.

Feder, J., Halahan, J., and Marmor, T. (eds) (1980) *National Health Insurance: Conflicting Goals and Policies*, Washington, DC: Urban Institute.

Flexner, A. (1910) *Medical Education in the United States and Canada: A Report to the Carnegie Foundation for the Advancement of Teaching*, New York: Carnegie Foundation.

Hanghurst, C.C. (1982) *Deregulating the Health Care Industry; Planning for Competition*, Cambridge, Mass: Ballinger.

Hyman, H.H. (1975) *Health Planning: A Systematic Approach*, Germantown, Md: Aspen.

Institute of Medicine, Committee on Controlling the Supply of Short-Term General Hospitals (1976) *General Hospitals in The United States: A Policy Statement*, Publication IOM: 76–03, Washington, DC: National Academy of Sciences.

Lave, J.R. and Lave, L.B. (1974) *The Hospital Construction Act: An Evaluation of the Hill-Burton Program, 1948–1973*, Washington, DC: American Enterprise Institute for Public Policy Research.

Litman, T.J. and Robins, L.S. (1984) *Health Politics and Policy*, New York: Wiley.

Ludmerer, K.M. (1985) *Learning to Heal: The Development of American Medical Education*, New York: Basic Books.

Marmor, T.R. and Marmor, J.S. (1970) *The Politics of Medicare*, London: Routledge & Kegan Paul.

May, J. (1967) *Health Planning, Its Past and Potential*, Health Administration Perspectives no. A5, Chicago, Ill: Center for Health Administration Studies, Graduate School of Business, University of Chicago.

Newhouse, J.P. *et al.* (1982) "Where have all the doctors gone?", *Journal of the American Medical Association* 247: 2,392–6.

Raffel, M.W. (1985) *Comparative Health Systems: Descriptive Analysis of Fourteen National Health Systems*, University Park, PA: Pennsylvania State University Press.

Rosen, G. (1958) *A History of Public Health*, New York: MD Publications.

Shryock, R.H. (1948) *The Development of Modern Medicine: An Interpretation of the Social and Economic and Scientific Factors Involved*, London: Gollancz.

Smillie, W.G. (1955) *Public Health, Its Promise for the Future; A Chronicle of the Development of Public Health in the United States, 1707–1914*, New York: Macmillan.

Soltow, L. (1975) *Men and Wealth in the United States, 1850–1870*, New Haven, Conn: Yale University Press.

Starr, P. (1982) *The Social Transformation of American Medicine; The Rise of a Sovereign Profession and the Making of a Vast Industry*, New York: Basic Books.

Stevens, Robert and Stevens, Rosemary (1974) *Welfare Medicine in America: A Case Study of Medicaid*, New York: Free Press.

Stevens, Rosemary (1971) *American Medicine and the Public Interest*, New Haven, Conn: Yale University Press.

Sundquist, J.L. (1968) *Politics and Policy: The Eisenhower, Kennedy, and Johnson Years*, Washington, DC: Brookings Institution.

Weisbrod, B.A. (1977) *The Voluntary Nonprofit Sector: An Economic Analysis*, Toronto. Heath.

Part Two

Insurance/social security
health systems

Three

New Zealand health services

Marshall W. Raffel

New Zealand is a small country, and for most North Americans and Europeans it is literally at the other end of the earth, located in the south-west Pacific, one thousand miles south-east of Australia. Its 3.3 million people live on two main islands – the North Island and the South Island – separated by the Cook Strait. The land is comparable in size to the British Isles, running approximately 960 miles from north to south, its width varying but at its greatest point it is 270 miles wide.

It is for Europeans a relatively new country, the first white settlement occurring in the early nineteenth century, although there was already a Polynesian population there – the Maoris – for some 800 or 900 years prior to the white man's arrival. The population today is predominantly of European origin (85.8 per cent); 8.9 per cent are Maoris, and 2.8 per cent are more recent Polynesian immigrants from the nearby Pacific islands.

The South Island is slightly larger in size but its population is decreasing as more and more people move to the North Island with its slightly milder climate, greater urbanization, and economic opportunities. Approximately 73 per cent of the New Zealand population now resides on the North Island.

Its economy is overwhelmingly agricultural, its principal

exports being meat, dairy products, wool, fruits and vegetables, and wood products (*New Zealand Official Yearbook* 1985: 624); 70 per cent of its exports can be assigned to these categories. The significance of this is that New Zealand is heavily dependent on agricultural earnings to finance the purchase of cars, airplanes, machinery, oil, medical equipment, and so on. Nearly the same percentage of imports are for manufactured goods. When the price of wool falls or when its entrée to European or other markets for meat and dairy products is curtailed, New Zealand has less money to purchase needed manufactured goods and other essentials. As we shall see, this has considerable significance for the development of its health services.

Its health system, while influenced by and bearing many similarities to other developed nations, is organizationally an outgrowth of the country's history and social philosophy. New Zealand historian, Keith Sinclair (1959), put it this way:

> New Zealand's social security system was shaped by the ideal of equality; it made men more free. Only a fortunate country could have afforded it, but it was not merely a by-product of reviving prosperity. It was created by the general will – a will which had sought expression from the earliest days; . . . inspired, in the colonial period, by the humanitarianism of the missionaries and by the utilitarian creed, "the greatest good of the greatest number" . . .
>
> "Welfare" – "insulation" – meant the State. Perhaps that is the most striking feature of New Zealand's history. From the beginning the settlers have sought to achieve their aspirations through the medium of government activity. Farmers' governments or workers' governments alike have extended their sphere of action. Slumps and wars alike led to further centralization of power.
>
> (Sinclair 1959: 263, 265)

The benchmark for the present health system is the Social Security Act, 1938, introduced by the first Labour government, which held power initially from 1935 to 1949. As Henry Lang, former Secretary of Treasury, put it, the Labour government sought to "make hospital and other health services universally available to all New Zealanders in a publicly funded health care program with no direct charge to the patient" (Lang 1987: 143). In democratic societies – and New Zealand is one – what a political party sees as needed may not be fully accomplished even when it has a parliamentary majority. Compromises are made, and so they were in New Zealand. What emerged was a publicly financed hospital service providing in-patient and out-patient care by salaried specialists without direct charge to the patient. Hospital specialists, however, had the option of limited private practice in their private consulting rooms and in private hospitals, and could charge a fee for such care. There was to be no private care in public hospitals as is the case in British public hospitals. Primary care was to be provided by general practitioners (GPs) mostly on a fee-for-service basis with the government paying a portion of the fee.

Primary care

Over half of the GPs are in solo practice, and over one-third are in group practice (Mackay 1984: 424). The remainder practice in health centers run or subsidized by locally elected hospital boards. The prevailing mechanism for paying for care is fee-for-service except in a few special hardship areas (fifteen in 1984) where a salaried general practitioner service is available without direct charge to the patient. In 1986 GP fees fell in the $12–20 range, government paying only $1.25 of that amount. (All $ references are to New Zealand dollars.) The discrepancy between the doctor's charge and the government's General Medical Service (GMS) payment has been one of the principal stimuli for many taking out private health insurance, and it has also led to pressure from some medical practitioners for government to raise the payment because it was believed that costs were preventing some people from seeing the doctor when they should.

When the Social Security Act, 1938, was passed the medical profession vigorously fought the idea of a general practitioner service which could not charge the patient for service: the profession did not want government control over what it could charge. After some years of spirited negotiation, government gave in to the medical profession and agreed to pay 7s 6d (75 cents) for each patient visit. At the time (1941) this covered 75–100 per cent of the prevailing charge. Despite inflation no change in this payment occurred for thirty-one years when, in 1972, the payment was raised to $1.25 where it has remained, as of 1986, for fourteen years. In retrospect the medical profession could argue that this justifies the profession's reluctance and refusal to agree initially to a scheme whereby government payments would be accepted as full payment for their services. Conversely government could argue that since the profession was free to raise its fees, there was no reason or pressure for government to increase the GMS benefit unless the extra patient payments proved burdensome and/or deterred some from seeking medical advice, which is what some practitioners are now saying occurs.

Supportive of the medical profession's position is the experience of general practitioners who handle obstetric cases. Although there is a general practitioner agreement to accept the government payment as full payment for maternity services with the understanding that the government payment would be renegotiated periodically, some GPs feel that the renegotiation has not taken place as frequently as it should and that the current payment for obstetric care is much too low. One GP told the author that the payment for an obstetric visit is half what he charges for a regular office visit, and as a result he is cutting back on the number of obstetric cases he will handle.

The "saving grace" for the GPs in providing routine non-obstetric care has been their freedom to raise their fees as inflation took its toll on the economy, and raise them they did over the years to their current level. As fees rose, however, more and more people took out private health insurance, which covered 80 per cent of the portion not paid for by the government subsidy. In 1986 an estimated 40 per cent of the population had private health insurance.

There were, however, a few special adjustments in the above payment schedule. In 1969 when the GMS payment was 75 cents, government doubled the payment to $1.50 for beneficiaries (pensioners and their dependants). In 1972 when the GMS payment was raised to $1.25, a special payment of $2 was introduced for children, and the beneficiary allowance was also raised to this level. In 1974 the payment was increased to $3 for pensioners and children, and the chronically ill were also included to receive this added contribution towards the doctor's fee per consultation. In 1978 the payment was increased to $4.75 for children only. Lang (1987: 152) points out that during this period inflation was "reasonably substantial." In 1984 the Labour government proposed to raise the payment for children's

visits to $9.50 with some added adjustments for urgent consulta-
tions and home visits. This would be financed by a $1 per
prescription charge except for those under 16, beneficiaries, and
the chronically ill, and for the purchase of contraceptives. The
proposed added payment would be contingent on the doctors'
agreeing to limit their fees, to charge only a set amount for each
child's visit over and above the proposed payment. As in the
beginning, some forty-six years earlier, controversy with the
profession erupted and, as before, government capitulated by
agreeing to pay $10.25 per visit, and leaving doctors free to
charge whatever they wished but with a fee complaint mechanism for families who felt the additional doctor's charge excessive. The complaint mechanism "would comprise a Fees
Complaint Officer (a doctor) plus 2 other doctors and one lay
person nominated by the Minister in each of the 21 divisions of
the Medical Association" (Lang 1987: 153). Given the New
Zealand egalitarian social ethic which pervades the society,
including the medical profession, it would be rash – indeed,
unfair – to suggest that this mechanism is like having the fox
protect the chickens. What is perhaps the weakness of the
mechanism is its seeming failure to recognize that patients will
generally be reluctant to file complaints against a doctor with
whom they may feel they need to maintain a relationship.

Shortly after the above agreement, significant salary increases
were granted by government to doctors employed by the public
hospitals, leading some GPs to increase their usual charges
substantially. If this fee jump becomes universal, public pressure
on government to raise the regular GMS allowance of $1.25 is
likely to develop because the lower socio-economic population
will find the added cost inhibiting their access to care and the
more affluent will resent the added charges because of the likely
increase in private health insurance premium rates. Partial
payment of the doctor's fee by the patient can, of course, be an
effective and, many would say, an appropriate mechanism for
containing costs by deterring frivolous visits to the doctor such
as for conditions we would normally expect patients to deal with
on their own at home, the common cold for instance. The
experiences of insurance programs in the United States have
amply demonstrated that when full payment is made to the
doctor by the insurance policy, visits to the doctor are more
frequent and the costs of insurance considerably higher. But if
co-payments are too large they can deter a patient from seeing

the doctor when a visit ought to be made for sound medical reasons. The appropriate level of co-payment is, however, not easily decided upon. The sum might deter a low-income person, but not one with a higher income. If the co-payment is lowered to strike a better balance for the low-income person, the lower co-payment can be an inducement for the increased utilization by higher-income people. Thus the co-payment mechanism poses dilemmas not only for patients but also for insurers, and – in New Zealand – for government. The dilemmas are not easily resolved.

Securing access to care

When a New Zealander wants a medical consultation he or she normally goes to the general practitioner's office, though home visits by the GP sometimes occur. Some people seek primary care at the emergency department of the few urban hospitals which have staffed emergency rooms. As Joan Mackay (1984: 429) pointed out in her description of the New Zealand health system, the use of emergency rooms is common among recent Pacific island immigrants who customarily secured such care on the islands, and also by those who want to avoid paying a portion of the general practitioner's fee.

If treatment by the GP requires medication, the patient takes the prescription to a private pharmacy and, except in the cases cited earlier, a patient charge of $1 is now made and the government pays the balance. If the GP feels that further medical consultation is necessary the patient is referred to the hospital out-patient department where specialist consultation is provided without charge. The patient may prefer, however, to have a private consultation in which event the government will pay a specialist consultation benefit, the patient paying the balance of the specialist's charge. Emergency or urgently needed consultations are handled promptly but when not urgent there may be a delay at public hospital, the length of delay depending on the clinical department's workload, which is affected by the availability of clinicians, nurses, technicians, space, and equipment. The waiting list for consultation induces many patients to seek private consultation.

Where hospitalization is necessary the patient may be admitted to the public hospital where the care is provided without any direct charge to the patient, or the patient may elect to go to a private hospital where the patient will receive a hospital bill and a private doctor's bill. In private hospital, government pays a portion of the cost and the patient or patient's insurance covers the rest. Urgent cases are promptly admitted to public hospital, but when not urgent the patient may be put on a waiting list; the waiting time varies depending on the availability of beds, surgical theatre time, nurses, specialists, existing workload, and so on. As in many countries the waiting lists are most common in non-emergency surgical areas, and the waiting times may sometimes stretch to two years or longer. In the extreme, a patient may thus have a long wait for an out-patient consultation, and then another wait for admission to the hospital for treatment. This, along with the desire of many patients to have surgery when most convenient to them and/or to have a particular surgeon, has encouraged the development of private hospitals and of private health insurance.

As of 31 March 1984 there were 42,972 on the surgical waiting lists in New Zealand (*Hospital Management Data, Year Ended 31 March 1984*: Table 5). The clinical specialty breakdown illustrates the nature and extent of the blockage:

General surgery	9,278
Orthopaedic surgery	8,490
ENT surgery	8,462
Ophthalmology	3,380
Gynecology	5,468
Urology	2,191
Plastic surgery	4,449
Dental surgery	285
Neurosurgery	100
	42,103

That represents 1.3 per cent of the population (3,265,500) on that date, and the number also represents an increase of 7.2 per cent from the preceding year. Some of the people on the waiting list undoubtedly had their surgery performed in private hospitals, some perhaps died while waiting (probably from other conditions, because if the condition for which they were waiting deteriorated, they would have been moved into the hospital promptly), and a number – as Mackay notes – can be deleted for other reasons as, for example,

> a number of orthopaedic cases after a time refuse operation either because they have learned to live with their disability or have improved sufficiently to do so, and such outcome is frequently anticipated at the time their names are put on the list.
> (Mackay 1984: 430)

Notwithstanding, the size of the lists and their growth spotlight a problem and represent a forced rationing of care particularly for those who do not have private health insurance: rationing in the sense that access to non-emergency surgical care is parceled out in a democratic way, each waiting one's turn on the waiting list, putting up with decreased mobility or other inconvenience until the needed procedure can be fitted in to the hospital's schedule, a schedule affected by various kinds of shortages – personnel, equipment, space. There is no black market, no getting ahead of the line unless there is a deterioration in the patient's condition. But there is a white market, represented by the private hospitals. Thus patients may wait for public hospital care to avoid paying whereas others will pay for care in private hospital to avoid waiting.

Hospitals

For health services New Zealand is divided into twenty-nine hospital board areas and eighteen health districts. The hospital boards are elected by the people in their area, and each board is responsible for planning and managing all publicly owned institutional services in its area – general hospitals, mental and other special hospitals, and old people's homes. All finance, however, comes from the central government. Turnout for the hospital board elections is very small. The health districts, which are not conterminous with the hospital boards, are responsible for the traditional public health functions which normally fall under the heading of environmental protection and community prevention services. Voluntary agencies also play an important role in this area. Of particular note is the Plunket Society which provides most of the well-baby care with considerable subsidy from government. The district health offices are directly responsible to the central government's Department of Health. Current policy encourages, but does not require, hospital boards to merge with health districts to form area health boards, and to bring the non-governmental sector into the planning process. It is believed that by planning together through "service development groups", that is by the type of services to be provided (e.g. geriatric care, child care, specialty services, etc.), there will be improved coordination in the development and delivery of services, and that also with formal responsibility for community services these area health boards will be able to bring about a more appropriate allocation of resources between hospital and community services. Such efforts have been advocated in most countries in recent years, but seldom has the rhetoric been translated into the balance of expenditures between hospital and community services. As of mid-1986, three area health boards have been established.

It should be noted that while prevention activities can have a major impact on future health status, except in a few discrete areas such as accident prevention and immunizations, prevention does not have an immediate impact on the demand for medical care services nor does it deal effectively with the growing volume of chronic problems affecting the elderly, conditions which are costly to treat.

The hospital boards are products of history. Many serve small populations and were appropriate in earlier times when knowledge of clinical treatment was limited. However, getting the smaller boards to join other boards to make larger units more capable of providing for current needs has not been easy. Regional pride, and concern that their population will not be as well taken care of, have combined over the years to make a rationalization of the board areas extremely difficult. While many reasons can be, and are, advanced to eliminate the very small boards, there is some evidence – albeit fragmentary and anecdotal – which supports the hesitancy of local boards to change. One of the best examples occurred in England a few years ago: at one large hospital in the neonatal intensive care unit the registrar went to the senior consultant to say that the unit was full and yet there was a child who needed admission. At one point the consultant asked where the child was from, from the immediate area or outside? When told that the child was from the immediate area, the consultant said that the registrar should do all he can to find space for the child for it "would be disastrous" not to admit it. The message was clear: if you are from the immediate area you have a much better chance of securing access than if you are from the hinterland. Thus, those who resist joining forces with others to make larger, more efficient, and more effective units may indeed have that gut feeling that as good as the rationale is, they may be better off staying as they are and have more direct control over their health resources. It is worth noting that this is essentially the argument for local control which most developed countries are returning to after frustrations with central control. To be sure, *too* local can be *too* much, but compromise on the principle of local control needs stronger justification and assurance than is often given. Central control often evolved, it might be noted, because of local inability or unwillingness to carry out certain needed functions from lack of money, expertise, or will. As time and circumstances changed, however, and as it became feasible for local units to resume responsibility, central authorities often resisted, for bureaucracies tend not to give up power without a struggle. Facilitating the decentralization process in many countries today is recognition by central authorities that they are unable to solve some of the local problems they thought initially that they could solve, and hence there is an increased willingness to redelegate to the local units. This is not meant to suggest that reducing the number of hospital boards in New Zealand isn't a good idea but rather that resistance of some boards to integration is based on more personal concerns and cannot be overcome simply by verbal assurances.

As of 31 March 1984 New Zealand public hospitals had 12,853 acute, general hospital beds (*Hospital Management Data, Year Ended 31 March 1984*: Tables 3 and 4). These and other beds were distributed as follows:

Surgery	4,801
Medicine	4,280
Pediatrics	1,601
Maternity	2,171
	12,853
Geriatrics, long–term	2,974

Assessment and rehabilitation	642
Rehabilitation	207
Psychopaedic (child psychiatry)	2,837
Psychiatric	5,361
Frail ambulant	909
	12,930
Grand Total:	25,783

Private hospital beds came to 5,809, and were distributed as follows:

Surgery	1,232
Medicine	205
Maternity	44
Geriatric	4,319
Psychiatric	9
	5,809

As noted earlier, money for operating the public institutions in New Zealand is given to each board by the central government. Until recently each board's allocation was "largely the result of historical accident and political pressures from local areas on central government" (Lang 1987: 151). This did not always take into account the changing age structure of the board's population, the movements of people to other areas, or the need for, and efficient use of, new technology. A new mechanism was introduced in the 1980s to allocate money on a formula basis which would take into account these and other factors. New Zealand thus decided to follow the British example of adjusting its regional allocations by what is believed to be a more equitable, population-based funding formula. The process, as in Britain, is both controversial and – for some boards – painful. For the 1981–2 year, for example, if the formula had been implemented that early, Auckland would have received a 7.8 per cent increase in its budget; the capital city board of Wellington would have had a 10.8 per cent budget decrease; and the South Island's city of Dunedin where the nation's first medical school is located, would have a budget decreased by 15.5 per cent

(Hyslop *et al*. 1983). To minimize the pain, the formula is being implemented in stages so as to lessen the fiscal impact on the boards which are slated to lose money.

The significance of this new funding mechanism can be readily seen. Wellington, for example, will not have enough money to replace equipment, to take advantage of new technological advances, or to increase its staff. It is also closing hospital wards which the board chairperson said would result in fewer operations being performed, and thus a lengthening of the surgical waiting list (personal interview 1985). In Dunedin a decreasing population and now a decreasing budget raise serious questions as to the ability of the hospital board to maintain the medical school hospital and to sustain its level of clinical expertise given the high cost technological requirements necessitated by modern medical education processes. (There are presently two medical schools in New Zealand – in Dunedin and in Auckland, and two clinical schools – in Christchurch and in Wellington – that provide clinical training for students from the other two schools. The medical education process is similar to that in Britain.) In addition to the in-patient services, hospital boards also provide a range of out-patient services, and some community domiciliary services.

Private hospitals

Private hospitals represent an important component on the New Zealand health scene. Government provides these institutions with a subsidy: of $26.50 a day for surgical care, $20.50 for medical (including psychiatric) treatment, $25.50 a day for geriatric treatment and long-stay medical cases, and $28.50 a day for maternity cases in 1984 (*New Zealand Official Yearbook* 1985: 171). In addition, government will sometimes provide loan money toward the construction or renovation of private hospitals (*New Zealand Official Yearbook* 1985: 180). Without private hospitals government would be forced to spend considerably more in the health sector. Approximately 10.3 per cent of the nation's 14,334 general acute beds (including maternity beds) are in private hospitals, and these private beds are used overwhelmingly for non-emergency surgery – hip replacements, hernias, coronary by-passes, and so on (*Hospital Manage-*

ment Data, Year Ended 31 March 1984: Table 4). According to a spokesperson for the Private Hospital Association, 23.2 per cent of all hospital operations in New Zeäland are done in a private hospital. This represents 31.3 per cent of all hip replacements, 29.5 per cent of all transurethral prostatectomies, 70.5 per cent of the vasectomies, 73.6 per cent of the semilunar knee cartilage excisions, and 40.9 per cent of the inguinal hernia repairs (personal interview 1985). Many of the orthopedic and hernia cases were paid for by the Accident Compensation Corporation which is discussed later. The private hospital, to be sure, weakens the commitment to equality by providing a way out for those who can pay. On the other hand, as I have pointed elsewhere (Raffel, 1984: 597 600), an equalitarian approach with no outlet for those who can pay can also be unjust. There is no simple answer to this except to note two things. First, no country has been able to provide economically or politically a fully equitable service; compromises on the ideal have always had to be made, and the ability of some to use their money has proved to be an essential part of social equity. Second, without a private sector it is difficult to maintain excellence in the public sector for it is the challenge of a competing system which keeps each in a state of excellence.

Without these private beds, the surgical waiting lists to public hospitals would be much longer, and the resultant pressure much greater on government to do something about them. The private general hospital thus represents a political safety valve for government, reducing pressure for increased public expenditures while drawing to the health sector additional community monies without resort to taxation.

Most of the private, acute hospitals are small, and voluntary or church sponsored. The classification of private hospitals in New Zealand is, however, somewhat inexact so that one has to be careful in looking at the data on these institutions. The imprecision stems from the fact that the category of "private hospital" covers 170 such institutions with some 5,809 beds. However, as noted earlier, only 25.5 per cent of those beds are acute hospital beds. The rest are nearly all in geriatric, long-stay institutions. Some of these latter hospitals are also voluntary or church sponsored, but most are for-profit institutions. Few, if any, specialists devote their full time to private practice. Care in private hospitals is instead provided by public hospital doctors when not on public hospital duty.

Geriatric long-term care

As in the United States, the private sector dominates the field of long-term institutional care: hospital boards have 2,974 geriatric, long-term care beds whereas private hospitals have 4,319 beds or 59 per cent of all geriatric beds. Nearly all of the private beds are in the private hospital classification. For government to pay for long-term care in a private institution, the patient must first go through an A&R (Assessment and Rehabilitation) review to determine the need for such care as against the potential for rehabilitation or need simply for a rest home. If rehabilitation is appropriate an A&R unit will provide or coordinate it. If a rest home (a home which does not provide nursing care) is appropriate, then the patient goes to one of the 909 frail ambulant beds in public hospital, or to a rest or residential home run by some voluntary or other private agency. If the patient can manage at home with some support services, those services are provided by the hospital board, the district health office, or by a private agency. The hospital and/or district office will often pay for all or part of the private agency services depending on the patient's income.

Community services

One finds in New Zealand basically the same range and variety of services as one finds in most developed countries. As in other countries, whether the services are publicly or privately owned will vary as will the manner of payment for these services, though when provided by public bodies there is generally no direct charge to the patient.

Being a relatively small country it should be noted that services tend to be well coordinated, for to a remarkable degree in each community or city, everyone knows each other.

Accident Compensation Corporation (ACC)

New Zealand introduced in 1974 a scheme to deal with accidents of all kinds – work, highway, playground, home, and so on. Its "basic premise," in the words of former Prime Minister Sir Wallace Rowling, "is that the laying of blame, or determination of fault, is often a time wasting exercise which delays an adequate resolution of the victim's problems. This premise arises from a fundamental philosophy of community responsibility" (Rowling 1987: 140). One should not interpret this as simply another social welfare program, for at its base was the conviction that, as Rowling put it, "it makes absolute sense to ensure an early and healthy return of an accident victim to full and productive participation in the workforce, if this is at all possible." All New Zealanders, as well as visitors to the country, are protected by this program.

Under this program the Accident Compensation Corporation provides compensation for earning losses and dependent allowances for permanent physical disabilities. Although public hospital treatments are provided without charge, the ACC will pay medical, hospital, dental, and rehabilitation expenses for treatment in the private sector if public sector care cannot be secured promptly. The moneys are not part of the health budget but rather come from a separate line item appropriation, supplemented by levies on employers on a risk-related scale and on motor vehicles. Hospital boards are not pleased with the refusal of the ACC to pay for accident care in public institutions. If the wait for public hospital admission is longer than three months for someone who has filed a claim with the ACC, the ACC will approve care in private hospital. In 1983-4 the payments by the ACC for medical expenses represented close to 4 per cent of what the Department of Health spent for similar services.

The economics behind health

Britain in 1950 was New Zealand's chief trading partner, taking 66 per cent of its exports (*New Zealand Official Yearbook* 1985: 610). But the sword of Damocles was over New Zealand, and it fell with Britain's entrée to the European Community with the consequent obligations to the Community, and New Zealand's preferential trade arrangements with Britain began to decline. By 1984 Britain accounted for only 13 per cent of New Zealand's exports. New or enlarged markets for its agricultural products had to be found, and they were – in the Middle East, Asia (especially Japan), the United States, and Australia. In some instances formal trade restrictions existed and had to be overcome. US trade is a case in point where "trade is circumscribed by various quantitative restrictions imposed on beef, mutton, veal, and dairy products" (*New Zealand Official Yearbook* 1985: 608). In the search for new markets, New Zealand had its good years and its bad years, and along with the impact of world market price fluctuations on its exports, its purchases abroad were affected. The nation had frequent balance of payment crises with accompanying feasts and famines on the import of manufactured goods, with feasts in recent years maintained by heavy borrowing on the international money markets. The *New Zealand Official Yearbook* (1985: 758) records what is at least a ten-year high for its external debt.

Rowling (1987: 139) noted that "In New Zealand we seem to have a habit, every thirty or forty years, of picking up our society, putting it under the microscope and evolving new policies to replace those which have become inequitable or inefficient." And the time came again in 1984 with an Economic Summit Conference to which was invited the leadership from all sections of the New Zealand community. Lang quotes from the briefing paper prepared for that conference:

> Over the last twenty years, New Zealand's economic performance has been poor and deteriorating. There are four main measures of economic success which, provided income is fairly distributed, give an indication of economic well-being. The measures are: the rate of economic growth (which determines the standard of living), the level of unemployment, the rate of inflation, and the balance of payments. These have improved from time to time in New Zealand over the last two decades, but by and large the picture has been one of steady deterioration (Lang, 1987: 145).

Lang goes on to say:

> The major conclusion of the Conference was that improved economic performance required a willingness to accept much more rapid change, to adjust to a changing world environment and to take on the risk of the international market place. This required a consistent policy framework that encompasses all the interrelated elements of the economy instead of addressing one objective at a time.
> The Government's policy in the 18 months since the Con-

ference has involved major changes. From being one of the most regulated and restricted economies, New Zealand is rapidly turning into one of the most free. Controls on financial institutions have been substantially abolished; exchange controls have been eliminated and the exchange rate is allowed to float freely; subsidies to farming and other industries are being quickly phased out, as are quantitative restrictions on imports; taxes are being restructured and social welfare benefits revised to target more adequately towards need. Policy is made within a coherent framework based on the view that the market provides better signals and information than a bunch of bureaucrats. The process is of course not painless. In the short run the farming industry which was the basis of an export oriented economy is facing major difficulties; the economic boomlet of the last year or so is turning into mild recession while the adjustments for more economic growth in the future are made. However, it is clear that substantial improvement in our economic performance cannot be expected in the short term and this has obvious implications for the constraint that government is under generally and in the field of health care in particular.

To lend credence to this economic forecast he notes that unemployment in March 1984 was up to 4 per cent in a nation accustomed to 1 per cent, and that consumer prices for the year had risen 13 per cent.

The new government policies referred to by Lang were instituted by the newly elected (1984) Labour government which has become one of the most conservative governments in terms of economic policy in recent history. The government began to institute policies reflecting the prevailing view that "government spending has been too fast and that the aim should be to reduce growth sufficiently to bring about a decline in the share of the public sector relative to the national product" (New Zealand Planning Council 1979, quoted by Lang 1987: 146).

Cost control/containment

When belt-tightening was necessary the health sector could and did adjust by slowing down its investment in new technology, replacement of aging equipment, and maintenance. These have been time-honored practices in New Zealand when resources are scarce, as they are in other countries, but in recent years these practices have intensified. Hospital boards, for example, "were required to accept a 1-per cent reduction in their allocation of funds in 1979–80, 1980–81, and again in 1981–82" (*New Zealand Official Yearbook* 1985: 178). The subsequent population-based funding formula also contributed to some budget difficulties at some hospital boards, particularly cutting heavily into three of the four largest population areas – Dunedin with its medical school (15.5 per cent budget reduction initially projected), Wellington with its clinical school (11.8 per cent), and Christchurch with its clinical school a more moderate reduction (1.1 per cent) (Hyslop *et al.* 1983: 160). These budget cuts under the formula are particularly severe because these urban center teaching hospitals get many referrals from other hospital boards, generally the more complicated and more expensive cases to treat but the payment by the sending hospital board is the receiving board's average per diem cost, not its actual cost. Thus the boards centered in Dunedin, Christchurch, and Wellington are forced to subsidize the care provided to patients from the outlying boards. The aging of the equipment and the inability or difficulty in securing replacements, not to mention the latest advanced technology, are the cause of considerable professional dissatisfaction. While there is an appreciation for the nation's economic plight, the frustration of many medical doctors over their inability to meet the health needs of the population in the best professional manner has become acute.

People need motivation. For some it is money. For others it is the work environment – the collegiality, the physical surroundings, the life-style one is able to maintain. Professional people, while responding to these factors in varying degrees, often tend to be more concerned with professional satisfaction. What seems to be occurring in New Zealand is growing professional dissatisfaction due in large part to the scarcity of resources, and some exodus – particularly to Australia where the professional climate is more hospitable and the pay considerably higher. Loss of just one or two specialists in some areas can create havoc, impacting the entire health system: in a recent visit, a senior health administrator expressed considerable frustration on hearing that very day that in one important specialty area two of the four doctors in New Zealand were leaving for Australia. While salary scales can and are sometimes adjusted, New Zealand can ill afford to match doctors' salaries common in Australia and the United States because to do so would create such enormous salary discrepancies *vis-à-vis* the rest of society that it would be socially and politically unacceptable. However, in interviews with surgeons and various medical specialists, including some who are moving and others who contemplate it, professional dissatisfaction appeared to be the dominant reason. Factors contributing to this dissatisfaction were: nurses are in short supply, equipment may not be available, scarcity of up-to-date equipment in hospitals, needed support medical specialists frequently not available, and facilities are not adequate.

The nurse shortage stems from the fact that nursing is still a low paying profession at the very time when women have greater opportunities in other fields for which the rewards are higher, and from the fact that hospital training programs are being phased out and replaced by more academically oriented programs in technical colleges and universities which have lower enrollment capacities. Doctors are thus frustrated when they are unable to work at full capacity because procedures are limited and beds closed due to the shortage of nurses.

CT scans illustrate the equipment problem. New Zealand in 1985 had seven scanners – six in public hospitals, one in a private hospital. The waiting time for a scan in one urban center was reported as being fourteen weeks, and up to two years in another center. This can be frustrating to the doctor who believes that a scan would be diagnostically desirable, particularly if it obviates the need for a more risky invasive procedure. Exacerbating the situation is the shortage of radiologists, positions going unfilled because there are no suitable applicants. In many of the specialties the applicants come from overseas. The New Zealand positions are often unattractive because they pay less than for comparable posts in other countries, an important factor in the eyes of those who are not familiar with New Zealand, and the doctors quickly recognize that they will not oftentimes have the latest equipment available to them. The New Zealander going overseas for advanced training, however, may not be as concerned about the salary because he or she is familiar and comfortable with the New Zealand life-style, and hence would be more inclined to focus attention on the professional climate. One hospital board administrator lamented the training of New Zealanders in the United States because of the type of equipment they become accustomed to, which – he felt – New Zealand could not afford given its limited resources for medical technology.

Equipment maintenance and replacement were cited by a number of specialists: since budgets are being cut, maintenance is one of the first items on which expenditures are deferred. Radiologists, and those who depend upon radiologic procedures, are a case in point.

Along with equipment goes the availability of adequate facilities, be that a bed shortage in certain specialties or a persistent shortage of operating theater time for a surgeon. All these factors have both short- and long-term implications for patient care. On the short-term basis non-emergency surgical waiting lists get longer, and some patients do not have access to some types of care. The wait for a CT scan, for example, can skew the diagnostic process toward invasive diagnostic work which can sometimes be more expensive and also place the patient at greater risk. As one radiologist put it, if there is a long wait for a CT scan, the doctor may elect to do a reticulogram which is both more costly and of greater discomfort for the patient. Also, as doctors become aware of the long waiting time for diagnostic and treatment procedures, they may encourage private care or advise the patients to live with their problems. The latter was the case in Britain with regard to renal dialysis for patients over 55 (Aaron and Schwartz 1984). Rationing of dialysis in Britain, of course, means an earlier patient death, although it must be borne in mind that for many of these elderly patients, given their medical complications, dialysis may or may not prolong life but – if prolonged – it may be a life of markedly decreased quality.

Cost considerations almost certainly have had an effect on renal care in New Zealand. The treatment rates in New Zealand are less than those of most European countries. In 1983 the New Zealand rate was twenty-eight per million, a drop from previous years and the lowest since 1979 (Disney 1984). The age of patients is also of interest. In Australia, for example, 22 per cent of the patients were in the 60–79 age group whereas in New Zealand only 12 per cent were in that group. There is reason to believe on the basis of such data and from discussions with doctors that patients in New Zealand over age 70 are not normally accepted for dialysis, though each case is reportedly evaluated on an individual basis. If those over age 70 were handled more frequently as is the case in many European and

North American countries, the rate in New Zealand would rise from twenty-eight to over forty per million – at least a 43 per cent increase. That would have of course an enormous cost impact since it was estimated that to train and maintain a patient on home dialysis costs $20,000 a year. In 1983 there were 335 patients on dialysis at an annual cost of $6.7 million. A 43 per cent increase would raise the outlay to at least $9.6 million, a significant sum for a nation of 3.3 million people. The current rate of dialysis is able to be sustained because of a predominant reliance on continuous ambulatory peritoneal dialysis (CAPD) which is carried on outside of the hospital. In at least one urban center CAPD is used almost exclusively. Also, it is believed that many GPs do not refer cases knowing, as in Britain, that certain types of cases are not likely to be accepted. A third factor is that some GPs are reported to be reluctant to refer cases likely to end up on home dialysis because they are reluctant to handle the follow up on what many believe to be very difficult cases. Finally, "the painful prescription" is necessitated by renal specialists and referring doctors because of the limited capacity for dialysis mandated by the available resources: additional moneys must come from the hospital board's budget and yet in New Zealand four out of the five boards which provide dialysis are slated for budget cuts. Those boards, moreover, have other pressing needs to consider, such as facilities for the elderly, new equipment and maintenance of existing equipment, new operating theaters, additional specialists to work off the backlog of surgical cases, and so on. Hard choices have to be made and there is no objective way to make them which will prevent dispute. Consequently hospital boards tend, as do our legislatures, to spread the resources – a little here, a little there, put out a fire somewhere else. This contributes to social harmony by defusing pressures from those who demand everything at the cost of denying resources to others.

In cardiac surgery, only those cases urgently requiring coronary by-pass surgery are placed on the waiting list (Lawrie 1984). In the three public hospital cardiac surgical units, cardiac operations of all types were performed at an overall rate of 41.2 per 100,000 population in 1983. This rate also includes those cases handled in the then one private hospital cardiac unit. At the end of the year, 485 people were waiting for cardiac surgery. All but three of those patients were waiting for public hospital. Of the 485, almost half had waited less than three months, but 54 persons had been waiting at least one year, including 28 for over two years (*Cardiac Surgery 1983 Registrations* nd). But, an unknown number of patients were not on the public hospital waiting list for by-pass surgery because they did not meet the criterion of urgency, though they might have been appropriate candidates for surgery under more liberal criteria. In one unit the number of operations performed each week was reportedly below capacity largely because of a lack of support staff.

To relieve the situation with regard to cardiac surgery, there are now two private hospital cardiac surgical units – one in Auckland, and a newer one in Wellington. One can surmise, however, not only that the long waiting list keeps some patients off the public hospital waiting list who could benefit in terms of improved quality of life from surgery but also that the cost of private care will deter some patients from seeking it if they do not have private health insurance.

The long-term effect on New Zealand of these cutbacks is that the nation will lose some of the highly trained specialists that it will need in the future. Moreover, as it allows its physical plant to deteriorate through deferred maintenance, and as it fails to acquire new technology it will fall further and further behind. With an aging population with their orthopedic, ophthal-mologic, and other chronic conditions, many of which are amenable to treatment, the crisis in New Zealand will get more critical. John Campbell (1987: 188) notes that from 1981 to the year 2001 the number of persons over 60 years of age will increase 33 per cent, from 445,800 to 593,600; but more critical is that those over 80 years of age – the group which is particularly dependent – will double from 53,892 to 107,100.

Health status of the population

Despite the economic constraints on the health system, the health of the New Zealand population is very good. Although it spends less on health than most other developed countries, its health profile is similar in large part due to its socio-economic status. It is a well educated, comfortably housed nation with high public and environmental health standards, and a long-standing egalitarian tradition.

New Zealand is affected by the same major diseases as the rest of the developed world. Its principal causes of death in 1982 per 100,000 population were: heart disease (27.3), malignant neoplasms (179.8), cerebrovascular disease (88.2), accidents (45.3), and pneumonia (33.5) (*New Zealand Official Yearbook* 1985: 141). Its infant mortality rate was 13 per 1,000 live births in 1980 which was comparable to West Germany (12.7), the United States (12.5), and England (12), but considerably higher than the Scandinavian countries whose rates ranged from 6.9 to 8.4 (*New Zealand Official Yearbook* 1984: 140; Raffel 1984: 245, 319, 570). In 1982, the New Zealand rate was down to 12 (*New Zealand Official Yearbook* 1985: 144).

The Maori population has a poorer health profile than the rest of the New Zealanders. The death-rate for Maoris overall is nearly double that of non-Maoris. "Maori deaths from asthma, obesity, cancer (except bowel), renal disease and diabetes are all well in excess" of the non-Maori population (Durie 1987: 201). The Maori infant mortality rate in 1982 was 19 compared to the non-Maori rate of 11 (*New Zealand Official Yearbook* 1985: 144). A variety of factors contribute to the lower health status of the Maori, only some of which have been identified. However, improving Maori health is a high priority for the government as is evidenced by its financial support, including its willingness to support Maori-initiated health programs that differ from traditional western-style health services.

Conclusion

The budget crunch is real. New Zealand has discovered, along with every other developed country, that in today's world it is not economically feasible for any state to provide the highest quality of health care to all people in a timely manner. As Lang (1987: 146) noted,

> there is . . . and always will be some scope for making health care delivery within a given volume of resources more effective but the scope for this is not enough to enable New Zealanders to take advantage of the continual technological developments.

Choices have to be made, and the choices in publicly funded programs are particularly difficult in democratic societies for they translate into some form of politically mandated health care rationing: denial of care – and sometimes thereby shortening life – waiting for care, or charging for care.

New Zealand is fortunate that its strong public sector has had a mitigating safety valve in the private sector. But there is a limit. The private sector is no longer permitted to expand at will without coordination with the resources in the public sector. The private sector in the past proved to be a challenging force on the public sector, and it is *challenge* that brings forth innovative solutions to problems as well as keeping the skills sharp of those in the competitive game.

None the less, the very presence of the private sector is a moderating force which gives New Zealand *time* as the economic pressures force a change in society's expectations of the role of the state in health care. The economic pressures are most keenly felt because of New Zealand's precarious economic position in the world where its earnings, primarily from agricultural products, make the nation dependent on the vagaries of world market conditions, affecting the nation's ability to pay for the importation of manufactured goods, including medical technology, and of its ability to retain highly skilled personnel. There is an increasing acceptance in New Zealand of the view that the general principles underlying the entire social security system must be reappraised and a new overall health policy developed that will meet the current financial and social needs of the country.

Happily, New Zealand's political parties are not so ideologically bound that they cannot adapt to the exigencies of the changing world. The Labour government, though egalitarian in principle (as are the other parties) and the originator of key social welfare programs in the country, is changing its course, not abandoning the spirit of social democracy and equality, but rather showing a willingness to modify its social and economic policies to meet the needs of the present day. In March 1986 a Royal Commission on Social Policy was appointed and in announcing its appointment the Prime Minister noted that "there is a substantial and growing evidence that the social services do not serve the purposes for which they were intended or meet the expectations which the community has of them now" (quoted by Lang 1987: 148). After noting the shortcomings of current policies he concluded:

> All must be remedied. None of them ultimately can be remedied by a piecemeal approach, or by an approach which leaves vested interests undisturbed. What is required is a

thoroughgoing assessment of the principles on which social policy is based.

The Royal Commission will presumably address the desirability of establishing a new comprehensive national health policy, which many feel is necessary. But acceptance and implementation of a new policy is fraught with difficulties. The necessity for economic constraint which limits the amount, type, and quality of health care, and the importance of retaining highly skilled professionals, are issues which will not be easily resolved either in the formulation or implementation of a new policy because there will be the inevitable tradeoffs to which all parties will have to be reconciled. There will be the temptation to handle some of the more difficult problems through incremental changes, by adjustments here and there, to try to balance the scene until better days or solutions arrive, as was done in the recent attempt to raise the GMS allowance for child care. Historically this has been the near-universal style of democratic governments as they sought to balance conflicting interests to maintain domestic peace, if not harmony. A governor of Pennsylvania illustrated this approach when he said, "I don't solve problems; I handle them!"

Whatever proposals come from the Royal Commission, politicians will need to be courageous enough to disturb, if necessary, vested interests and not yield to a piecemeal approach that will not solve the basic problems, and skilfull enough to build a strong national consensus if there is to be major change. Without a strong national consensus in support of new policy proposals, they will be politically unacceptable, and the piecemeal approach will have to continue as on most occasions in the past when incremental, piecemeal steps were the only realistic game in town.

New Zealand, a small nation with its relative affluence and high educational level, is once again presented with one of those rare opportunities to make a successful great leap forward, as it has done on several occasions in its history.

References

Aaron, A.J. and Schwartz, W.B. (1984) *The Painful Prescription*, Washington, DC: Brookings Institution.

Campbell, J. (1987) "Implications of health policy for the elderly in New Zealand," in M.W. Raffel and N.K. Raffel (eds) *Perspectives on Health Policy: Australia, New Zealand, United States*, Chichester: Wiley.

Cardiac Surgery 1983 Registrations (nd) Wellington: Department of Health.

Disney, A.P.S. (1984) *Seventh Report of the Australian and New Zealand Dialysis and Transplant Registry (ANZDATA)*, Woodville, South Australia: Queen Elizabeth Hospital.

Durie, M.H. (1987) "Maori health: contemporary issues and responses," in M.W. Raffel and N.K. Raffel (eds) *Perspectives on Health Policy: Australia, New Zealand, United States*, Chichester: Wiley.

Hospital Management Data, Year Ended 31 March 1984 (1984) Wellington: Department of Health.

Hyslop, J., Dowland, J., and Hickling, J. (1983) *Health Facts New Zealand*, Wellington: Department of Health.

Lang, H. (1987) "Health policy formulation in New Zealand," in M.W. Raffel and N.K. Raffel (eds) *Perspectives on Health Policy: Australia, New Zealand, United States*, Chichester: Wiley.

Lawrie, T. (1984) *Review of Waiting List Management Processes*, Department of Health, Wellington (unpublished).

Mackay, B.J. (1984) "Health services in New Zealand," in M.W. Raffel (ed.) *Comparative Health Systems*, University Park, Pa, and London: Pennsylvania State University Press.

New Zealand Official Yearbook (1984) Wellington: Government Printer.
—— (1985) Wellington: Government Printer.

New Zealand Planning Council (1979) *The Welfare State? Social Policy in the 1980s*, Wellington: New Zealand Planning Council.

Raffel, M.W. (1984) *Comparative Health Systems*, University Park, Pa, and London: Pennsylvania State University Press.

Rowling, W. (1987) "Accident compensation corporation," in M.W. Raffel and N.K. Raffel (eds) *Perspectives on Health Policy: Australia, New Zealand, United States*, Chichester: Wiley.

Sinclair, K. (1959) *A History of New Zealand*, Harmondsworth: Penguin.

Four

Health care and the
Japanese state

William E. Steslicke

As they look to the future, the Japanese people have a long and colorful past upon which to reflect – both in joy and sorrow! A strong sense of their own history is a basic component of contemporary Japanese consciousness and the intermingling of past and present seems to pervade the daily lives of the people. However, it is not so much stories of the past as the spinning of future scenarios that has aroused greatest popular interest and concern during the 1980s (Social Policy Bureau, Economic Planning Agency 1982). A growing awareness of having reached a critical turning-point in modern Japanese history has also affected public policy discussions in various sectors of society including health and medical care. Clearly the Japanese state is unlikely to "wither away" in the coming decades, but the form, style, and content of state intervention is likely to change in response to the changing domestic and international environment of the 1990s and beyond.[1] Since the Meiji Restoration of 1868, Japanese national government officials have played a major role in shaping the way in which health care services have been organized and delivered (Steslicke 1972; Saguchi 1985). As in other sectors, they have been strongly influenced by western models, especially German, British, and American. Unfortunately Japanese public policy-makers no longer have the kinds of road maps to lead them into the twenty-first century that were available to their predecessors (Steslicke 1982a). As noted by one elite group of futurists:

> Over a period of about 100 years since the Meiji Restoration, Japan has followed the model provided by the West in order to attain the objective of catching up with the advanced Western countries. Under the present circumstances, however, Japan can no longer find any models to follow outside the country, but has to create on its own a new life style best suited to its nature, climate, history and society.
> (Subcommittee on the Long-Term Projection, Economic Welfare Council 1979: 3–4)

The point has been repeated often during the 1980s and it seems to be the premise for most serious discussions of the future role of the Japanese state. What the state should or should not do with respect to the creation of a "new life-style" best suited to Japanese circumstances is being hotly debated in the health care community as well as in other public policy sectors. Although they continue to be avid observers of foreign experiences, it seems widely accepted that "Japan must take a renewed look at its existing systems and customs, work out new mechanisms, and steadily build up its social environment in order to realize a society comfortable for the people to live in" (Long-Term Outlook Committee, Economic Council 1983: 179).

Recent economic and demographic developments have given special urgency to the reexamination of health care organization and delivery in the 1980s (Tominaga 1983; Ogawa 1982). Of course, the past has provided a frame of reference for such reexamination and Japanese public policy-makers realize that the existing system has served the nation admirably since the end of the Second World War. Moreover, the existing pattern of policies and programs enjoy considerable popular support and serve as a constraint that must be taken into account. Nevertheless, it is apparent that responsible national government officials are determined not to follow the path of "business-as-usual" into the 1990s and beyond (JICWELS 1983). Japan's changing domestic and international economic position as well as the pressures of a rapidly aging society dictate basic re-examination of health care organizations, delivery, and financing (Steslicke

1982b). As in other sectors, health policy-makers are being urged to exploit the "vitality of the private sector" as a mechanism for change. Even so, it remains widely accepted that state intervention and guidance should continue to play an important role in the creation of a new "Japanese-style welfare state."[2]

The context of health policy in the 1980s

As Japan entered the 1980s, its economic performance remained outstanding. Although the "economic miracle" and the era of 10 per cent annual growth of the 1960s and early 1970s had ended, Japan managed to survive the oil-price and other economic shocks of the 1970s and to remain competitive in the international market-place. According to one authoritative assessment of Japan's comparative economic performance prepared by the Organization for Economic Cooperation and Development (OECD), it was "at or near the top for 1983" (OECD 1984: 1). The assessment was graphically stated as follows:

> As a rough indicator of economic performance, OECD's economists use a diamond-like object . . . which links four points representing rises in GNP, productivity (GDP/ employment), consumer prices . . . and the unemployment rate . . . The bigger and more regular the diamond, the better. Japan has the best diamond among the six largest countries.
>
> (OECD 1984: 1)

The combination of high GDP and productivity and low inflation and unemployment was not attributed to new economic miracles. Rather, the OECD analysts concluded:

> The key to this performance in the face of adversity seems to hinge on Japan's resilience, its ability to adapt its economy to change, whatever the source – oil shocks, increased competition from newly industrializing countries (NICs), new market opportunities (products and countries) as well as new dead-ends, changing exchange rates and terms of trade and even, perhaps, protectionism.
>
> (OECD 1984: 5)

As one might expect of a nation with the "best diamond," the general standard of well-being enjoyed by the Japanese people was at or near the top of OECD members in the early 1980s. That included health status. Successful economic performance and improved health status seem to go hand-in-hand (WHO 1980; Abel-Smith 1976). In terms of commonly accepted indicators, the Japanese state-of-health in the early 1980s was among the highest in the world. For example the estimated life expectancy at birth in 1945 for males was 23.9 years and for females 37.5 years. By 1980, the average life expectancy for males had increased to 73.32 years and for females to 78.83 years. The figures were the highest in the world in 1980. Japan continued as "Number One" in that regard in 1984 as the life expectancy for males increased to 74.54 years and 80.18 years for females (Kosei Tokei Kyokai 1985: 79). Among the lowest in the world in 1980 was Japan's infant mortality rate of 7.5 per 1,000 births (down from 90.0 in 1940 and 76.7 in 1947). Other health statistics also indicate that a virtual "health miracle" has taken place since the Second World War in Japan (Steslicke 1987).

It should be noted that national surveys suggest that Japanese citizens place a very high priority on good health and access to medical services. For example, in a survey conducted by the Economic Planning Agency in 1981, 35.3 per cent of the national sample selected health and medical care as the top priority "at present and in the future" (Economic Planning Agency 1981). More than 80 per cent included health and medical care among their top five priorities. More recent surveys indicate similar findings. In brief, it appears that the Japanese people have attained a relatively high level of well-being and that they expect to live long and healthy lives. Such expectations must be taken into account by those who seek to establish and implement national priorities (Steslicke 1982c, 1988).

One of two persons born in 1980 could expect to live to 80 years of age. However, in that year 722,792 Japanese died of various causes. The fluctuation in the death rate per 1,000 persons between 1955 and 1980 was slight (from 7.8 to 6.2 per 1,000 persons), but the age distribution changed markedly. Of 690,000 deaths in 1955, 17.3 per cent were 14 years of age or below. By 1980, the ratio dropped to 2.9 per cent, and there was a corresponding decrease in the mortality rate in those aged 15 to 64 over the same period from 38.6 per cent to 27.5 per cent.

Thus by 1980, 69.6 per cent of the deaths were among persons 65 years or older, as compared with 44.1 per cent in 1955. This drastically changed distribution reflects demographic changes in Japanese society as well as the sharp decrease in infant mortality and in tuberculosis-related deaths in people aged between 15 and 64.

With respect to causes of death in contemporary Japan, there has been a remarkable increase in the so-called "adult diseases" (cerebrovascular disease, hypertensive disease, neoplasms, heart disease, and cirrhosis of the liver), especially of cancer, heart disease, and cirrhosis of the liver. Between 1960 and 1980 cerebrovascular and hypertensive disease as causes of death increased by 8.1 per cent and 5.3 per cent respectively – but cancer deaths increased by 72.4 per cent, heart disease by 80.5 per cent and cirrhosis of the liver by 81.6 per cent. In 1982 cancer became the leading cause of death in Japan and accounted for about 24 per cent of all deaths. As a result, there have been increased efforts at education and screening as well as research and training of specialists funded both publicly and privately. As noted by one observer:

> Japan has declared war on cancer. In the past, Japanese health authorities have concentrated on detecting and treating cancer in its earliest stages. Now, emboldened by recent advances in molecular biology, the Japanese are taking the offensive. In April 1984, the government launched a 10-year cancer programme, commonly known as the Nakasone project after its initiator, the Prime Minister, Yasuhiro Nakasone. The goal is to clarify the mechanisms of carcinogenesis – the biological processes that lead to cancer – by spending more money on research and by trying just a little bit harder.
>
> (Johnstone 1985: 30)

Responsibility for implementation of the "Comprehensive 10 Year Strategy for Cancer Control" has been assigned to a special Cabinet Council for Cancer Countermeasures that includes the Ministry of Health and Welfare, the Ministry of Education, Science and Culture, and the Science and Technology Agency. National government ministries in Japan are not noted for their interdepartmental cooperation and "departmentalism" is regarded as a serious problem by Japanese political scientists (Tsuji 1984: 6–7). Moreover, it is unusual for a Japanese prime minister personally to promote a health-related program. In keeping with recent trends, the Japanese "war on cancer" also has an *international* dimension centered on interchange of information and researchers between the National Cancer Center of Japan and the National Cancer Center of the United States. While it is too early to evaluate this ambitious cancer control strategy, it provides one illustration of Japan's "resilience" in the health policy arena ("in the face of adversity" to paraphrase the previously mentioned OECD report). Given the economic and demographic context of the 1980s and the emerging pattern of health and sickness within the population, health policy-makers will need to demonstrate that kind of resilience and determination in other cases. As stated in the most recent of Japan's national economic and social plans of August 1983 titled *Outlook and Guidelines for the Economy and Society in the 1980s*:

> With the aging of the population, the change in the disease structure and the progress in medical science, great changes are occurring in the environment surrounding health and medical care, and the demand for health and medical services is increasing and diversifying. Under these circumstances, it is important to provide the people with necessary health and medical services adapted to these changes, intensively and efficiently.
>
> (Economic Planning Agency 1983: 67)

Japan's national planners, *circa* 1983, in keeping with the "indicative" nature of their task (Steslicke 1982b), went on to suggest a health policy agenda as follows:

> the Government will encourage the people to build up their health throughout their life cycle, while promoting health service projects for the elderly, and organize an integrated system for providing health and medical services including prevention and rehabilitation. Research on cancer, now the number-one cause of death in Japan, will be promoted to find out the true nature of the disease, and research results will be used to prevent, diagnose and cure the disease. The measures for rationalization on both the demand and supply will be taken to keep the growth in the nation's medical expenditure, now growing faster than the national income, within proper limits, so that the medical costs will not unduly strain the

national economy. It is necessary to review the way the
medical insurance system is coordinated, while rationalizing
benefits and contributions, reforming National Health Insurance System and Day-Laborer's Health Insurance System
whose financial foundations are weak, and studying the
establishment of the retirees' medical system.

(Economic Planning Agency 1983: 67)

Before taking ¿ closer look at this health policy agenda, it is
necessary to examine the organization of the Japanese state and
the nature of governmental intervention in the health sector
since the Second World War. It will be seen that a wide range of
groups and individuals enjoy access to public policy-making
circles and that a kind of "limited pluralism" tends to prevail
(Fukui 1972; 1977; Steslicke 1982c). However, health policy-
makinᵣ 's also a top-down enterprise that is constrained by
prioritiᵤs articulated by Japan's political–economic–administrative elite.

The health policy-making process

Although the bulk of personal health services are provided
through the private sector in contemporary Japan, the system is
subject to a wide range of state interventions related to
organization, delivery, and financing.[3] The legitimacy of state
intervention is widely accepted even though specific interventions may be highly controversial. The frequency and intensity
of controversy have been high during the 1980s and it is unlikely
that policy-makers will encounter greater tranquility in the near
future. The issues are complex and the stakes are high.
Organized interest groups are alert and aggressive, and ordinary
Japanese citizens display a growing sense of entitlement to
accessible, high quality, and relatively inexpensive medical care.
As in other OECD countries, Japanese medical care has become
highly politicized.

Also as in other OECD countries, public health services in
Japan have been provided by government agencies at national,
prefectural, and local levels. The privatization movement has
had little impact on such services and the increased governmental activity is relatively non-controversial. Japan is divided
into forty-seven prefectures, which are further subdivided into

cities, towns, and villages. Within these units, public health services are provided through a network of health centers in accordance with the Health Center Law of 1947. All prefectures and thirty larger municipal governments are required to establish and maintain health centers on the basis of one health center per 100,000 persons. In 1980 the actual rate was one per 136,000 persons and a total of 855 health centers were in operation staffed by health professionals, most of whom have received advanced, specialized training at the National Institute for Public Health in Tokyo. The institute was established in 1938; there are no separate schools of public health.

The legally prescribed duties of the health centers include: (1) control of communicable diseases including preventive vaccinations; (2) prevention of tuberculosis; (3) control of venereal diseases; (4) control of various other parasitic and degenerative diseases; (5) mental health promotion; (6) maternal and child health programs; (7) consultation on eugenic protection; (8) dental hygiene; (9) improvement of nutrition; (10) food, meat and milk sanitation; (11) rabies prevention; (12) environmental sanitation programs; (13) environmental pollution activities; (14) medical affairs; (15) public health nursing activities; (16) medical social work; (17) public health laboratory services; (18) maintenance of health and vital statistics; (19) public health education (Ministry of Health and Welfare 1981: 12). The public health center network was especially important immediately after the Second World War and made a significant contribution to the Japanese "health miracle." It is anticipated that the network will also play an important role in the future and public health professionals hope to enhance their own status and influence in the health policy arena (Hashimoto 1984). They constitute an interest group that policy-makers will look to for information, support, and leadership in coordinating and integrating public health with personal health, and welfare services and programs.

Article 25 of the Japanese Constitution adopted in 1947 guarantees all citizens "the right to maintain the minimum standards of wholesome and cultured living." Article 25 goes on to declare: "In all spheres of life, the state shall use its endeavors for the promotion and extension of social welfare and security, and of public health." Although the Japanese were regarded as "welfare laggards" during the first two decades of economic recovery and development following the end of the Second World War, during the 1970s a Japanese version of the welfare

Table 4.1   *Social security expenditures in Japan 1970–83 (Unit: 100 million yen)*

| Fiscal Year | Social security benefit[1] | | | | Ratio of social security to national income |
	Total	Medical care	Pension[2]	Other[3]	
1970	35,239	20,758	8,562	5,920	5.8
	(100)[4]	(58.9)	(24.3)	(16.8)	
1975	116,726	56,881	39,316	20,529	9.4
	(100)	(48.7)	(33.7)	(17.6)	
1980	246,044	106,582	104,709	34,753	12.3
	(100)	(43.3)	(42.5)	(14.1)	
1983	319,016	129,931	144,966	44,120	14.1
	(100)	(40.7)	(45.4)	(13.8)	

Source: Ministry of Health and Welfare (KOSEISHO) 1986: 5

Notes: [1] Social security benefit conforms with that as laid down in the ILO social security system. It is calculated on domestic social security benefit expenditure for each scheme on settlement basis and does not include patient cost-sharing.

[2] Pension includes retirement pension.

[3] "Other" refers to public assistance, sickness and injury allowance, unemployment benefits, etc.

[4] Figures in brackets are percentages.

state came into being. As indicated in Table 4.1, national social security expenditures (including social insurance, public assistance, public health and medical care, and social welfare services) were only 5.8 per cent of national income in 1970. These expenditures increased to 9.4 per cent of national income in 1975, to 12.3 per cent in 1980 and to 14.1 per cent in 1983. Not only was the constitutional prescription being filled but also some critics insisted that Japan had become a "welfare superstate" and warned of the dangers of incipient "English disease." As might be expected, an extensive apparatus for state intervention in health and welfare also came into being at both national and regional levels. The Ministry of Health and Welfare, which was established as a result of pressure from the Japanese military in 1938 and reorganized under the aegis of the Supreme Commander of the Allied Powers during the Occupation of Japan following her defeat in the Second World War, has been assigned major responsibility for health and welfare administration.

Figure 4.1 depicts the organization of the ministry in 1986. Headed by a minister of cabinet rank, it consists of nine bureaux,

Figure 4.1 *Ministry of Health and Welfare organization 1986*

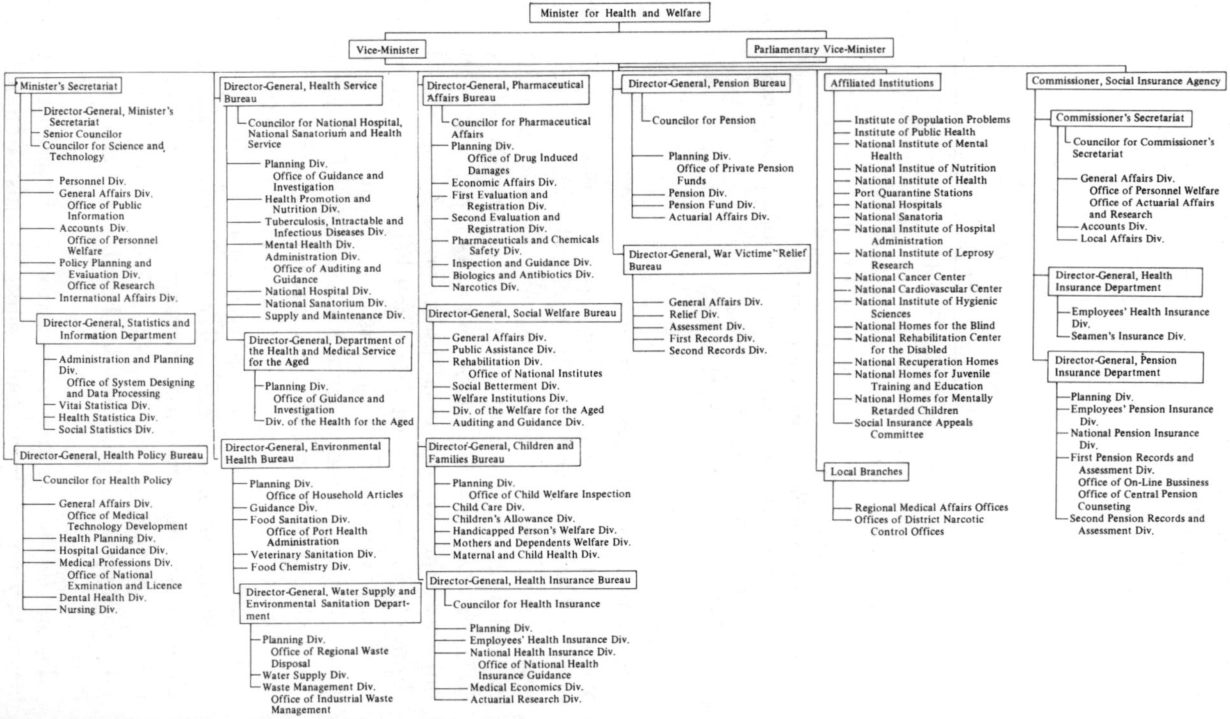

Minister for Health and Welfare

- Vice-Minister
- Parliamentary Vice-Minister

Minister's Secretariat
- Director-General, Minister's Secretariat
- Senior Councilor
- Councilor for Science and Technology
  - Personnel Div.
  - General Affairs Div.
  - Office of Public Information
  - Accounts Div.
  - Office of Personnel Welfare
  - Policy Planning and Evaluation Div.
  - Office of Research
  - International Affairs Div.

Director-General, Statistics and Information Department
- Administration and Planning Div.
- Office of System Designing and Data Processing
- Vital Statistics Div.
- Health Statistics Div.
- Social Statistics Div.

Director-General, Health Policy Bureau
- Councilor for Health Policy
  - General Affairs Div.
  - Office of Medical Technology Development
  - Health Planning Div.
  - Hospital Guidance Div.
  - Medical Professions Div.
  - Office of National Examination and Licence
  - Dental Health Div.
  - Nursing Div.

Director-General, Health Service Bureau
- Councilor for National Hospital, National Sanatorium and Health Service
  - Planning Div.
  - Office of Guidance and Investigation
  - Health Promotion and Nutrition Div.
  - Tuberculosis, Intractable and Infectious Diseases Div.
  - Mental Health Div.
  - Administration Div.
  - Office of Auditing and Guidance
  - National Hospital Div.
  - National Sanatorium Div.
  - Supply and Maintenance Div.

Director-General, Department of the Health and Medical Service for the Aged
- Planning Div.
- Office of Guidance and Investigation
- Div. of the Health for the Aged

Director-General, Environmental Health Bureau
- Planning Div.
- Office of Household Articles
- Guidance Div.
- Food Sanitation Div.
- Office of Port Health Administration
- Veterinary Sanitation Div.
- Food Chemistry Div.

Director-General, Water Supply and Environmental Sanitation Department
- Planning Div.
- Office of Regional Waste Disposal
- Water Supply Div.
- Waste Management Div.
- Office of Industrial Waste Management

Director-General, Pharmaceutical Affairs Bureau
- Councilor for Pharmaceutical Affairs
  - Planning Div.
  - Office of Drug Induced Damages
  - Economic Affairs Div.
  - First Evaluation and Registration Div.
  - Second Evaluation and Registration Div.
  - Pharmaceuticals and Chemicals Safety Div.
  - Inspection and Guidance Div.
  - Biologics and Antibiotics Div.
  - Narcotics Div.

Director-General, Social Welfare Bureau
- General Affairs Div.
- Public Assistance Div.
- Rehabilitation Div.
- Office of National Institutes Administration
- Social Betterment Div.
- Welfare Institutions Div.
- Div. of the Welfare for the Aged
- Auditing and Guidance Div.

Director-General, Children and Families Bureau
- Planning Div.
- Office of Child Welfare Inspection
- Child Care Div.
- Children's Allowance Div.
- Handicapped Person's Welfare Div.
- Mothers and Dependants Welfare Div.
- Maternal and Child Health Div.

Director-General, Health Insurance Bureau
- Councilor for Health Insurance
  - Planning Div.
  - Employees' Health Insurance Div.
  - National Health Insurance Div.
  - Office of National Health Insurance Guidance
  - Medical Economics Div.
  - Actuarial Research Div.

Director-General, Pension Bureau
- Councilor for Pension
  - Planning Div.
  - Office of Private Pension Funds
  - Pension Div.
  - Pension Fund Div.
  - Actuarial Affairs Div.

Director-General, War Victims' "Relief" Bureau
- General Affairs Div.
- Relief Div.
- Assessment Div.
- First Records Div.
- Second Records Div.

Affiliated Institutions
- Institute of Population Problems
- Institute of Public Health
- National Institute of Mental Health
- National Institute of Nutrition
- National Institute of Health
- Port Quarantine Stations
- National Hospitals
- National Sanatoria
- National Institute of Hospital Administration
- National Institute of Leprosy Research
- National Cancer Center
- National Cardiovascular Center
- National Institute of Hygienic Sciences
- National Homes for the Blind
- National Rehabilitation Center for the Disabled
- Office of National Training and Education
- National Recuperation Homes for Juvenile
- National Homes for Mentally Retarded Children
- Social Insurance Appeals Committee

Local Branches
- Regional Medical Affairs Offices
- Offices of District Narcotic Control Offices

Commissioner, Social Insurance Agency
- Commissioner's Secretariat
- Councilor for Commissioner's Secretariat
  - General Affairs Div.
  - Office of Personnel Welfare
  - Office of Actuarial Affairs and Research
  - Accounts Div.
  - Local Affairs Div.

Director-General, Health Insurance Department
- Employees' Health Insurance Div.
- Seamen's Insurance Div.

Director-General, Pension Insurance Department
- Planning Div.
- Employees' Pension Insurance Div.
- National Pension Insurance Div.
- First Pension Records and Assessment Div.
- Office of On-Line Business
- Office of Central Pension Counseling
- Second Pension Records and Assessment Div.

Source: Ministry of Health and Welfare (KOSEISHO) 1986, 69

two departments, a separate Social Insurance Agency, nineteen "affiliated institutions," as well as regional and local branch agencies. The Ministry of Health and Welfare engages in four basic activities, that is public health and medical care, social welfare and public aid, social insurance, and education, research, and information gathering. It oversees the administrative and programmatic activities of prefectural and city, town and village governments in the public health-medical care sector, including the network of health centers. The ministry also plays a major role in health planning and policy development at the national and regional levels and is the most visible and concrete manifestation of the Japanese state in public health and medical care. Ministry officials are responsible for integration and coordination of public health and medical care with other state activities and priorities. Even though they are not in a very good

Table 4.2   *Ministry of Health and Welfare budget 1981–5 (Unit: million yen)*

Fiscal Year	1981	1982	1983	1984	1985
Public Assistance	991,886	1,045,640	1,085,811	1,139,446	1,081,537
Social welfare	1,495,882	1,719,958	1,918,418	1,999,189	2,004,211
Social insurance	5,493,282	5,442,868	5,259,167	5,263,705	5,569,386
Health and hygiene	409,775	423,155	424,226	464,992	461,207
Scientific and technological promotion	20,435	22,499	22,665	25,016	26,333
Assistance for survivors and unrepatriated families	147,146	154,530	141,644	144,476	148,429
Maintenance of sewerage system and environmental sanitation facilities	157,127	157,164	157,364	156,454	154,834
Economic cooperation	4,564	5,114	5,552	6,005	6,220
Other	44,150	45,907	46,621	49,856	50,606
KOSEISHO general accounts budget total	8,764,247	9,016,835	9,061,468	9,249,141	9,502,763
General accounts budget total	46,788,131	49,680,837	50,379,603	50,627,214	52,499,643

Source: Ministry of Health and Welfare (KOSEISHO) 1986: 4

position to determine basic national priorities, they seek to articulate those priorities within their own sphere of influence and to promote the role of the ministry in the overall governmental process and their own role as managers of state intervention in public health and medical affairs.

Within the broader social policy arena, Health and Welfare ministry officials have expanded their influence and prestige as well as their share of the national budget – from 13.9 per cent in 1970, to 18.4 per cent in 1975, to 19.1 per cent in 1980. Recent trends in ministry expenditures are shown in Table 4.2. Note that the largest single line item in the 1980s is social insurance expenditures, the cornerstone of the Japanese welfare state and the foundation upon which contemporary social policies have been developed. Still, ministry officials are not paramount in the social policy field and they share jurisdiction with a number of other powerful agencies of national government, including the Ministry of Finance, the Ministry of Education, Science, and Culture, the Ministry of Labor, the Ministry of Construction, the Ministry of Home Affairs, the Economic Planning Agency, the Environment Agency, and the National Land Agency. The Social Security System Council attached to the Office of the Prime Minister and the Economic Council of the Economic Planning Agency also participate in the public health and medical care policy-making process as do a number of advisory councils within the Ministry of Health and Welfare (e.g. Social Insurance Council, Central Social Insurance Medical Council, Central Pharmaceutical Affairs Council, Medical Service Council, Medical Service Facilities Council, Public Health Council, and others).

It should be noted that Japanese national government is constitutionally divided into legislative, executive, and judicial branches.[4] All three are involved in public health and medical care policy-making in varying degrees. The bi-cameral National Diet is composed of a House of Representatives and a House of Councilors, elected from separate constituencies, and both have subject-matter committees that handle the legislative workload. Health-related legislation is normally introduced by the government and considered in the Social-Labor Committees of each house. Since the Diet is designated "the highest organ of state power" and "the sole lawmaking organ of the State" by the constitution, what happens in the Social-Labor Committees has a significant bearing on health policy. However, the constitution also provides separately for a cabinet in which "executive power shall be vested." It is what is usually referred to as a strong cabinet system and it is headed by a prime minister who also heads the majority party in the Diet. Since 1955 the conservative Liberal-Democratic Party (LDP) has held a majority in both houses. T.J. Pempel has aptly labeled the resulting pattern of public policies that has emerged during this period as "creative conservatism." Taking note of the strong emphasis on private sector initiative by the dominant conservative coalition in contemporary Japan, Pempel points out that "when the government chose, or was politically forced to act . . . it set goals and accomplished specific improvements with impressive speed, clarity, and effectiveness." He concludes.

> The secondary consequences of many of these actions may be open to criticism, particularly in terms of the value choices they represent. But the general efficiency of Japanese public policies in terms of meeting stated government objectives is undeniable. In this regard, Japan stands in marked contrast to many other countries, especially Britain, France, and the United States, where the opposite result has occurred.
>
> (Pempel 1982: 300)

In summary, by 1980 the Japanese state (dominated by a conservative coalition acting through the LDP) was engaged in the following basic activities related to public health and medical care:

1 development of plans, programs, and policies;
2 regulation of services and providers;
3 provision of services;
4 financing and subsidization of services and providers;
5 research, education, and information-gathering;
6 integration and coordination of public health and medical affairs with other state activities and priorities.

Comparative evaluation of what Pempel refers to as the "secondary consequences" of such activities is difficult. However, it is clear that a variant of "creative conservatism" in the health policy arena contributed positively to the relatively high level of well-being of the Japanese people and to the system of accessible, high-quality medical services – for considerably less than what was being spent in the United States and a number of other OECD countries.[5] Whether it can muster the determination and resilience of meeting the objectives stated in *Outlook and Guidelines for the Economy and Society in the 1980s* (Economic Planning Agency 1983), and in other such policy statement in the economic and demographic circumstances of the late 1980s, remains to be seen. A review of Japan's "health insurance for the whole nation" policies and programs and recently developed health and medical services for the elderly will suggest some of the major problems and issues and the challenges to "creative conservatism" in the 1990s.

Health insurance for the whole nation

Social insurance provides the foundation upon which the contemporary Japanese version of the welfare state has been erected and health insurance is the oldest and most highly developed part of the overall structure. Beginning with the Health Insurance Law, 1922 (the first of its kind in Asia) the system has grown incrementally to include other employment-based schemes for seamen, day laborers, teachers, and government workers. Citizens not covered by one of the employment-based schemes are entitled to coverage under the National Health Insurance Law, 1958, which requires that every city, town, or village in Japan offers health insurance to residents and collects a special tax from those who are covered. Insurees are expected to share the costs of benefits with the community insurer and the national treasury.

Implementation of the National Health Insurance Law in April 1961 was part of the "Health Insurance for the Whole Nation" policy adopted by Prime Minister Nobusuke Kishi in the late 1950s and embraced by successive Japanese governments (Saguchi 1985). Implementation of the National Health Insurance Law, a revision of the original 1938 legislation, meant extending health insurance coverage to 25 million persons (roughly 30 per cent of the population) not already covered. Since that time, Japan has had a system of universal, comprehensive, and compulsory health insurance that covers virtually the entire citizenry as well as the bulk of resident aliens. Even though the system contained glaring inequities and imbalances, it was warmly embraced by the Japanese people and it continues to enjoy widespread support in the 1980s.

From the standpoint of the individual citizen, the system offers relatively free access to medical services on an in-patient as well as on an out-patient basis and assurances that financial crisis will not be the automatic result of medical crisis. A much greater measure of medical security is thus available to the average Japanese citizen than to his or her American counterpart. From the standpoint of the provider, there is assurance not only that fees for service will be covered, but also that customers will be encouraged to enter the market for services quite freely. Indeed, over-utilization of services has been a major problem over the years. Although the system has been more or less continuously under attack by the Japan Medical Association (JMA), medical care providers have benefited enormously by the system.

The major features of the health insurance system are outlined in Table 4.3. It is unnecessary to go into details regarding the various plans here except to note that there have been many modifications of the system that have not seriously comprom-ised the integrity of the social insurance model.[6] Until the late 1970s private life and casualty insurance companies were not permitted to offer health insurance coverage. However, in keeping with the recent emphasis on utilizing the "vitality of the private sector," private companies are now permitted to offer supplementary coverage. It is not clear to what extent this will alter the basic thrust of the system and the government's decision to open the market was quite controversial. Govern-ment officials insist that social insurance will continue as the basis of the medical security system. Skeptics suggest that it was not so much the malfunctioning of the social insurance system as pressure coming from the domestic private insurance industry to create new investment opportunities as well as from the United States to open Japan markets to outsiders that led to the decision.

This is not to suggest that the social insurance system has not had its problems. However, it was not until the early 1980s that serious reform efforts were taken by government officials with respect to the social security system in general (Liu 1987). In the health insurance branch of social security, increasing costs as well as imbalances in payments and benefits provided the impetus for the ongoing reform effort. Cost containment and rationalization of costs and benefits has been the target of numerous investigations and reports and a far-reaching strategy

Table 4.3 Japanese health insurance system in 1986

Scheme			Insurer (as of March 31, 1984)	Number of Insured Persons (As of March 31, 1984) insured persons dependents Unit: 1,000 persons	Insurance benefits		
					Medical care benefits		
					Medical benefits	Dependents' medical expenses	High-cost medical expenses
Employees' Health Insurance	Health Insurance — Regular Employees	Government-Managed Health Insurance	National Government	31,928 (15,119 / 16,809)	90 % *80 % from day follow · g Diet approval	· Inpatient 80 % · Outpatient 70 %	Patient maximum deductible: ¥ 51,000 (¥30,000 for low income persons)
		Society-Managed Health Insurance	Health Insurance Societies 1,711	28,620 (12,150 / 16,470)		Same as above (additional benefits available)	*Total medical expenses per household (When 2 or more payments exceeding ¥30,000 each
		Day Laborers Health Insurance	National Government	413 (247 / 166)	*Deductible will be ¥100, ¥200 or ¥800 depending on cost of medical treatment provided at desired facility, total bill not to exceed ¥3,500.	· Inpatient 80 % · Outpatient 70 %	(¥21,000 each for low income households) are made, benefits cover the total expense.)
		Seamen's Insurance	National Government	632 (196 / 436)		Same as above	Abatement for households with repeated applications (Patient deductible is lowered to ¥30,000 (¥21,000 low income households) from the 4th application made in 12 months.)
	Mutual Aid Association Insurance	National Public Service MAAs	27 MAAs	12,533 (5,287 / 7,246) (As of March 31, 1983)		Same as above (additional benefits available)	
		Local Public Service MAAs	54 MAAs				
		Private School Teachers and Employees MAA	1 MAA				
National Health Insurance		Agricultural Workers Self-employed, etc.	Cities, towns, villages 3,272 National Health Insurance Associations 169	44,838 Cities, towns, villages 41,428		70 %	Abatement for patients suffering from diseases requiring costly treatment (Patient deductible is ¥ 10,000 for hemophiliacs and those suffering from chronic insufficiency of the kidneys requiring regular dialysis.)
		Retirees from Employees' Insurance	Cities, Towns, Villages National Health Insurance Associations 3,410		Insured person: 80 % Dependents: inpatient 80 % outpatient 70 %		

	[Operating entity]	7,346 Employees Insurance 2,558 National Health Insurance 4,788	Patient cost sharing Outpatient: ¥ 400 per month Inpatient : ¥ 300 per day [maximum two months]	Provided by each insurer of health insurance	[Share of costs]
Health and Medical Services for the Aged	Head of city, town, or village				· National government 2/10 · Local governments 0.5/10 0.5/10 · Insurers of each health insurance 7/10

Source: Ministry of Health and Welfare (KOSEISHO) 1986: 19

Cash benefits	Financial resources insurance Contribution	National government subsidy	Percentage receiving health and medical services for the aged (%) (as of March 31, 1984)
· Injury and sickness allowance · Maternity allowance · Delivery expenses, etc.	8.4 % Special insurance contribution 1 % (Since March, 1984)	16.4 % of benefit costs	4.1
Same as above (additional benefits available)	8.057 % (Average for all societies, as of March 31, 1983)	¥ 1,300 million as benefit cost assistance (Fiscal 1984)	2.8
Same as above	Grade I ¥ 120 per day Grade II ¥ 1,670 per day	Equivalent to 35 % of benefit costs at fixed rate and fixed sum	12.1
	8.2 % (Since April, 1982)	¥ 2,700 million as benefit costs at fixed rate and fixed sum	5.4
Same as above (additional benefits available)	6.05 – 12.86 % (As of April, 1984)	None	3.7 (As of March 31, 1983)
· Midwifery expenses · Funeral expenses · Nursing allowances, etc. (Optional)	Contribution based on individual income, assets etc.	50 % of benefit costs 32 % – 52 % of benefit costs None	11.3

of change is now underway (Kosei Tokei Kyokai 1985). Health policy-makers insist that their strategy is proving successful in containing costs and they are able to offer evidence to support their claim. They are also able to point with pride to a number of measures that have addressed the imbalances between the various schemes and to reorganization efforts that promote rationalization and efficiency. One such measure was the creation of a new scheme for retired persons as a special branch of the National Health Insurance plan.[7] The most remarkable reform, however, was the enactment of the Health and Medical Services for the Aged Law in 1982.

Health and medical services for the elderly

Even more remarkable than the 1982 reform, perhaps, were a number of reforms implemented by Japanese social policy-makers in 1973, often referred to as "the first year of the welfare era." In particular, as a consequence of a 1972 amendment of the Old-Age Welfare Law of 1963, all Japanese citizens of 70 years of age and older (bedridden 65 years and over) became entitled to virtually free medical services through the health insurance system. The cost-sharing of that segment of the population was assumed by the various insurers, public and private. However, the burden fell especially heavy on the public sector and the National Health Insurance scheme in particular. The proportion of elderly citizens being twice that of all other schemes combined, the National Health Insurance scheme increased its share of medical costs for the elderly from 20.8 per cent in 1973 to 32.0 per cent in 1981. As indicated in Table 4.4, the distribution of the burden of medical care costs for the elderly within the health insurance system was uneven and a mechanism for more equitable distribution was lacking. The distress felt by national and local government officials in charge of National Health Insurance schemes was intense and soon was seen as a threat to the integrity of the overall system. That, plus the increased ratio of medical costs for the elderly from 10.8 per cent of total medical costs in 1973 to 19.4 per cent in 1982 contributed to the climate for change that developed in the late 1970s and into the early 1980s. Japan's experiment with "free medical care for the elderly" thus came to an end in 1983 with the implementation of Health and Medical Services for the Aged Law (Steslicke 1984).

Table 4.4 Distribution of medical care costs for the elderly

Year	Government-managed health insurance	Society-managed health insurance	Mutual aid associations	Day laborers' health insurance	Seamen's insurance	National health insurance	All medical care insurance
	%	%	%	%	%	%	%
1973	6.5	7.3	10.5	5.4	9.5	20.8	12.7
1974	7.7	8.6	12.4	6.2	11.0	23.0	14.3
1975	8.8	9.6	13.6	6.7	12.1	24.2	15.5
1976	9.3	10.1	14.5	7.0	12.6	25.0	16.2
1977	10.0	10.8	15.3	7.4	13.5	26.3	17.2
1978	10.6	11.4	15.6	8.0	14.6	27.7	18.3
1979	11.1	11.8	16.1	8.5	15.9	29.1	19.2
1980	11.6	11.9	15.9	9.1	16.4	30.5	20.0
1981	12.4	12.5	16.8	9.5	17.7	32.0	21.2

Source: Social Insurance Agency, Government of Japan 1986: 53
Note: These ratios are calculated based on medical care costs from April of one year to March of the next.

Figure 4.2   *Health services for the elderly in Japan 1986*

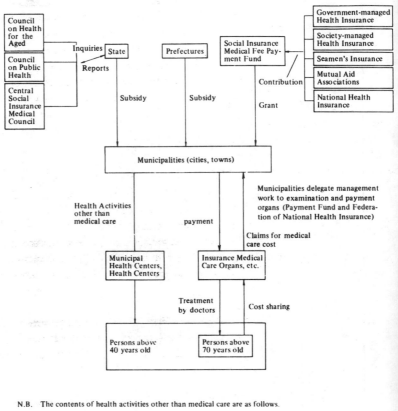

N.B.   The contents of health activities other than medical care are as follows.

        Issuance of Health Notebooks
        Health education
        Health consultation
        Health examination – General health examination – Cancer examination
                                  (Routine examination   (Stomach cancer
                                    Detailed examination   (Uterine cancer
                                 \ Visiting health examination
        Therapy
        Visiting guidance

Source: Ministry of Health and Welfare (KOSEISHO) 1986: 25

The fact that the 1982 Law instituted a measure of cost-sharing by elderly patients, even though it was slight, created a good deal of consternation in Japan that has not been put to rest. Cost-sharing remains controversial and this feature of the broader reform strategy has tended to deflect attention from what are the more significant aspects of the new system. More specifically, the new system of health and medical services for the elderly not only addresses the cost–sharing and rationalization of health insurance financing but also seeks to implement a comprehensive health program as indicated in Figure 4.2. It is comprehensive in that it incorporates prevention, treatment, and rehabilitation services for the aging population, with welfare services in general. Thus the goal is not only to integrate and coordinate personal and public health services but also to overcome the separation and fragmentation of social services that prevails in the west.[8] Viewed from that perspective, the cost–sharing features seem less onerous. However, it must be emphasized that the new system is still very much in the development stage and subject to both internal and external pressures (Steslicke and Kimura 1985). Integrated social policy measures have been the subject of considerable discussion among policy-makers in OECD countries and Japan's bold move in that direction is noteworthy (OECD 1977). Many Japanese and foreign observers see serious problems and question the capacity for Japanese institutions and vested interests to absorb the redistribution of functions and rewards implicit in the new strategy. But many also share the ethos expressed in a recent report of the Long-Term Outlook Committee of the Economic Planning Agency that declared:

It is necessary for us not to be excessively pessimistic about problems when we run into unknown variations. The shift towards an aging society in the future will force both social and economic fields, and others, to come up with various accommodations. However, we have so far conquered the changes in various domestic and external conditions. It is fully possible for us to carry out a smooth transfer if we grasp the problems correctly and make appropriate responses, given the long-term trend we are now facing.

(Long-Term Outlook Committee,
Economic Council 1983: 118)

Such expressions of "determination" and the need for "resilience" are pervasive in the health policy arena, even though held with varying degrees of conviction. For example, there is a growing concern among ordinary Japanese citizens that what many had come to see as amenities of life in an advanced industrial society may be threatened. Indeed, there is a growing sense of entitlement to accessible, high-quality, and relatively inexpensive health services. Concerned groups and individuals are by no means quiescent and are becoming increasingly active at both national and local levels. Thus health policy entrepreneurs are finding that in order to "grasp the problems correctly and make appropriate responses," they need to take into account the bottom–up reluctance to give-up the gains of the recent past.

Health policy and "creative conservatism" in the 1990s

What the state should or should not do with respect to the organization, financing, and delivery of health services in the 1990s and into the twenty-first century remains unsettled in contemporary Japan. The issue has been assigned a much higher priority on the national policy agenda during the early 1980s than at any other time since the end of the Second World War. However, national policy-makers have been preoccupied with various other issues related to defense, trade, and the changing domestic and international economies. Under the circumstances, health policy issues have been somewhat less compelling than might otherwise have been the case. Therefore various options and alternatives continue to be studied.

This is not to suggest that public and private sector participants in the conservative coalition that has governed Japan in the past few decades are sanguine about the impact of economic and demographic changes on the health care system. The fact that the health status of the Japanese people is among the highest in the world and that the health services system has been relatively effective and efficient is of some comfort. Also widespread dissatisfaction among consumers and providers of health services has not been a major problem, as in the United States, and the level of political conflict within the system has been quite low since the early 1960s. Still, there has been a growing appreciation of the complexities of the Japanese situation and that the rapid aging of the population is not an illusion. Coming to grips with the profound changes in the environment in which the health system operates is regarded as a necessity. Failure "to grasp the problems correctly and make appropriate responses" could have dire consequences for health care consumers and providers. Moreover, major disturbances in the system could also impact on other sectors of the society and economy and thereby compound the problem of Japanese survival in a highly competitive and changing international market-place. Those high-level policy-makers who deal with the fundamental problem of survival of Japan as an independent and affluent member of the international order are reluctant to intervene in the lower-level policy-making process operative in the health sector and they would prefer to entrust the task of policy development, coordination, and management to those who have accepted the challenge in the past. Thus far, the collection of government officials associated with the Ministry of Health and Welfare and other national ministries having some responsibility for health policy and administration together with representatives of "interested" groups and associations, insurers, providers, and various academic experts have demonstrated some capacity to deal with the issues.

For example in October 1982, the Ministry of Health and Welfare instituted a "Headquarters of Promotion Comprehensive Measures for National Medical Care Costs Rationalization" headed by the Vice-Minister of Health and Welfare (JICWELS 1983). The mission of the "headquarters" was to coordinate the medical care cost-containment effort from both a long-term and a short-term standpoint and to serve as the "nerve-center" for reforming the health insurance system. The effort not only was successful in articulating a reform agenda and strategy but also led to legislative and administrative actions that tended to promote the cause of cost containment and thereby enhance the prestige of ministry officials. As a result, the ministry has embarked on a comprehensive review of health policy issues and the formulation of a tentative plan for dealing with these issues in the 1990s and beyond.

To be sure, these and other reform agendas have stirred a good deal of opposition from provider groups, insurers, labor unions, and opposition political parties – as well as from ordinary Japanese citizens who see a threat to the services to which they have become accustomed. As indicated earlier, rising expectations and a growing sense of entitlement to high-quality health services within the populace has added another new dimension to the field-of-forces confronting health policy-makers. Therefore it would be premature to celebrate the victory of "creative conservatism" in dealing with the health policy issues of the 1980s and the 1990s. Whether it is possible to direct "the vitality of the private sector" so as to meet the needs and demands of Japan's rapidly aging society remains to be seen. Nevertheless, it is clear that, whatever the outcome, the Japanese state will continue to play a leading role in setting the health policy agenda in the 1990s and in determining how Japanese health services will be organized, financed, and delivered. Such state intervention will have not only widespread acceptance within Japan but also a rich heritage of past accomplishments upon which to build.

In conclusion, it should be emphasized that health care policy is no longer a purely domestic concern for those nations that compete in the international market-place for goods and services. The Japanese case illustrates that the way in which particular nations organize, finance, and deliver health services has a significant bearing on productive capacity and costs. Japanese leaders would very much like to maintain the relative advantage the nation has had in that respect and "to polish the Japanese diamond," so to speak. To the extent that increasing health care costs, especially those related to the rapid aging of the populace, are perceived as contributing to the deterioration of Japan's competitive position internationally – even greater "resilience" in the formulation of health policies for the 1990s can be expected. The challenge will be not only to contain costs but also to maintain the relatively high health status of the work-force that has served as an important basis for Japanese economic accomplishments of the past.

Notes

1 For a discussion of the changing role of the Japanese state during the past century, see Johnson 1982, especially chapter 1.
2 One vision of the "Japanese-style Welfare State" was incorporated into the *New Economic and Social Seven-Year Plan* of 1979 (Economic Planning Agency 1979: 162–6).
3 For more detailed description of the Japanese health care system,

see Hashimoto 1984; Steslicke 1987a; 1987b; Ohnuki-Tierney 1984; Lock 1980; and Ohtani 1971.

4 A recent, brief description of the governmental system is presented in Kishimoto 1982 and Pempel 1982.

5 The point is argued forcefully by Macrae 1984.

6 For a review of the social insurance system in English (updated annually) see Social Insurance Agency, Government of Japan 1986.

7 Institution of the new health insurance scheme for retired persons is described in National Federation of Health Insurance Societies (KEMPOREN) 1986: 33–5.

8 Writing in 1975, Steven Jonas quite accurately observed: "The Japanese health services system is a complex one. It bears many similarities to the health care systems of the large western capitalist countries. At the same time, as one would expect, there are significant differences as well. For the most part, as in the west, there is a rather high degree of organizational and functional separation between the preventive, treatment, and rehabilitative services" (Jonas 1975: 58).

References

Abel-Smith, B. (1976) *Value for Money in Health Services: A Comparative Study*, London: Heinemann.

Economic Planning Agency (1979) *New Economic and Social Seven Year Plan*, Tokyo: Ministry of Finance, Government of Japan.

—— (1981) *In Search of a Good Quality of Life: Annual Report on National Life 1981*, Tokyo: Ministry of Finance, Government of Japan.

—— (1983) *Outlook and Guidelines for the Economy and Society in the 1980s*, Tokyo: Ministry of Finance, Government of Japan.

Fukui, H. (1972) "Economic planning in postwar Japan: a case study in policy making," *Asian Survey* 12: 327–48.

—— (1977) "Studies in policy-making: a review of the literature," in T.J. Pempel (ed.) *Policy-Making in Contemporary Japan*, Ithaca, NY: Cornell University Press.

Hashimoto, M. (1984) "Health services in Japan," in *Comparative Health Systems*, University Park, Pa, and London: Pennsylvania State University Press.

JICWELS (Japan International Corporation of Welfare Services) (1983) *Trends of Policies of Health Care Services in Japan: Rationalizing Medical Care Costs*, Tokyo: JICWELS.

Johnson, C. (1982) *MITI and the Japanese Miracle: The Growth of Industrial Policy, 1925–1975*, Stanford, Calif: Stanford University Press.

Johnstone, B. (1985) "Yen for basic research in cancer," *New Scientist* 1,464: 30–2.

Jonas, S. (1975) "The district health center in Japan: history, services, and future development," *American Journal of Public Health* 65: 58–62.

Kishimoto, K. (1982) *Politics in Modern Japan: Development and Organization*, Tokyo: Japan Echo.

Kosei Tokei Kyokai (1985) *Kokumin eisei no doko* (*Trends in National Public Health*) Tokyo: Kosei Tokei Kyokai.

Liu, L. (1987) "Social Security Reforms in Japan," *Social Security Bulletin* 50: 29–34.

Lock, M. (1980) *East Asian Medicine in Urban Japan*, Berkeley, Calif: University of California Press.

Long-Term Outlook Committee, Economic Council (1983) *Japan in the Year 2000: Preparing Japan for an Age of Internationalization, the Aging Society and Maturity*, Economic Planning Agency, Tokyo: Japan Times.

Macrae, N. (1984) "Health care international," *Economist* 291: 17–35.

Ministry of Health and Welfare (KOSEISHO) (1981) *Guide to Health and Welfare Services in Japan*, Tokyo: Health and Welfare Problems Research, Inc.

—— (1986) *Health and Welfare Services in Japan*, Tokyo: Japan International Corporation of Welfare Services.

National Federation of Health Insurance Societies (KEMPOREN) (1986) *Health Insurance and Health Insurance Societies in Japan*, Tokyo: KEMPOREN.

OECD (Organization for Economic Cooperation and Development) (1977) *Towards an integrated social policy in Japan*, Paris: OECD.

—— (1984) *Japan: then . . . and now*, OECD Observer, 3: 3–16.

Ogawa, N. (1982) "Economic implications of Japan's aging population: a macro-economic demographic modelling approach," *International Labor Review* 12: 117–33.

Ohnuki-Tierney, E. (1984) *Illness and Culture in Japan: An Anthropological View*, Cambridge: Cambridge University Press.

Ohtani, F. (1971) *One hundred years of health progress in Japan*. Tokyo: International Medical Foundation of Japan.

Pempel, T.J. (1982) *Policy and Politics in Japan: Creative Conservatism*, Philadelphia, Pa: Temple University Press.

Saguchi, T. (1985) "Nihon no iryo-hoken to iryo seido" (Japan's health insurance and medical care system), in Tokyo daigaku shakai kagaku kenkyu-jo (eds) *Fukushi Kokka 5: Nihon no keizai to Fukushi* (*The Welfare State 5: Japan's Economy and Welfare*), Tokyo: Tokyo Daigaku.

Social Insurance Agency, Government of Japan (1986) *Outline of Social Insurance in Japan 1985*, Tokyo: Yoshida Finance and Social Security Law Institute.

Social Policy Bureau, Economic Planning Agency (1982) *Scenarios 1990*, Japan: Ministry of Finance, Government of Japan.

Steslicke, W.E. (1972) "Doctors, patients, and government in modern Japan," *Asian Survey* 12: 913–31.

—— (1982a) "Development of health insurance policy in Japan," *Journal of Health Politics, Policy and Law* 7: 197–226.

—— (1982b) "National health policy in Japan: from the 'age of flow' to the 'age of stocks'," *Bulletin of the Institute for Public Health* 31:1–35.

—— (1982c) "Medical care in Japan: the political context," *Journal of Ambulatory Care Management* 5: 65–77.

—— (1984) "Medical care for Japan's aging population: an introduction," *Pacific Affairs* 57: 45–52.

—— (1987) "The Japanese state-of-health in the 1980s: a political-economic perspective," in M. Lock (ed.) *Health and Medical Care in Japan*, Honolulu: University of Hawaii Press.

—— (1988) "Health care in Japan," in R.B. Saltman (ed.) *International Handbook of Health Care Systems*, Westport, Conn: Greenwood Press.

Steslicke, W.E. and Kimura, R. (1985) "Medical technology for the elderly in Japan," *International Journal of Technology Assessment in Health Care* 1: 27–9.

Subcommittee on the Long-Term Projection, Economic Welfare Council (1979) *National Life in the 21st Century – Toward a Society being Full of Humanity*, Tokyo: Economic Planning Agency, Japan.

Tominaga, K. (1983) "Japan's industrial society at a critical turn: advantages are fading," *Oriental Economist* 1983: 32–9.

Tsuji, K. (1984) *Public Administration in Japan*, Tokyo: Tokyo University Press.

WHO (World Health Organisation) (1980) *Sixth Report on the World Health Situation 1973–1977, part I: global analysis*, Geneva: WHO.

Five

The health system in Spain

Jesús M. de Miguel and
Mauro F. Guillén

Spain is a case study in the early creation of a public and extensive – but deficiently organized – health sector, which coincides with high health levels of the population. The Spanish health system (which may be characterized by its unbalances, disorganization, and lack of adequate planning) does not prevent the population from enjoying good health, although public health problems such as infections, diseases, cleanliness, poisonings, and epidemics still exist. An objective analysis of the problems of the Spanish health system leads the researcher towards variables other than those related to health care resources to explain the satisfactory health levels. It seems possible that once a certain degree of health development is achieved, health levels depend more on other (structural) variables.

Our hypothesis is that health levels therefore do *not* depend directly on either existing health care resources or their utilization. Health inequalities are, however, the discouraging side of this rather contradictory situation in Spain. The public health sector still plays the main role in the attainment of a better distributed health status. In this study, we analyze the relationships between (1) health indicators (including health inequalities); (2) health care resources and their distribution; (3) health system reforms, especially those of the public sector; and (4) structural factors that influence (1), (2), and (3). The case of Spain as a changing, many-faceted, inequitable society presents both new ideas and new facts for analyzing these relationships.

Is Spain really different?

Covering most of the Iberian Peninsula, Spain is a vast, mountainous, low-density country compared with the rest of Europe. The relationship between size and low population density has produced a model in which the population concentrates in six specific areas (creating a hexagon), giving Spain one of the highest urbanization rates in Europe. Spain shares features of both Europe (low birth-rates, moderate economic development) and Latin America (late industrialization, high urbanization). The population is relatively young: 26 per cent are less than 15 years old according to the *1981 Census*, and the proportion of persons 65 and older is still low (11 per cent). But in the 1980s birth-rates are decreasing rapidly, so Spain – although a Catholic country – will soon resemble low-natality Central European countries. This aging trend will bring not only an increased demand for health care, but also changes in the distribution of health care and personnel resources. Spain is still a prototype of a country with late, partial industrialization processes; with a market-driven economy that coexists with more traditional social structures; and with enormous differences by social class, region, rural-urban state, and sex.

Spain is also a case study in early state building and late peripheral nationalism (mainly the Basque country and Catalonia), which together reinforce the image of an invertebrate country. In spite of the many civil wars, *pronunciamientos*, and *guerillas*, the state is still centralist-oriented, and the health system is no exception to this rule (at least not until the 1980s). The Civil War of 1936–9 was the most important political event, bringing a sudden halt to all social processes except urbanization. During the resulting theocratic Franco regime, an extensive and powerful health system was developed. The stabilization program of 1959 set the conditions for the years of growth and prosperity that lasted until the dictator's death in 1975. The country smoothly transformed its institutions, approved a new

Table 5.1 *Evolution of the Spanish public health sector*

Period (in years)	General structure	Financing	Legitimacy	Actual beneficiaries	Prospective model
1908–35	The *Instituto Nacional de Previsión* coordinates social insurance programs	State and personal fees	Anti-revolutionary, Catholic interest groups	Certain groups of manual workers	A global system of social insurance programs
1936–43	Health aid during the Civil War; more insurance programs are created	*Ley de Seguridad Social* (Social Security Act)	Each side in the Civil War	Soldiers and civilians	A coordination of the public sector under the Ministry of Labor
1944–66	*Seguro Obligatorio de Enfermedad*, based on the *Ley de Bases de la Seguridad Social*	Unions Social Program fees and mutual benefit societies	The *Falange*, and since 1964 the politicians in charge of the *Plan de Desarrollo*	Ministry of Labor, leaders of the *Movimiento*, and the "economically weak" workers	A system for industrial workers

1967–75	Health care under the social security, as established by the *Ley de Bases de la Seguridad Social*	Workers and employers	The *Movimiento*, and the Bureau for Development Planning	Professional groups, hospital care institutions, the pharmaceutical industry and *conciertos*	A system comprising the entire active population (beginning with laborers, and the urban middle classes)
1976–81	A Governmental Commission, the Health Reform, and in 1978 the INSALUD	Growing fees of employers	Ministry of Health (since 1977), and the 1978 Constitution	Pharmaceutical industry and *conciertos*	Two competing models: privatization (promoted by the government), and NHS (promoted by the Socialist opposition)
1982–85	INSALUD, designing a national health service, with control over the private sector	Growing state fees	First Socialist government, and legislators of the *Ley General de Sanidad*	Corruption recedes, and there is a halt in the privatization process	Unification of the public sector, with a control over expenditure and emphasis on PHC
1986–90	*Ley General de Sanidad* (1986) and the national health system	State general budget (in the long run)	Second Socialist government	The health system, and population	Coverage of the entire population Decentralization of the public sector

democratic Constitution in 1978; and, in 1982, elected a socialist government. But the health system suffered a crisis between 1975 and 1982: a dilemma of whether it should go private or public. The first socialist government (1982–6) not only designed a unified model for the public sector that covered the entire population, but also organized a decentralization process with the *Ley General de Sanidad* (LGS) or General Health Law of 1986. The second socialist government (1986–90) is now coping with the problems of implementing that law, a reform that has been delayed for decades because of political reasons. Precisely at this moment problems and hopes come together.

The Spanish health system has undergone various reforms during this century, culminating in the creation of the *Seguro Obligatorio de Enfermedad* (SOE) in 1944. Three later reorganizations developed in the form of the *Asistencia Sanitaria de la Seguridad Social* (ASSS) in 1967, the *Instituto Nacional de la Salud* (INSALUD) in 1978, and finally the modern *Sistema Nacional de Salud* (SNS) in 1985 (see Table 5.1). At the present time the Spanish public sector is called the "National Health System." Nevertheless it is an intermediate model between a national health *service* and a national health *system*. The public sector covers approximately a quarter of the ambulatory health care, and runs a quarter of all hospital beds in the country; it is also a health insurance system which accounts for three-quarters of total health care expenditure. Thus it works both as an insurance system and as a health care service at the same time. What is peculiar is that public health care resources are of a better quality than those of the private sector.

Spain's present health system originated in 1908 with the creation of the *Instituto Nacional de Previsión* (INP). This institution coordinated the various social insurance programs: retirement, illness, disability, maternity, and accidents-at-work. Conservative governments before the Constitution of 1931 (which recognized the right to health insurance) tried to counterbalance social movements (especially those of the working class) by enlarging these insurance programs. Put into practice after 1939, the idea was to satisfy the (industrial) working class and to restore workers' ill health.

In the years of hardship shortly after the Civil War, 1941–4, a *Ley de Bases de la Sanidad Nacional* and a *Seguro Obligatorio de Enfermedad* (SOE) or Compulsory Health Insurance were created. Both laws were a continuation of the Catholic reformism characterizing the INP, but were now backed by the falangist component of the early Franco governments. The SOE was an invention of the powerful Minister of Labor, José A. Girón – an extreme falangist who ran both the health system and the vertical trade unions from 1941 until 1957. As a falangist project created during a military dictatorship, the SOE is a rare invention that brought about a large public health system.

Since the 1940s the public sector (including hospitals and out-patient services) has changed little, although it has been gradually enlarged and has taken on new responsibilities. The SOE, which had been designed for industrial workers, grew during the following twenty years to cover a larger proportion of the population: 25 per cent in 1944; 45 per cent in 1963. But only one out of every ten beds belonged to SOE at that time. The government then decided to establish a more comprehensive model: *Asistencia Sanitaria de la Seguridad Social* with the *Ley de Bases de Seguridad Social* (1967). That model increased the rate of population coverage from 53 per cent to 84 per cent and gained control over 23 per cent of the country's beds. In the early 1970s (and especially after the dictator's death), the system went into a crisis, and ultimately was reorganized as INSALUD. Seven years later under the socialists' rule, the formerly falangist project was transformed into a *Sistema Nacional de Salud* (SNS) or National Health System. By 1982 INSALUD covered 86 per cent of the population and maintained 26 per cent of the country's (best) hospital beds. The new LGS (1986) seeks the total protection of the population, but it does not substantially change the organization of the public sector.

The decade prior to the crisis of the 1970s saw the most intense expansion of the public system, covering an increasing percentage of the population, from industrial workers to all salaried workers. These years represent the maximum rate of hospital-building and enlargement of physician-hiring (85 per cent of the total), and of pharmaceutical expenditures (the public sector paid up to 76 per cent of those costs). This public sector served essentially the interests of health personnel, the pharmaceutical industry, the contracted private sector (*conciertos*), and the political establishment. It took the first Socialist government most of its stay in office to understand and evaluate the situation and to pass a law designing a *Sistema Nacional de Salud*. This reform involves (1) unifying the public sector; (2) protecting the entire population (86 per cent was protected before the socialists came to power); and above all, (3) decentralizing health care resources. The second Socialist government is supposed to implement the law (García Vargas 1986).

The problem concerning the lack of coordination between INSALUD and the Ministry of Health (MSC) remains unresolved. The former INP, and presently INSALUD, is an extensive bureaucratic institution, with a huge power share, an arrogant administrative style, and relative autonomy. The second Socialist government reorganized the public sector in such a way that INSALUD is reduced to a mere resource administrator, deprived of planning and economic programming powers. INSALUD's budget for 1987 has risen to 1,200 billion pesetas, representing an 11 per cent increase compared with 1986 and 28 per cent of all social security expenditure. The state's share in this budget (25 per cent in 1987) is also increasing. Using 55 per cent of INSALUD budget, hospital care is the most significant expenditure. The Socialist government cannot further enlarge the public sector (partly due to resources scarcity), but may attempt changes in the health system's organization.

Studies about the Spanish health system are recent but sparse. The first empirical work (financed by the FOESSA Foundation) was published in 1970 as Chapter 13 of the *Informe sociológico sobre la situación social de España 1970* (Sociological Report on Spain's Social Situation 1970) by Amando de Miguel *et al.* (1970: 752–831). The Catholic-oriented FOESSA Foundation also promoted two later studies: in 1975 (by Adolfo Serigó) and in 1983 (by Enrique Martín). These three reports combine basic statistics with the first health surveys of both the general population and health care personnel. The first analyses of the Francoist health system appeared in the 1970s with a critical account of the Social Security system by Felip Soler-Sabarís (1971), from a Catalonian perspective and in a radical style. After Franco's death, a period of polemics gave birth to several studies on the possibility of a health care reform. The most official of these is the *Libro Blanco* (Subsecretaría de la Seguridad Social 1977). Three other conservative, although imaginative, interpretations by Gerardo Clavero (1977), Adolfo Serigó (1979), and Manuel Evangelista (1981) also belong to this period. A critical opposition that promotes the *Servicio Nacional de Salud* (a Spanish version of the British National Health Service) presents alternative models such as those of the

Catalonian socialists (Reventós 1977), the report on health care planning and reform by Jesús M. de Miguel (1978), and the study by Javier Yuste (1982). The first Socialist government began in 1983 with a series of analytical studies such as the book on health sector structures (J.M. de Miguel 1983; 1986). The first comparative studies appear during the 1980s: Josep A. Rodríguez (1986); Pedro J. Saturno (1988). But there is still no single study on the Spanish health system at present, and our understanding of the private sector in particular is limited.

The government has yet to conduct a health survey of the population, although both the preliminary study and the design of the survey instrument have already been made. Official statistics (essentially of the *Instituto Nacional de Estadística*) provide data on hospital care (from a hospital census), hospital morbidity (an annual survey), death causes (in the yearly issue of *Movimiento Natural de la Población*), and health care personnel distribution. INSALUD publishes important information in both its *Memoria anual* and its *Información económico-funcional de las instituciones sanitarias*, but with considerable delay, some confusion, and a lack of reliability. The decentralization processes of the 1980s have permitted some regional studies, especially in Catalonia (Departament de Sanitat i Assistència Social 1980) and in the Basque Country (Departamento de Sanidad y Seguridad Social del Gobierno Vasco 1982). These reports have emerged from the continuous political strains between Spain's center and periphery

The Spanish health system is the result of an initiative by the falangist faction of Franco's regime. The structural evolution of the health system has legitimized the various groups in power without taking the population's needs into account. However, year by year the proportion of the population covered by the public system increased. During the last decade, the system has achieved a protection rate of nine out of every ten Spaniards, and unification of the public sector under the model of a *Sistema Nacional de Salud* has been proposed by the socialists (1982–86; 1986–90). But neither that increase in the protection rate nor the improvement of the bed-to-person ratio explains the continually increasing health levels.

Health system resources

The health system in Spain lacks many resources and entails a relatively low expenditure. Spaniards typically consider the public sector an extensive, or even excessive, system (partly because of the urban expansion of INSALUD hospitals). But in reality, institutional resources are still scarce, fractionated, and insufficient. Spain spends only 6.3 per cent of its national income on health care. The health system is not expensive: it represents 85 per cent of OECD's average health care expenditure. The trend, however, is to mimic most developed countries, which have doubled their expenditure over the last decades as well as augmented the proportion of the public share of expenditure. Maintaining a low public share of health care expenditure (73 per cent in 1982) compared with the average of other OECD countries (78 per cent) (Table 5.2), Spain is below average in both trends, but rapidly closing the gap. The 70/30 pattern (70 per cent public resources and 30 per cent private resources) has changed little over decades, despite both socio-political shifts and health care reforms. The proportion of the population covered by INSALUD has reached a maximum of 86 per cent in 1983, but the proportion of INSALUD beds is just 27 per cent. The peculiarity of the Spanish health care system is that the public sector is more modern, efficient, and developed than the private sector.

Table 5.2   *Health expenditure and importance of the public health sector*

Country[1]	Health expenditure as a percentage of national income			% of public (health) sector		
	1960	1970	1982	1960	1970	1982
Greece	2.9	3.9	4.4	59	56	77
Portugal	—	—	5.7	—	—	70
United Kingdom	3.9	4.5	5.9	87	87	88
Belgium	3.4	4.1	6.2	62	85	94
Spain	—	4.1	6.3	—	56	73
Japan	3.0	4.6	6.6	60	65	73
Italy	3.9	5.5	7.2	82	87	85
Australia	5.1	5.7	7.6	47	56	63
West Germany	4.8	5.6	8.2	67	75	80
Canada	5.5	7.2	8.2	44	71	74
Netherlands	3.9	6.0	8.7	33	85	79
France	4.3	6.1	9.3	58	70	71
Sweden	4.7	7.2	9.7	72	86	92
USA	5.3	7.6	10.6	25	37	42
OECD average	4.1	5.6	7.4	61	71	78

Source: OECD 1985: 12

Note: [1] In increasing order of percentage of health expenditure in 1982.

Table 5.3 Health sector resources in 1982

Country[1]	Population per physician	Per hospital bed		Hospital admission rate (% of population)	Average length of stay (in days)	In-patient care (in days per person)
		population	personnel[2]			
Greece	394	162	0.92	11.9	13.0	1.6
Portugal	454	195	1.18[3]	9.6	14.4	1.4
United Kingdom	775	124	—	12.7	18.6	2.4
Belgium	384	106	—	13.9	13.5	2.8
Spain	362	185	1.34	9.2	14.6	1.3
Japan	738	84	0.76	6.4	56.1	3.6
Italy	798	127	1.13[3]	15.6	12.4	2.2
Australia	509	91	3.27	21.0	7.4	3.2
West Germany	422	90	1.11	18.1	18.7	3.4
Canada	520	145	2.11	14.7	13.3	2.1
Netherlands	497	83	—	11.9	34.1	4.0
France	480	90	1.29	12.1	14.1	3.1
Sweden	427	71	1.68	18.9	22.9	4.8
USA	498	169	2.69	17.0	9.0	1.7

Source: OECD 1985: 15, 115
Notes: [1] In increasing order of percentage of health expenditure in 1982.
[2] 1981.
[3] 1980.

Spanish health care resources follow a precarious pattern: an excessive number of physicians and a general lack of hospital beds. This requires several qualifications, but summarizes adequately the structural problems within the health system. With a national health system similar to the British NHS, Spain has fewer than half the number of people per physician than Britain, and even much less than another, culturally closer Southern European country such as Italy (Table 5.3). Spain is one of the most developed countries with the worst provision of hospital beds but one of the best physician-to-person ratios. Existing hospital beds fail to cover population needs adequately because a significant proportion is devoted to emergency services and to chronic and mental patients. Changes in the age structure (mainly aging of the population) are causing additional difficulties. The problem lies in bed scarcity and long average hospital stays (14.6 days) rather than in understaffing (1.34 personnel per hospital bed). As a result, only 9.2 per cent of the population is admitted to a hospital each year, so the average number of hospital days per inhabitant per year is 1.3.

All the studies about the Spanish health system – as well as the latest available data – suggest that the public sector is large, but also is disorganized and functionally defective, lacks planning, and has an uneven distribution of resources. The excessive number of physicians and the relative lack of hospital beds worsens the situation. Additionally, corruption is pervasive, and public/private boundaries are blurred. Taking all this into account, the high health level of the population – even higher than in many western countries such as the United Kingdom, Italy, and West Germany (Table 5.4) – is most surprising. The data support our hypothesis that after a certain level of health development is reached, the health system has little to do with either the actual health level of the population or its distribution among different population groups. (This second hypothesis requires further analysis for which adequate data are lacking.)

With a life expectancy at birth of 76 years for women and 72 years for men, in 1980 Spain surpasses other developed countries that have more sophisticated health systems: the United Kingdom, Belgium, Italy, West Germany, and even the United States. The significant difference between women and men (6.5 years) provides evidence for the idea of the modernity of this pattern. Remembering that Spain is predominantly Catholic with high (although decreasing) birth-rates, infant mortality is

Table 5.4 *Health indicators in 1980*

Country[1]	Life expectancy at birth (in years)			Mortality: (% of live births)		Percentage of population in private households with:	
	females	*males*	*difference*	*infant*	*perinatal*	*piped water*	*flush toilet*
Greece	77.8	73.2	4.6	1.79	2.12	—	—
Portugal	75.0	67.0	8.0	2.60	2.55	—	—
United Kingdom	75.9	70.2	5.7	1.21	1.34	92	94
Belgium	75.5	69.8	5.7	1.10	1.40	99	81
Spain	78.0	71.5	6.5	1.11	1.57	88[2]	84[2]
Japan	79.2	73.7	5.5	0.75	1.20	93[4]	46[4]
Italy	77.4	70.7	6.7	1.43	1.75	92[4]	89[4]
Australia	78.0	70.9	7.1	1.07	1.40	100	96
West Germany	76.5	69.7	6.8	1.27	1.16	—	93[3]
Canada	79.0	71.0	8.0	1.04	1.20	—	98[3]
Netherlands	79.2	72.5	6.7	0.86	1.10	100[4]	100[4]
France	78.3	70.1	8.2	1.01	1.29	99	83
Sweden	78.9	72.6	6.3	0.69	0.90	98[3]	96[3]
USA	76.7	69.6	7.1	1.26	1.32	97[4]	97[4]

Sources: OECD 1985: 131; OECD 1986: 139

Notes: [1] In increasing order of percentage of health expenditure in 1982.
[2] 1975.
[3] Percentage of private households.
[4] Percentage of dwellings.

unexpectedly low at 1.11 per cent – lower than in West Germany, Britain, and the United States. Prenatal mortality could still decrease, but in 1980 it corresponds to a pattern of countries with large numbers of illegal abortions rather than with low health level. Furthermore, if we consider other structural and health variables, Spain shows a comparative disadvantage. This mystery's only solution can be that health levels also depend on other factors uncorrelated with the health system, or at least with the public system.

How can we explain such a favorable situation? Which variables have produced such an accelerated progress? In three decades the Spanish female population's life expectancy has increased by 14 years, the male population's by 12 years (in 1950, women's life expectancy at birth was only 64 years, and men's was barely 60 years). In just twenty years infant mortality rates have been reduced to a quarter of what they had been (from 4.37 per cent in 1960 to 1.11 per cent in 1980). In 1982 the rate decreased even more (to below 0.96 per cent). The change has been so rapid that no clear explanations have arisen, although falling birth-rates might be a contributing factor.

We may mention a few non-health aspects that contribute to high health levels in Spain: (1) a low proportion of women working (only 18 per cent of women of working age are employed outside the home); (2) high urbanization rates which facilitate health care actions; (3) a good basic health education and knowledge of the population, mainly of mothers and grandmothers, which means that children are well taken care of; and finally (4) the traditional Spanish diet which is rich in vegetables, fruit, and carbohydrates (potatoes, bread, rice), while at the same time the consumption of meat and milk-fat is not so high. Nevertheless, there are some other structural factors that do not favor good health levels: housing and sanitary equipment are deficient, consumption of pork is still high, and alcohol and tobacco consumptions are high and still increasing. The favorable variables do not fully explain recent improvements in health levels. Therefore, further research efforts are needed in order to explain the situation.

In Spain there are not only few hospital admissions (3.5 million per year, and 50 million days of stay), but also few deaths (fewer than 300,000 annually). We suspect that persons falling ill, persons being admitted to hospitals, and persons who die are different. Mental patients have the largest share of days of stay (13 million days), but only a thousand people die of mental diseases each year. Reproductive processes are responsible for nearly 600,000 women being admitted to hospitals annually, but fewer than a hundred of those die. The data in Table 5.5 show that Spanish hospitals admit many persons who do not die during their stay: 29 per cent of all stays correspond to mental patients, 19 per cent to women who are admitted for normal deliveries (14 per cent of all admitted patients); 13 per cent to patients with digestive problems; and 10 per cent to patients with fractures or other external injuries. Persons who die do not represent a high percentage of admissions; the probable explanation is that hospitals are reluctant to admit terminal cases. Deaths due to heart or cerebrovascular diseases account for 41 per cent of the total number, cancer deaths for 20 per cent. These two categories together represent 62 per cent of all death causes but only 16 per cent of hospital admissions, which explains why only 2.5 per cent of those admitted die in Spanish hospitals.

Table 5.5 *Causes of morbidity and death in Spain*

Diagnosis	Deaths in 1979	Hospital admissions in 1984	
		Patients	Days of stay
	%	%	%
Circulatory system	41.4	8.4	8.3
Tumors	20.5	7.4	7.2
Neoplasms	*20.4*	*4.6*	*5.2*
Respiratory system	6.3	9.2	5.8
External causes	5.7	10.1	7.3
Digestive system	4.2	12.7	9.5
Perinatal	2.4	2.5	3.0
Infective and parasitic			
diseases	1.9	2.9	4.0
Mental disorders	0.4	2.8	28.7
Reproduction (females)	0.02	19.1	5.6
Normal delivery	—	*13.8*	*3.8*
Others	17.1	23.4	20.5
Total of defined cases	100	100	100
	(279,054)	(3,002,187)	(45,476,613)
Ill-defined conditions	4.2	14.4	9.7
Total	(291,213)	(3,490,395)	(50,346,116)

Sources: INE 1983; INE 1986

Thus it is paradoxical that health levels are so comparatively high in a country that has moderate economic development; that is undergoing intense economic stagnation; and whose health system is small, disorganized, and characterized by unbalances in its resource distribution (too many physicians, too few beds). This state of affairs suggests that at high levels of health care development, health levels depend on other social, structural variables than just on health care expenditures.

Impact of technology on health care

Like that of many other countries, the Spanish health system has undergone a process of technical improvement, specialization, and price increases. Health care has developed at two poles: the primary health center (or *ambulatorio*) and the modern hospital. Josep A. Rodríguez (1986) has analyzed the seven processes of change in Spain's health care, especially in the hospital system:

1 Concentration of beds in a decreasing number of hospitals;
2 First period of a public sector centralization;
3 Relative privatization of health care;
4 Structural lack of hospital beds;
5 Scarcity and inadequacy of resources;
6 Defective utilization of resources, with multiple corruption levels;
7 Persistence of several types of health inequalities, e.g. social, biological, and regional.

The various reforms have intended to improve the network of health care, but the processes of technologization and institutionalization are so strong that the outcome has been a reinforcement of the hospital system, especially the public system included in INSALUD. That hospital network (70 per cent of which is public) is the core of health care. One reason for the reinforcement of the hospital system is its low starting-point: the lack of hospital beds in Spain is so noticeable that special efforts need to be devoted to improving and expanding that network. This goal, however, remains unattained despite the rise in hospital expenditure. A second reason is that some hospitals have been increasingly allocating resources to primary health care (PHC), with a continuous climb in the number of

Table 5.6 *Evolution of hospitals in Spain*

Hospital characteristics	1949	1963	1972	1980	1982	1982 Index 1949 = 100
Number of hospitals	1,622	1,648	1,287	1,084	1,050	65
Number of beds[1]	127,343	156,819	177,385	201,035	206,567	162
Annual average number of new beds	—	2,105	2,285	2,956	2,766	131[2]
Average hospital size (beds per hospital)	78	95	138	186	197	253
Beds per 10,000 inhabitants	44.5	49.3	51.6	53.8	49.9	112
Beds in the public sector (%)	69.9	66.8	69.7	68.0	68.2	98
Out-patient visits per bed	—	—	75	101	99	—
Personnel per bed	0.34	0.48	0.77	1.35	1.52	447
Registered nurses per bed	0.06	0.11	0.14	0.32	0.37	617
Hospital occupation rate (%)	68	—	70	70	73	107
Hospital admission rate (% of population)	—	—	—	9.3	9.1	—
Average length of stay (in days)	—	—	—	14.8	14.6	—
Autopsies per 100 deaths	—	—	—	9.7	8.7	—
Daily operations per operation room	—	—	—	—	1.5	—
Daily deliveries per delivery room	—	—	—	—	1.4	—

Sources: Instituto Nacional de Estadística, *Estadística de establecimientos sanitarios con régimen de internado*, Madrid: INE. Years 1949, 1966, 1972, 1980, and 1982

Notes: [1] After 1972, data include incubators.
[2] 1963 = 100.

both out-patient services offered and emergency admissions. The final result is the worst: the public hospital system has not actually expanded; public beds are still unevenly distributed geographically; resources have been taken away from PHC; and the best primary-care consultations are now being held in hospitals (the so-called *consultas externas*).

Table 5.6 shows that despite the creation of a public system (from SOE to SNS) that eventually covered the entire population, hospital bed rates have only slightly increased (4.4 beds per 1,000 inhabitants in 1949 and only 5.0 in 1982). Many small hospitals (35 per cent) have disappeared in these years, most of them private and traditional. This balance is surprising considering both the notorious scarcity of beds and the high resource concentration. In spite of this lack of (public) beds, the public system has been operating at low performance levels: with long average stays (15 days) and filled to only 73 per cent of capacity. This situation should favor an expansion of the private sector, but it prefers to concentrate on private medical consultations and marginal activities related to hospital care, creating a model in which public hospitals and INSALUD are subsidiaries of private medicine.

The outcome is discouraging: just 9 per cent of the population receives hospital care yearly, the number of deliveries per delivery unit and day is especially low (1.4), the number of surgical operations per operating room and day is equally low (1.5), and the number of autopsies is exceedingly low (9 per cent). The problem is not that these indicators do not improve rapidly (some even worsen), but rather that they seem to stagnate. All these data support the hypothesis that the basic structure of the health system resists both changes and reforms, and even remains insensitive to them. Structural changes are exasperatingly slow, and the impact of governmental policies (from different ideological backgrounds) is almost imperceptible.

In 1983 INSALUD maintains over a thousand PHC centers and employs approximately 45 per cent of all personnel. Ambulatory services are primarily in the hands of the public sector, which serves not only as a first-selection institution (conducting middle-class patients to the private sector and chronic or difficult cases to the public sector), but also as a PHC service for the lower classes. The ambulatory care system (which is the most widely spread) sends away a patient every

Table 5.7 Health establishments of INSALUD in 1983

Operations	Total INSALUD[2]	National hospitals	Hospital complexes	General hospitals	Diagnosis and treatment centers	Out-patient clinics	Dispensaries
				Types of hospitals			
Centers in service	1,128	6	12	108	3	312	489
Personnel	155,665	10,527	44,897	58,530	695	14,875	3,959
Time (in mins and secs)							
General consultations	3'55"	—	—	—	2'42"	3'01"	3'08"
Specialties	11'05"	40'19"	45'25"	21'24"	29'27"	6'50"	5'28"
Radiology	4'37"	9'19"	10'12"	3'59"	4'27"	2'31"	—
Tests	44"	47"	2'03"	41"	37"	20"	—
Costs (in 1983 pesetas)							
Per hospital day of stay[1]	16,893	19,906	18,376	15,716	—	—	—
General consultations	110	—	—	—	106	120	101
Specialties	616	2,770	3,404	1,918	2,277	285	182
Radiology	493	2,218	808	555	770	254	—
Tests	63	90	146	75	123	34	—

Source: INSALUD 1985b

Notes: [1] Includes teaching and research expenditure.
[2] Includes also emergency services (142), special emergency services (15) and work-place accident and occupational disease out-patient clinics (41).

three minutes in general consultations and every seven minutes in specialty consultations. It seems clear that in such a short time, complete diagnosis and treatment are impossible. The out-patient services in INSALUD hospitals actually play the role of the PHC, devoting twenty-one minutes to every patient (Table 5.7).

Technology and hospital expansion have produced a general disorder in the health care system: out-patient services in hospitals are really PHC consultations; specialty consultations are general medicine consultations, and general medicine consultations are bureaucratic mechanisms distributing patients within the public sector once the most profitable patients have been screened out. The duplicity in private and public jobs of those persons working for the public sector (especially physicians) allows for an efficient transfer of patients from one sector to the other. Many physicians in the public sector solicit patients to come to see them privately. The ambulatory system is cheap (a consultation there costs one-seventh of that in a hospital), but of poor quality. The worse its quality and the greater the number of patients to deal with, the better for the private-consultations sector (and especially for physicians working for both sectors).

The growth of hospital care at the expense of PHC is a double-discriminatory process; reinforcing technologization while raising health care costs, it aggravates social inequalities. The fact that consultations last only two or three minutes and that hospitals are scarce and unevenly distributed does not justify their deficient utilization, their operation at low capacity, or the long stays. The technological impact has been unexpected: public PHC has been impoverished and has deteriorated, and public hospitals still need to be developed, improved, and made more flexible.

Private versus public

Is there an actual privatization of the Spanish health system? This question has no simple answer. There is an extensive public sector (70 per cent) and a private sector (30 per cent), proportions that have hardly changed over decades despite the creation of SOE, SS, INSALUD, and finally SNS. No particular tension or conflict seems to exist between the two

Table 5.8 *Evolution of hospital bed ownership*

Hospital ownership	Years				Index 1982 1949 = 100
	1949	1963	1972	1982	
	%	%	%	%	
Public sector	69.9	66.8	69.7	68.2	98
Local administration	38.4	30.3	28.7	22.8	59
Provincial	29.1	25.8	25.3	20.4	70
Municipal	9.4	3.2	3.1	2.3	24
INSALUD[1]	2.9	9.1	18.7	27.4	945
Central state administration	28.7	27.4	21.4	17.8	62
AISNA[2]	14.3	18.2	10.8	6.8	48
Ministry of Defense	14.3	9.1	7.3	6.1	43
Ministry of Education	—	—	2.8	4.9	—
Others	—	—	0.4	0.3	—
Private sector	30.0	33.2	30.2	31.8	106
Private	18.6	21.0	14.3	19.0	102
Church	10.2	10.8	9.1	6.6	65
Charity[3]	—	—	5.1	4.4	—
Red Cross	1.2	1.3	.6	1.8	150
Others	—	0.1	—	—	—
Total	100				
	(127,343)	(156,819)	(177,385)	(206,567)	162
Public beds (per 10,000 inhabitants)	31.1	32.9	36.0	34.0	109
Private beds (per 10,000 inhabitants)	13.3	16.4	15.6	15.9	120

Sources: Instituto Nacional de Estadística, *Estadística de establecimientos sanitarios con régimen de internado*, Madrid: INE, years 1949, 1963, 1972, and 1982
Notes: [1] Before 1977, *Seguridad Social.*
[2] The groups *Education* and *Others* are not specified in some cases and we assume that they are included in the category AISNA (Institutional Administration of National Health Care), which before 1977 was called *Gobernación* (Department of Interior).
[3] The groups *Charity* and *Others* are not specified in some cases and we assume that they are included in the category *Private*.

sectors; in fact, overlapping between them is pronounced. The public sector mimics the organizations, patterns, structure, and goals of the private sector, while the private sector takes advantage of public patients and resources for its own interests. This two-sided process coincides with the aforementioned three processes: (1) public sector deterioration, (2) slow institutional privatization, and (3) rapid health care internationalization with equipment and standards set abroad influencing local procedures and health care.

In thirty-three years public sector hospitals have decreased their share of total beds by only 2.4 per cent (69.8 per cent in 1949, and 68.2 per cent in 1983). To postulate a *process of hospital privatization* regarding bed ownership, however, is inappropriate at this time. Only during the 1960s and the 1980s has the private sector progressed slightly, while the 1970s represent the apogee of the public sector. A modern SNS has been created in the mean time, but at the expense of both local and state administration beds (except for those owned by the Ministry of Education and Science, which runs the teaching hospitals). When the private sector grows, neither the charity nor the church hospitals expand, but rather the private hospitals and, to a lesser extent, those of the Red Cross (which are likely to be transferred to the public sector in 1987). Table 5.8 indicates how the Spanish hospital sector changes to remain the same (in a structural way), and how the aggregate increase in the number of beds is close to zero. Again, the structure is insensitive to reforms.

The Spanish health system is confusing: the public sector takes care of many private patients, and private sector health care is paid primarily by the public sector. Fewer than 10 per cent of admitted patients pay for their care. In local administration hospitals this percentage rises to 18 per cent (even greater than that of patients who pay for themselves in the private sector). In most private hospitals only 18 per cent of all patients pay directly. On the other hand, the largest proportion of patients (22 per cent) pay directly in the Red Cross hospitals. Nearly 8.2 per cent of patients admitted to private hospitals are supported by another institution: either the social security (52 per cent) or the so-called voluntary insurance agencies (25 per cent). That is to say, the SNS runs only 27 per cent of total beds, but accounts for 41 per cent of hospital admissions, and pays for 70 per cent of all hospital health care. In brief, the public sector is disorganized

Table 5.9 Institutions that covered hospital costs in 1982 (in percentages of hospitalized patients)

| Person or institution which covered the cost | Total[1] | Hospital which provides health care | | | |
		INSALUD	public charity[2]	private charity[3]	private
	%	%	%	%	%
Patients (totally or partially)	9.7	2.9	11.9	12.6	17.7
The hospital	0.9	—	—	3.8	1.8
Private insurance agencies	10.1	1.4	2.5	14.6	29.5
Social security	69.6	94.7	53.3	63.4	46.1
Provincial and local administration	7.1	0.2	28.9	2.6	0.6
Others	2.6	0.9	3.3	3.1	4.2
Total	100				
	(3,445,830)	(1,404,561)	(796,642)	(401,351)	(841,756)
% of total hospitalized patients	100	40.8	23.	11.6	24.4

Source: Instituto Nacional de Estadística (1986) Estadística de establecimientos sanitarios con régimen de internado: 1982, Madrid: INE
Notes: [1] Includes 1,520 other admissions.
[2] Includes local and state administration except for INSALUD.
[3] Includes private charity, church, and Spanish Red Cross.

and corrupt, and the private sector lives on resources of the public system.

Table 5.9 clarifies these relationships. The social security (INSALUD in 1982, and now SNS) pays for 70 per cent of all patients. The remaining 30 per cent is shared equally by other public institutions, by voluntary insurance agencies, and by the patients themselves. Within the public sector INSALUD is a radically different system, with its own financial instruments and just 5 per cent private patients. The rest of the public sector (25 per cent of all patients) is quite similar to the so-called private charity sector (which includes charity, church, and Red Cross hospitals and accounts for 12 per cent of all patients), and is even similar to the private hospital sector. In the three cases of the private–charity sector, private patients constitute between 12 per cent and 18 per cent, and the social security pays for between 46 per cent and 63 per cent of them. The only difference is that private hospitals depend on voluntary insurance agencies to a greater extent (30 per cent of the patients versus the average 10 per cent).

The hospital system – for which we fortunately have data – is an image of that confusing structure common to the whole health system, where health care, costs, and control are in different hands. The outcome is apparently disorganized, but actually effective and rational: the health system (private or public) serves private interests (institutional or personal), but rarely considers the needs of either the users of the system or the population in general.

Medicalization of society

The Spanish health system has been reorganized several times, but its basic structure is largely the same. Both an unprecedented expansion of health personnel and a halt in the creation of new health care centers have been allowed. For each new center or bed created, another disappears. Health personnel have led the way for the health system's improvement, lobbying at INSALUD/SNS, at the Ministry of Health, and the hospitals. Under the shadow of an expanding public sector (with resources and equipment), the power share of professionals and expert physicians has been tremendous. Within the context of both the health system and the health sector personnel, the power of the medical profession was unlimited until 1982.

Table 5.10 Health care personnel

	1960				1970				1980				1984			
	Total	Per 10,000 inhab-itants	% of females	% in province capitals	Total	Per 10,000 inhab-itants	% of females	% in province capitals	Total	Per 10,000 inhab-itants	% of females	% in province capitals	Total	Per 10,000 inhab-itants	% of females	% in province capitals
Physicians	35,228	11	1	43	45,235	13	4	48	86,253	23	17	68	121,362	32	24	67
Dentists	2,783	1	4	63	3,361	1	4	66	3,946	1	6	70	4,682	1	13	68
Pharmacists	10,254	3	28	50	15,963	5	34	49	23,299	5	47	54	28,748	7	55	53
Veterinarians	7,128	2	0.2	17	7,661	2	0.2	21	8,178	2	2	39	8,660	2	3	40
Nurses	—	—	—	—	—	—	—	—	125,313	33	73	68	142,542	37	73	65
Physiotherapists	—	—	—	—	—	—	—	—	2,149	0.6	50	77	2,962	0.8	49	75
Medical assistants	21,932	7	17	49	22,634	7	20	56	—	—	—	—	—	—	—	—
Midwives	5,117	2	100	46	4,123	1	100	52	4,192	1	100	56	5,770	2	100	60
Total health personnel	82,442	26	15	44	90,077	29	16	48	253,500	67	48	66	314,726	82	50	64
Total personnel	—	—	—	—	—	—	—	—	298,000	79	61	—	357,900	93	62	—

Sources: Instituto Nacional de Estadística, Anuario Estadístico de España, Madrid: INE, years 1961, 1971, 1981, and 1985; Instituto Nacional de Estadística, Encuesta de población activa. Octubre-noviembre-diciembre, Madrid: INE, years 1980 and 1984

The advantages of a health system that alters its external appearance without changing internally are seemingly innumerable and far-reaching. The public sector has been hiring fewer and fewer physicians every year, accounting now for 60 per cent of the total; a few years before the rate was 85 per cent. That percentage will continue to decrease. In the midst of an economic recession, the private sector cannot afford to hire additional physicians. So both under-employment and unemployment will rise considerably.

The public sector aids employment expansion, hiring most of the country's doctors (85 per cent of all physicians in the 1970s). Since 1976 the sector began hiring nurses and later other types of personnel. The situation until that year was peculiar: more physicians than nurses, more medical students than physicians. Furthermore Spain had the world's lowest proportion of female doctors. At the end of the 1970s (and for the first time) the system employed more nurses than doctors. The 1970s brought another considerable increase in female employment, of both nurses and physicians. By 1984 women constituted almost 25 per cent of all physicians, the majority of pharmacists, half of the health personnel, and 62 per cent of all health sector personnel (Table 5.10).

Contrary to some stereotypes, Spain has one of the highest urbanization rates in Europe. Over a third (36 per cent) of the population lives in one of the fifty province capitals. Resources are concentrated in urban areas: 64 per cent of all health personnel work in those fifty cities. Concentration is more intense regarding physiotherapists (75 per cent), dentists (68 per cent), and nurses (65 per cent). The urbanization rate of health resources between 1980 and 1984, however, seems to have decreased. None of the health system versions – SOE, SS, INSALUD, SNS – has produced an adequate plan. Studies show that hospitals are even more poorly distributed than health care personnel.

In brief, feminization is still a strong trend (partly because of the low starting-point), but the urbanization of health care resources seems to have slowed, and in some cases has receded. Urban unemployment has forced new graduates to seek jobs outside the fifty capitals where jobs were once available due to the higher average age of personnel working in non-urban areas.

Both medical education and medical knowledge in Spain have undergone an internationalization process. But again, planning has been non-existent. The only important action was to create a *numerus clausus* program in medicine in 1979. The number of medical students has been reduced from almost 80,000 in 1980 to slightly less than 60,000 three years later. But academic failure has also diminished. Conversely the number of pharmacy and veterinary students has risen considerably. The number of veterinary students increased 6.8 times between 1970 and 1983, with more than a third (36 per cent) of all students being freshmen.

The power share of the medical profession is about to shrink because first, its relative number within health sciences gradu- ates is decreasing, bringing more competition from other careers, and second, a rapid feminization process is occurring. And this process continues at an even higher rate than that of all health professionals, meaning the feminization of other health personnel will follow its path. By 1983 46 per cent of all medical students and 68 per cent of pharmacy students were women. In veterinary medicine, which had previously been a male career, women now make up 35 per cent of the students and 25 per cent of the university teachers. Thus there is a double process in health careers: first, a decreasing number of university students (although parity exists between medicine and veterinary), and second, rapid feminization in all careers and at all levels.

The system is self-regulatory: the number of medical students has been reduced dramatically, but not that of new graduates. In 1950 fewer than a thousand students (898) graduated from medical schools; nine times that many, however, graduated three decades later (7,752 in 1980) and still more in 1983 (10,355). The *numerus clausus* has also achieved a better student- to-teacher ratio: 15.2 in 1980; 10.6 in 1983.

Again, the reforms implemented in the health system are insufficient to alter the structure. Perhaps the dominant groups know how to take advantage of those changes to obtain additional benefits. What seems evident is that health care – especially medical care – is good business.

Social and health inequalities

With the limited data available now in Spain, the task of measuring health inequalities has become understandably diffi- cult. The only serious attempts have been the study by M.

Angeles Duran (1983), the health survey in Barcelona (Antó 1984), and some partial studies (J.M. de Miguel 1976; 1985: 71–132; Alonso Hinojal 1977; Mayor Domingo 1977; and Pérez Peñasco 1983). Spain boasts a high health level, higher than that of some more developed Western countries. But health discrepancies do exist: in 1976, Jesús M. de Miguel defined the main factors of health inequality in Spain as: sex, age, social class, rural/urban strata, and regions. A decade later these inequality factors remain the same. The creation of SOE in 1944 solved some of the health problems of certain social groups, particularly industrial workers (which that law called "economically weak producers"). The reform of the social security, and later of INSALUD in 1978, consolidated a dual system of medical care, with a public system of social security for the lower classes and a system of technologically advanced (and private) medicine for the upper classes. Paradoxically INSALUD sometimes generates health imbalances rather than eliminating existing ones. Above all, this institution reinforces a model of two socially disparate health systems. This dual model is dealt with by the *Servicio Nacional de Salud* (national health *service*), which, after four years, of discussions and fights among pressure groups, was reduced to a national health *system* (SNS). As such, it merely attempts to unify the public sector. It will be difficult for that model to reduce the widespread health inequalities that exist in Spain.

Certain internal differences are notable. The upper classes seek health care at private hospitals in a proportion seven times greater than that of the lower classes, but they go to private physicians only three times more frequently than the latter. In part, these differences may be because a private physician is cheaper than a bed in a private hospital. The actual difference, however, is that it is more likely that the upper classes in Spain know how to utilize the best of both the private and public sectors (using the SNS when appropriate and probably without standing in line).

The problem is not a discrepancy in access to health care resources by social class, but the poor quality and low utilization of those resources, although medical care *is* quite different by class. As in many western countries with an extensive public sector, Spain's middle and lower classes (which are protected by the public sector) seek physician consultations and are admitted to hospitals more frequently than the upper classes, as shown in the Barcelona health survey (Antó 1984: 51). Medical consultations for the lower classes are quick (65 per cent last less than five minutes), but this is the case in only 5 per cent of upper-class consultations (Durán 1983: 112). Surveys reveal that most Spaniards (64 per cent) believe private hospitals to be the best (versus 20 per cent who prefer those of the social security). The same question addressed to physicians, however, points out the opposite relationship: only 33 per cent feel that health care is better at private hospitals (Mayor Domingo 1977: 815–16). The lower classes use the public sector, but the higher the social class, the more frequent the use of private insurance programs or a combination of both sectors. Differences by social class run deeper regarding PHC (4.6 times as many lower-class than upper-class patients go to INSALUD ambulatory services) than regarding hospitals (2.6 times as many lower-class than upper-class patients use INSALUD hospitals). Thus the discrimination intensity of Spain's health system resides in PHC and not so much in hospital utilization.

In some situations, however, health inequality processes seem to be reversed. For instance upper-class women give birth in private hospitals fourteen times more often than lower-class women, while the latter use public hospitals with a frequency seven times greater than the former. The data show that 48 per cent of lower-class mothers gave birth at home last time, and an additional 10 per cent without technical assistance. On the contrary, only 17 per cent of upper-class women gave birth at home, and none without technical help. Social inequality is still important, although disguised with a symbolic utilization of private hospitals as a social status indicator.

Tobacco and alcohol consumption provide a similar instance of health inequality processes, as pointed out in the health survey of Barcelona (Antó 1984: 84–95). Addictions are a good example of sexual inequalities, sometimes being more conspicuous than social inequalities. The higher the social class, the lower the proportion of men who consume tobacco and alcohol. The reverse is true for women, especially as far as cigarettes are concerned. The same survey (Antó 1984: 74–7) shows that dental health inequalities directly correlate with social class but not with dentist consultations. Consistently we find that health inequalities are structural (they depend on inequality factors such as social class and sex), but they do not depend on health care utilization (medical consultations and hospital care).

This relation holds even when we introduce a third variable: regional variations, which are especially influential in Spain. The differences in distributions of hospital beds and physicians by province are narrowing. The country's northern part has high rates, particularly in provinces specializing in psychiatric hospitals (such as Valencia, Teruel, and Tarragona). Map 5.1 shows that private-ownership patterns represent an even more important factor than economic development in explaining the uneven distribution of beds. It seems clear that even within the public sector, hospital planning is inadequate: frequently hospitals are built where they are not needed. The secular trend of lacking hospital beds appears to be unchanging in the southern part. The most surprising fact is that hospital-resources inequalities among regions are even more intense than those of physicians.

The medical profession originally concentrated in the northern section following the pattern of private ownership which was better distributed among the population than in the south. But thanks to increased mobility, in the last few years there has been a shift not only towards the periphery (especially towards the Mediterranean), but also to provinces with medical schools (Barcelona, Valencia, Granada, Seville, Salamanca, Vizcaya, Navarra). Both tendencies are now overlapping. Still, resource distribution has nothing to do with needs: the poorest parts of Spain have the fewest health care resources.

But these geographical inequalities in resource allocation surprisingly are not in accord with the health level of the population in certain areas. Mortality within the first twenty-four hours after birth correlates positively with hospital bed rates in poor areas (Orense, Caceres, Huelva), but less with bed rates in the coastal north and in the interior. In the latter, hospital beds are more important than physician availability; this explanation also holds for early neonatal mortality, but to a lesser extent. In Galicia (with the exception of La Coruña) there are many deaths due to both general economic underdevelopment and resource concentration in La Coruña. In some provinces with many psychiatric beds (not very useful for deliveries), there is a positive correlation between high infant mortality rate (IMR) and high bed rates.

Relationships between health resources and health levels are reasonably easy to establish when two such closely related variables as hospitals and babies born are taken into account.

Map 5.1   *Distribution of health sector resources (per 10,000 inhabitants)*

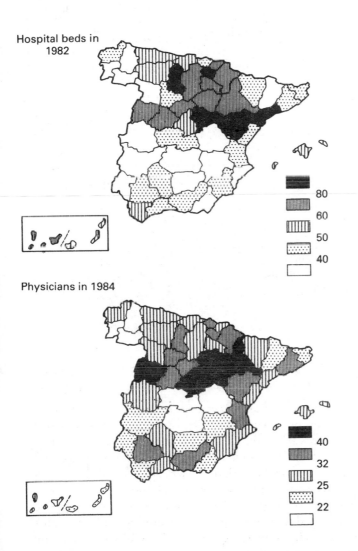

Hospital beds in 1982

Physicians in 1984

80
60
50
40

40
32
25
22

Sources: Instituto Nacional de Estadística (1986) *Estadística de estable-cimietos sanitarios con régimen de internado: 1982*, Madrid: INE; Instituto Nacional de Estadística (1986) *Anuario Estadístico de España: 1985*, Madrid: INE

But when the IMRs are analyzed, these relationships vanish. The south has high IMRs, partly due to the lack of both hospitals and physicians. But IMRs are also high in the north, especially on the northern coast, including the Basque Country (which is a well-developed area, although Catholic and with high birth-rates). Alicante has a low IMR despite its lack of beds and doctors. The plateau of Castile and Aragon (to the north and east of Madrid) also enjoys a low IMR, with the exception of Soria. In summary, IMR distribution is difficult to explain, and seems to be unrelated to either hospital or human resources. A series of structural factors may account for those differences: urbanization, Catholicism, rate of female workers, nutrition patterns, birth-rate, migrations, development of the periphery, economic development, population in schools, private ownership, and land ownership. And although more complicated, such structural factors offer more validity than health care resources variables. The Spanish government ignores not only how the health system may improve health levels, but also how to diminish health inequalities. The solutions to these problems, however, are implemented by organizational reforms and not by structural changes of social reality.

Crisis, what crisis?

In Spain health disasters have always brought about reforms of the health system: with last century's cholera pandemics and more recently with the oil poisoning ("toxic syndrome") of the 1980s. The reform of the *Ley General de Sanidad* (LGS: 1986) represents the first extensive political reform of the health system. A whole legislative term (1982–86) was needed to pass this law. But the second Socialist government (1986–90) is supposed both to develop the LGS and to implement the invention of the *Sistema Nacional de Salud*. Like any other socialist reform, two underlying goals are present: first, to increase the health level of the population, and second, to diminish social and health inequalities (Lluch 1983; García Vargas 1986).

These changes are sought by transforming three main factors: knowledge, power, and organization. Knowledge of the health status of the population is still weak. Public health in the contemporary sense has barely begun in Spain, and the first specialists in epidemiology (such as those in public health) are in a marginal position with respect to health care power centers, even those within academia. The obsession for health care decentralization and for resource transfer to regional administrations (the *Comunidades Autónomas*) has drawn attention to existing resources (the famous "health maps"), but not to either the availability and quality of those resources (public and private) or the social and health inequalities of the population. Knowledge about health education is scant, and negative outcomes are still erroneously being attributed more to a lack of "health culture" by the population than by the politicians or experts.

Meanwhile, power concentration has shifted from the medical profession towards the new managerial group. Thus a new health care class has emerged: managers and health economists (most of whom are men). It is true that health professions (even the medical profession) have become more feminine, but power is now held by a new masculine profession. The new managerial class is now in charge of decision-making and planning. The goals are to control health care expenditures strictly rather than to ameliorate health inequalities. No one seems to care about the population; there is no evaluation of its needs. The first four years of socialist rule were too brief to implement a "national health survey," and it remains to be seen whether the second Socialist government will be able to carry out and evaluate the survey, as well as to adapt its design to the actual needs of the population rather than to existing resources. The weakest aspect of the present reform is the absence of popular participation. Community participation (and population participation in general) seems weaker now than in the previous decade.

The most dramatic change has occurred in organization, although no analysis of its consequences on health levels has been undertaken; the LGS is regressive as compared to the preliminary projects. A national health *service* to control both the public and private sectors was intended in principle. But in the end, a national health *system* was adopted, which simply unifies the apparently dispersed public health care sector. A decentralization of the health system was carried out at the same time, implementing resource transfer to the seventeen regional governments (beginning with Catalonia, the Basque Country, and Andalusia). Another aim is to favor the PHC sector at the expense of the hospital system and to follow a public policy of health promotion. Thus far this goal has not been attempted: a good statement of purpose, it has had no effective reflection in the budget. Since the public sector seldom allocates enough resources to investments, the system is progressively deteriorating. The containment of economic cost has been successful, but at the expense of reducing health levels in certain population groups and in growing fees. The assumption that the greater the expenditure on health care, the higher the health level of the population seems to be false; but this realization must not lead us to deny that expenditure cuts may result in lower health levels, higher health inequalities among groups, or both. The problem is that the boundaries between spending too much and too little are not clear, as the Spanish case shows us.

The new *Sistema Nacional de Salud* (Figure 5.1) is a copy of the British NHS, although with the inclusion of some traditional Spanish institutions. The public sector is organized into concentric rings: state administration, health services of regional administrations, health areas, and basic health zones. At each level a health planning mechanism is designed, which is then combined with ones from other levels to form a *Plan Integrado de Salud* (PIS) or Integrated Health Plan. The population participates merely as a consultative organism and always in a minority position. All in all, the new organization produces no change (except for the nomenclature) consecrating what already exists. One advance is that the public sector is regrouped, unified, and made accessible to the entire population. These goals are necessary but do not represent a huge change. Again, reality is faster than reforms.

The history of Spain's health sector is a concatenation of forced reforms (due to epidemics or shifts in office) and models that have served to legitimize the groups that backed them. While health care resources (except for physicians) have been scarce over decades, health levels have increased, reaching truly high standards, even higher than in many countries with higher standards of living. Thus we find a health care system which is (1) unbalanced (too many physicians, too few beds); (2) disorganized, fragmented, and sometimes chaotic; (3) subsidiary to private interests (those of the professions, the pharmaceutical sector, and the multinationals); (4) concentrated in an expensive hospital health care system, compared to PHC; and (5) lacking adequate planning, but which paradoxically still allows favorable health levels.

Figure 5.1 *The Spanish national health system*

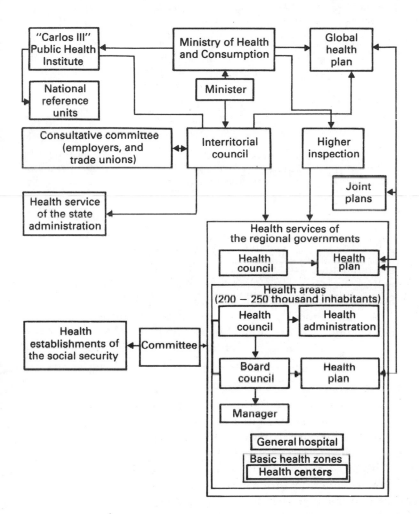

Source: Ley 14/1986, de 25 de abril, General de Sanidad, *Boletín Oficial del Estado* (April 29, 1986)

These high health levels are however unevenly distributed. Health inequalities are even more obvious than the high health level. Variables such as social class, sex, age, rural/urban strata, and province of residence underlie a structure in which not all the population shares the same health level; and only a small proportion may participate in health care planning. Our hypothesis that *health levels do not correlate with resources* seems to be true; nevertheless, it cannot be assumed that the (public) health sector has no part in eliminating health unbalances. This is why the alternative of promoting drastic budget cuts should be strongly criticized.

In Spain the question is not to improve the already high health level of the population by means of additional health care expenditure, but to diminish the inequality structure and lack of health care resources (PHC and hospital beds in particular). It seems doubtful that a higher health care budget, by itself, would ensure a better situation. But a reorganization of existing resources along with a rationalization that considers the needs of the population (and not just the interests of pressure groups) would certainly improve distributive problems. Although Spaniards' health does not seem to depend on health care resources, further deterioration of the health care system and/or indiscriminate cuts in health care expenditure might have disastrous consequences. Future health care reformers should analyze sociological and structural variables, and especially their impact on health levels. This is the lesson we learn by studying the Spanish case.

Acknowledgement

We gratefully acknowledge the technical help of Susan B. Greer and Alicia Martino.

References

Acarín, Nolasc *et al.* (1977) *El Servei Nacional de Salut: Una alternativa democrática*, Barcelona: Laia.

Alonso Hinojal, I. (1977) *Sociología de la medicina: Aspectos teóricos y empíricos*, Madrid: Tecnos.

Antó, J. M. *et al.* (1984) *Enquesta de salut de Barcelona 1983*, Barcelona: Ajuntament de Barcelona.

Clavero, G. (1977) *Análisis de la situación sanitaria española*, Madrid: Ministerio de Sanidad y Seguridad Social.

Council of Europe (1985) *Evolution démographique récente dans les états membres du Conseil de l'Europe*, Strasburg: Council of Europe.

De Miguel, A. *et al.* (1970) "Capítulo 14: Sanidad," in Fundación FOESSA (ed.) *Informe sociológico sobre la situación social de España 1970*, Madrid: Euramérica.

De Miguel, J. M. (1976) *Health in the Mediterranean Region: A Comparative Analysis of the Health Systems of Portugal, Spain, Italy and Yugoslavia*, New Haven, Conn: Yale University (doctoral dissertation).

—— (ed.) (1978) *Planificación y reforma sanitarias*, Madrid: Centro de Investigaciones Sociológicas.

—— (1980) *La sociedad enferma: Las bases sociales de la política sanitaria española*, Madrid: Akal.

—— (1983) *Estructura del sector sanitario*, Madrid: Tecnos.

—— (1985) *La salud pública del futuro*, Barcelona: Ariel.

—— (1986) "Health sector structures: the case of Spain," *Social Science and Medicine* 22, 2: 233–46.

Departament de Sanitat i Assistència Social (1980) *La sanitat a Catalunya: Anàlisi i propostes del Departament de Sanitat i Assistència Social*, Barcelona: Generalitat de Catalunya. (Normally referred to as *Libro Amarillo*.)

Departament de Sanitat i Seguretat Social de la Generalitat de Catalunya (1985) *Planificació sanitària pública a Catalunya: Desplegament del mapa sanitari de Catalunya 1983*, Barcelona: Generalitat de Catalunya.

Departamento de Sanidad y Seguridad Social del Gobierno Vasco (1982) *Mapa sanitario de la Comunidad Autónoma Vasca*, Bilbao: Departamento de la Presidencia del Gobierno Vasco.

Durán, M.A. (1983) *Desigualdad social y enfermedad*, Madrid: Tecnos.

Evangelista, M. (1981) *Medicina y sociedad: La reforma sanitaria*, Madrid: Instituto Nacional de la Salud.

García Vargas, J. (1986) *Discurso de la comparecencia del ministro de sanidad y consumo en la Comisión de Política Social y Empleo del Congreso de los Diputados*, Madrid: Congreso de los Diputados, 7 de octubre de 1986.

INE (Instituto Nacional de Estadística) (1983) *Movimiento natural de la población española. Ano 1979. Tomo III: Defunciones según la causa de muerte*, Madrid: INE.

—— (1986) *Encuesta de morbilidad hospitalaria: Ano 1984*, Madrid: INE.

INSALUD (Instituto Nacional de la Salud) (1985a) *Memoria 1983*, Madrid: Instituto Nacional de la Salud.

—— (1985b) *Información económico-funcional de las instituciones sanitarias 1983*, Madrid: Instituto Nacional de la Salud.

—— (1985c) *Anuario estadístico 1983*, Madrid: Instituto Nacional de la Salud.

Instituto Regional de Estudios de la Consejería de Salud y Bienestar Social de la Comunidad de Madrid (1986) *Mapa de salud y servicios sociales: Comunidad Autónoma de Madrid. Vol. I. Zonificación socio-sanitaria: Bases para una regionalizacíon de servicios*, Madrid: Comunidad de Madrid.

Lluch, E. (1983) *Política general del Ministerio de Sanidad y Consumo,*

Madrid: Secretaría General Técnica del Ministerio de Sanidad y Consumo.

Martín López, E. (1983) "Seguridad Social, Sanidad y servicios sociales en España 1975–1982," in Fundación FOESSA (ed.) *Informe sociológico sobre el cambio social en España 1975–1982. IV Informe FOESSA, Volumen II*, Madrid: Euramérica.

Mayor Domingo, F. (1977) *Investigación sobre la asistencia farmacéutica en España: Estudio socioeconómico sobre el conjunto de la asistencia sanitaria española*, Madrid: Instituto Nacional de Previsión.

Nadal, J. *et al.* (1984) *Oferta y demanda de médicos en España: Una primera aproximación*, Madrid: Secretaría General Técnica del Ministerio de Sanidad y Consumo.

OECD (Organization for Economic Cooperation and Development) (1985) *Measuring Health Care 1960–1983: Expenditure, Costs, and Performance*, Paris: OECD.

—— (1986) *Living Conditions in OECD Countries: A Compendium of Social Indicators*, Paris: OECD.

Pérez Peñasco, A. (ed.) (1983) *La sanidad española desde la perspectiva del usuario y la persona enferma*, Madrid: Ediciones Encuentro.

Reventós, J. *et al.* (1977) *Salut, sanitat i societat*, Barcelona: 7 × 7 Edicions.

Rodríguez Díaz, J.A. (1986) *Salud y Sociedad: Análisis sociológico de la estructura y la dinámica del sector sanitario español*, Oviedo: Facultad de Ciencias Económicas y Empresariales (doctoral dissertation) (1987), Madrid: Tecnos.

Saturno, P.J. (1988) "The health care system of Spain: on a wave of change," in R. Saltman (ed.) *International Handbook of Health Care Systems* (in press).

Serigó Segarra, A. (1975) "Sanidad y alimentación," in Fundación FOESSA (ed.) *Informe sociológico sobre la situación social de España: 1975*, Madrid: Euramérica.

—— (1979) *La crisis de la sanidad española*, Madrid: Artes Gráficas Gala.

Soler Sabarís, F. (1971) *Problemas de la Seguridad Social española*, Barcelona: Pulso.

Subsecretaría de la Seguridad Social (1977) *Libro blanco de la Seguridad Social*, Madrid: Ministerio de Trabajo. (Normally referred to as *Libro Blanco*.)

Yuste, F.J. (1982) *Apuntes para un libro negro de la Seguridad Social*, Madrid: Akal.

Six

Yugoslavia: health care under self-managing socialism

Donna E. Parmelee

According to critics of western "medicine under capitalism," socialist medicine holds forth the promise of an equitable and rational distribution of health resources according to need, a promise to be realized through decentralized, democratic control of the health sector by workers and citizens (e.g. Navarro 1976; Waitzkin 1983). The extent to which such an ideal can be realized has been subject to empirical test in various cases of actually existing socialism. With Sigerist's (1937) early optimism about the achievements of Soviet medicine tempered by later researchers (Field 1967; Navarro 1977), the case of Maoist China became for some the model of what medicine could and should be (Horn 1969; Sidel and Sidel 1973). Until recent counter-developments under the post-Mao leadership, there were indications in China that the delivery of medical and health care could be decentralized, democratized, and equalized, with corresponding improvements in the population's health (Sidel and Sidel 1982). Similarly the short-lived experiments of Allende's Chile and the ongoing commitment of Castro's Cuba to meet the health needs of their respective populations have also been singled out as models to be emulated (Navarro 1974; Danielson 1979; Waitzkin 1983).

In the context of such discussions of the theory and practice of socialist medicine, the case of Yugoslavia in the period since the Second World War clearly deserves greater attention than it has received to date. After first experimenting with the Soviet model of a centralized, state-controlled health sector, the Yugoslavs have attempted to decentralize, "de-étaticize,"[1] and democratize their health service and insurance systems in line with their evolving ideology and socio-economic system of self-managing socialism. To a certain extent they have succeeded. Thus the Yugoslav health sector arguably *is* now more decentralized, de-étaticized, and democratized than its counterparts in other existing socialist societies. With private medical practice virtually abolished, Yugoslav health institutions are conceived as neither state nor private but rather as "socially owned" organizations managed by workers' councils composed of their employees and community representatives. Health services are financed largely through a network of local "self-managing communities of interest"; that is, health insurance associations which are formally governed by assemblies composed of users and providers of health services. Yugoslavia would therefore seem an appropriate setting for examining the prospects and problems of socialist medicine.

Drawing upon extensive fieldwork and documentary analysis done in Yugoslavia during the period 1978–86, in this chapter I present a brief overview of the development of the health service and insurance system in Yugoslavia since the Second World War. Special attention is given to institution restructuring and innovation, essentially completed by the mid-1960s, which was designed to decentralize, "de-étaticize," and democratize control of the health sector. Against the backdrop of this discussion of the formal organization of the health sector, I then turn to an evaluation of Yugoslav efforts to address three interrelated problems:

1 Finding an "appropriate" mix among state, professional, and lay control over the health sector;
2 Balancing decentralization of the polity, economy, and social services against official promises to redress the historical legacy of regional and other inequalities, including health inequalities;
3 Balancing user and provider demands and concomitant rising costs against the financial possibilities of a moderately developed country.

Country profile

The Socialist Federal Republic of Yugoslavia is a country of 23 million people located on the Balkan peninsula of south-east Europe. It is composed of six socialist republics which roughly coincide with the major ethnic divisions in the population: Bosnia-Hercegovina, Croatia, Macedonia, Montenegro, Serbia, and Slovenia. The Republic of Serbia includes Serbia Proper and two autonomous provinces, Kosovo and Vojvodina, so distinguished because of their respective Albanian and Hungarian ethnic populations. Administratively the country is further divided into over 500 communes (analogous to counties in the United States). With an average of around 44,000 inhabitants, the commune represents the basic unit of local government (Federal Statistical Office 1986b). In 1980 Yugoslavia had an annual GNP per capita of $2,620 (US). Levels of socio-economic development, however, vary considerably along a north-west to south-east gradient, ranging from a high of $5,193 in Slovenia to a low of $812 in Kosovo. Such *interregional* disparities reflect the historical legacy of centuries of Austro-Hungarian and Ottoman Turkish domination of Yugoslav territories before the First World War, a legacy which has thus far proven to be a relatively intractable economic and a highly sensitive political problem for the Yugoslav Communities. Although less politically controversial, *intra*regional disparities are even greater, with variations in per capita income as high as 28:1 between urban industrialized and rural agricultural communes in Serbia Proper (World Bank 1983; Federal Statistical Office 1986b).

Transformation of the Yugoslav health sector under socialism[2]

Coming to power in a war-torn and devastated country in 1945, the Yugoslav Communists initially retained the tripartite system of organizing and financing health services which they inherited from the interwar monarchy. A *public (state) health service* financed through state budgets continued to provide limited free care for people afflicted with specific diseases (e.g. acute infectious diseases) and those in certain risk groups (young children, mothers, elderly people). Facilities owned and operated by social insurance funds to which employers and employees contributed offered care to the country's small but growing industrial working class (less than a quarter of the population was so covered). Given shortages of resources and the great need for care, *private practice* was permitted to continue, and indeed did so until abolished by federal legislation in the late 1950s.[3]

The new Communist regime soon took steps to reorganize this three-part system in ways deemed more consistent with socialist principles. With the Soviet Union at that time *the* model of proper socialist development, state intervention and centralized regulation of the health sector were strengthened. In 1948, for example, the social insurance facilities and personnel were merged with those of the state health service. Social insurance to finance health, disability, and pension benefits was made compulsory for blue-collar wage-earners and white-collar salaried employees and their respective dependents, and it was now administered through state social insurance institutes at the federal, republic, and district levels. Federal and republic ministries of health assumed responsibility for planning the expansion of health personnel and facilities under the country's first five-year plan (1947–51). Furthermore, in a policy which encountered resistance until it was abandoned in the early 1950s, ministries of health could assign health workers to areas where mass infectious diseases were rampant and shortages of health workers most acute (that is, the less developed regions of the south-east: Bosnia-Hercegovina, Kosovo, Macedonia, and Montenegro).

Yugoslavia's break with Stalin and the Cominform, however, led to a break with the country's early fascination with state or administrative socialism. After some initial floundering, the Yugoslavs began to develop their own model of socialist society, *self-managing socialism*, a model which they intended to be clearly distinguishable from that of the Soviet bloc. With varied emphasis and not without occasional setbacks, constitutional and legislative reforms after 1950 have been designed to transfer decision-making prerogatives from the federation to the republics/provinces and communes (*political decentralization*), and from government authorities at any level to health facilities themselves (Marx's "withering away of the state," or *de-étatization*, as the Yugoslavs call it). Simultaneously, there have been attempts to secure greater and more direct participation of health workers and citizens in the management of various aspects of the health sector (*democratization*).

These reforms aimed at the creation of a self-managed health sector can be illustrated by changes in the status of health facilities and health workers, and in the sources and administration of funding for health services and capital expenditures. With regard to the status of health facilities, in contrast to the early post-war years when they were under the direct jurisdiction of the central state administrative apparatus, health facilities gradually became relatively autonomous *vis-à-vis* the state and acquired the status of socially owned institutions managed ("self-managed") by their employees and community representatives. In the 1950s federal and republic ministries of health were replaced by councils (and in the late 1970s, by committees) of public health, their name changes and reduced staffing reflecting their more limited jurisdiction over the operations of health facilities (for example, regulating the legislative framework of the health sector, supervising matters of common interest such as the supply and quality of pharmaceuticals and implementing international health conventions).

As to the status of health workers under self-managing socialism, by the 1960s health workers were no longer state employees, and have since then been free to seek positions as they become available and are advertised. Like their counterparts in all Yugoslav socialized work organizations, these employees participate in the management of their work-places directly as members of "assemblies of workers" (all employees) and through referenda, and indirectly through their elected delegates in workers' councils. Initially mandated at the level of the entire health facility only, since the 1974 Constitution these assemblies and councils are also formed for separate departments or clinics, known in Yugoslav parlance as "basic organizations of associated labor" (or OOURs, to use the Serbo-Croatian acronym). These self-management bodies have acquired increasing control over the organization of work, hiring and firing, allocations of revenues, and setting of pay scales. To ensure representation of "broader social interests," community delegates have been included in self-management bodies in health institutions since their inception in 1953. However, in the 1960s these community representatives lost their majority membership in these bodies and, while still legally mandated, their involvement is often pro forma. In short, while democratization via community involvement has been weakened, democratization via health worker self-management has been enhanced.

Concomitant with these developments in the administration of health facilities, sources of funding for health services and capital expenditures have also changed. In the immediate post-war period, health facilities were funded through government budgets, compulsory social insurance contributions for blue- and white-collar workers in the socialized sector and direct patient fees (primarily from the large but declining number of uninsured private agricultural producers).[4] As part of broader processes of political decentralization during the 1950s, republics and especially local areas (districts and communes) assumed greater responsibility for financing health services. To illustrate, local budgets provided only 17 per cent of the combined expenditures for health and social welfare from 1947 to 1951; by 1960, this share had increased to over 54 per cent. By the 1960s, the share of total health expenditures financed from government budgets at any level had been reduced to a minimum. In 1965, for example, with virtually the entire population by then at least partially covered by compulsory health insurance, less than 5 per cent of total health expenditures came from government budgets, whereas 80 per cent was financed through local workers' and farmers' insurance associations. And, while government budgets had been the major source of capital investment funds during the 1950s, they accounted for only 20 per cent of these funds in 1965.

Trends towards decentralization, de-étatization, and democratization also affected the administration of the health insurance program. During the 1950s, the social insurance program (including health insurance) was removed from the competence of the state administrative apparatus, and acquired the status of a semi-autonomous public service managed by assemblies of insurees. The word "state" was dropped from the title of existing social insurance institutes which continued to implement the insurance provisions. After extension of compulsory insurance coverage from workers in the socialized sector to other categories of insured persons (to private farmers in 1959 and to self-employed craftworkers and professionals during the 1950s), Communal Insurance Associations for each category were founded in 1962. Communal (or at times intercommunal) associations were given autonomy to determine insurance benefits above and beyond minimum standards prescribed by federal law until 1974 and by republic law thereafter, provided they agreed to collect the necessary funds.[5] (Federal grants and republic-level "solidarity funds" assisted regions and communes unable to afford the basic level of services.) In addition to a professional staff, each communal association had an assembly composed of insuree-representatives formally charged with health planning and programming in the commune, negotiating contracts with provider institutions and determining the level of contributions from insurees and the types and range of benefits. In the 1974 Constitution, these insurance associations were rechristened "self-managing communities of interest" (SIZs in the Serbo-Croatian acronym) to reflect the fact that they would henceforth be co-managed by assemblies of user *and* provider delegates, and therefore settings where the interests of different social actors could be "harmonized," in theory, with minimal state involvement.

Balancing state, professional, and lay control over the health sector

Through numerous constitutional and legislative enactments, the Yugoslavs have attempted to transform central state bureaucratic control over the health sector into more decentralized, deétaticized, and democratized control in accordance with their evolving ideology of self-managing socialism. In other words, they have experimented with various mixes of state, professional, and lay control over health service delivery institutions and the health insurance program. It is one thing, of course, to prescribe organizational reforms though legal documents. It is quite another thing to implement these formal changes and yet another to have organizations then function as anticipated by reform architects. What, then, have been some of the results of the Yugoslavs' efforts to alter the balance of state, professional and lay control over the health sector?

Whither the state in health sector management?

While the decision-making prerogatives of the central state bureaucracy have been reduced, the Yugoslav state has certainly not yet withered away (cf. Zukin 1984). For example, in the context of the country's frequent economic crises since the 1960s (for example, problems with high inflation and unemployment, balance of payment deficits, and foreign indebtedness), the Federal Assembly (Parliament) and its executive body, the Federal Executive Council, have repeatedly intervened with *ad hoc* wage and price freezes or limits on the annual rate of contribution for health insurance, the setting of which is a formally prescribed prerogative of the local health insurance association assemblies. Similarly these latter assemblies are supposed to determine the range of benefits to be insured (expressed by the Yugoslavs as matching "local needs with local financial possibilities"). However, the scope of their decision-making has been restricted by federally-mandated and, since 1974, republic-mandated compulsory health care rights. The federal government also guarantees a certain measure of redistribution through grants-in-aid to the less developed regions of the country. And, not unimportantly, it has been the federal government which has orchestrated all of the various organizational reforms leading to the creation (and re-creation) of health facility self-management bodies and of health insurance associations.

In addition to the ongoing federal involvement in the health sector, the roles of the republic/provincial and communal authorities must also be considered. Indeed, some have argued that a reduction in the prerogatives of the federal government in post-Second-World-War Yugoslavia ("central statism") has been accompanied by the emergence of "pluralistic statism" at these lower levels of state administration. In effect, devolution of authority from the central state bureaucracy has meant partial de-étatization but, perhaps more importantly, political decentralization or "pluralistic statism" (e.g. Sekulić 1983).

Pluralistic statism appears in various ways in the health sector. To illustrate, as I have already noted, since 1974 republic and provincial legislation has prescribed the basic level of benefits which all communal health insurance associations must provide. Furthermore, while negotiations between the health insurance associations (since 1974, the SIZs) and health facilities regarding annual programs of health services are the subject of so-called "self-management agreements" which explicitly exclude direct state involvement, the government does have the legal right to intervene in the event that an agreement cannot be reached or if its contents are deemed "socially harmful" (Pejovich 1979). A more frequent and explicit case of state intervention is as a signatory to "social compacts." For example, although formally decisions on the allocation of health facility revenues and salary levels are entrusted to internal self-management bodies, the actual range of salaries for all work-places in a given commune or republic are set through social compacts negotiated among these work-places *and* the respective government authorities. And, for any major policy initiative of either the health SIZ or health facility (for example to introduce direct "out of pocket" payments for services or to call for a public referendum to raise funds for capital projects), it is necessary to have the support of various communal political structures, in particular the commune assembly and the local socio-political organizations (the trade union council, the Socialist Alliance, and the League of Communists).[6]

The shifting balance between lay and professional participation

Even with the state's (or, better to say, states') continued involvement in the health sector, the post-1950 evolution of self-managing socialism has allowed for some measure of lay and professional influence in the management of health facilities and the health insurance program. With regard to *health facility management*, legislation from 1953 mandated the formation of self-management boards in which community representatives would be in the majority. By 1960 some 20,969 persons were officially reported to be members of health facility self-management boards, having an average membership of 7.1 members per facility. Given an estimated population in 1960 of 18.4 million, this meant that more than 1 out of every 1,000 Yugoslavs was formally involved in health facility management. Of these self-management board members, around 57 per cent participated as citizens selected by local government authorities, 9 per cent represented the social insurance funds, 17 per cent were elected from the ranks of those employed in the facility, and 14 per cent served as *ex officio* members (e.g. health facility directors).[7] Out of the total membership, approximately 16 per cent were physicians and another 13 per cent were other medical workers. Despite the regime's proclaimed desire to bring specific categories of the population into the political process which had been previously excluded or underrepresented in "undemocratic" socialist or capitalist societies (e.g. blue-collar workers and women), the experience of these self-management

173

boards in health facilities in the 1950s is quite typical of difficulties encountered in self-management bodies more generally; namely, an overrepresentation of male white-collar workers (Parmelee 1983: 81–5).

As to the actual functioning of these early self-management boards, the evidence is woefully limited. However, two Yugoslav sources do provide some hints concerning actual practice (Juzbašić 1963; Georgievski 1972). For one thing, the presence of lay members in self-management boards apparently provoked considerable concern. Perhaps not surprisingly, health workers were not entirely pleased with the prospect of lay involvement in health facility management, particularly since such external representatives were not included in self-management bodies in economic enterprises. While unable to stop the formation of self-management boards with a majority of external members, some facilities reportedly slowed down the formation of these boards or even went so far as to strengthen the professional voice by having physicians from one institution nominated as external members of self-management boards in other health facilities. Moreover, during these early years, many of the issues formally within the self-management board's jurisdiction were still regulated by law (e.g. wage and salary scales) or had to be decided in conjunction with government authorities (e.g. prices of services). Finally, with directors (normally physicians) playing the major role in facility management, self-management board influence was apparently quite marginal.

During the 1960s two basic trends can be noted in health facility self-management bodies. On the one hand, health facilities became somewhat more autonomous *vis-à-vis* the state (i.e. de-étatization). For one thing, as noted earlier, a declining share of their revenues came from state budgets. For another, health personnel ceased to be state employees subject to state-determined pay scales, but rather became employees of their respective institutions with self-management rights to participate in setting pay scales and making personnel decisions (including hiring and firing of directors). On the other hand, professional dominance over lay members of self-management bodies in health facilities was formally legitimized. The first move in this direction came in 1960 when *new* self-management boards composed exclusively of health facility workers were mandated. These new self-management boards were to share decision-making prerogatives with new councils, at least half of whose members were to come from the community. According to legislation in 1965, however, these new councils could function with either a "broader" composition (including community representatives and staff members) when deciding such matters as the distribution of revenues or with a "narrower" composition of staff members only for other matters. Establishing a precedent which continues to the present day, this latter move seems to have further weakened lay participation in health facility management (for example, by 1970, community representatives constituted only around a quarter of the total membership in the councils) (Parmelee 1983: 118–25).[8]

As to the balance of lay vs. professional participation in the *management of the health insurance program*, the shift in composition of the insurance association assemblies from exclusively lay members in the 1950s and 1960s to bicameral assemblies of users and providers of health services in the 1970s and 1980s is not unimportant. Couched in the self-management rhetoric of decentralization, de-étatization, and democratization, formal management over the social insurance institutes was transferred from the state bureaucratic apparatus to assemblies of insurees organized at the local, district, republic/provincial, and federal levels during the 1950s. As of 1958, for example, some 11,582 insurees represented Yugoslavia's growing white- and blue-collar labor force and their families in 390 local and district social insurance assemblies. With the introduction of compulsory insurance coverage for farmers in 1959 and territorial redistricting of the units of local government in the early 1960s, by 1964 some 5,473 worker-insurees and 3,263 farmer-insurees represented their respective constituencies in 127 communal (or intercommunal) social insurance assemblies for workers and 92 assemblies for farmers. However, following further territorial redistricting and the creation of self-management communities of interest (SIZs) in 1974, bicameral health insurance assemblies included 10,053 delegates in chambers of users and 3,432 delegates in chambers of providers in 305 health SIZs in 1975.[9] Numerically at least, health providers now constituted one-quarter of the members of the health SIZ assemblies (Parmelee 1983: 94–7, 203).

At this point, it would seem appropriate to consider the actual influence these insurance assemblies have had in shaping insurance policies. With regard to the assemblies of the 1950s and 1960s with exclusive lay membership, the available evidence would suggest that their actual decision-making powers were rather limited. For as already noted, governmental authorities continued to regulate the rate of contribution for health and other forms of social insurance and to mandate minimum levels of benefits. Furthermore, insuree influence was further limited by the fact that assemblies were convened rather infrequently (reportedly only twice a year in the 1950s) (*Yugoslav Survey* 1960). While some measure of lay oversight was provided by executive boards which were elected from the ranks of the insuree assemblies and which met on a monthly basis, day-to-day operations were left in the hands of professional staffs of insurance administrators. If one takes seriously the critiques that insuree influence was inadequate and that the insurance program retained the character of a bureaucratic state structure despite its formally semi-autonomous status, then it would seem likely that these administrative staffs exercised considerable power in deciding matters not prescribed by legal regulations.

Reforms in the health insurance program in the 1970s were at least in part justified by calls for greater worker (i.e. lay) control over the allocation of the fruits of their labor, in this case over allocation of funds for health care. In theory, the bicameral SIZ assemblies were intended to bring users and providers of health services together so that they could directly negotiate annual health care programs without the need for the state or other bureaucratic intermediary. Without denigrating the fact that Yugoslav laypeople have a greater formal opportunity to participate in health care decision-making via SIZ assemblies than their counterparts in most other countries, their actual influence is limited relative to that wielded by insurance administrators, by providers, and as noted earlier by local political structures (the commune assembly and socio-political organizations).

That actual lay influence in health SIZ assemblies is lower than that which is formally prescribed is supported by my own case studies of three Croatian SIZ assemblies conducted in the late 1970s and in 1984 (Parmelee *et al.* 1979; Parmelee 1983), as well as by available Yugoslav reports (e.g. Šiber 1982). While the SIZ assemblies which I studied met more frequently than their counterparts from the 1950s (on the order of seven to ten times per year) and did not suffer from the frequently cited problem of SIZ assemblies more generally to get a quorum, the degree of

user influence was rather low. For their part, insurance administrative staffs continued to play an instrumental role in shaping
health SIZ activities through their responsibility to set assembly
agendas, to draw up often very complex contracts between
provider institutions and the health SIZs, and to formulate and
present most proposals for assembly consideration. Of the two
chambers, the chamber of providers appeared to be in a better
position to influence SIZ decisions, since their delegates were
more organized and generally were, as I was told, "the strongest
of the strong."[10] At meetings I observed of SIZ assemblies in
three communes in 1984, there was generally little opposition or
even discussion of agenda items, which were often presented in a
perfunctory manner by the SIZ executive secretary, followed by
a few supporting comments by another SIZ staff member or
medical professional, and then by a ritualistic show of hands.[11]
The pro forma character of assembly meetings in part reflects the
fact that items appearing on assembly agendas have already been
cleared through the assembly's executive body, the so-called
presidency, where somewhat greater discussion by user and
provider delegates was heard. Yet, as I was told by one
experienced and perceptive user delegate (actually a physician!),
to the extent that there was discussion at all it often focused on
relatively minor issues (e.g. the purchase of a specific piece of
equipment by a health facility or of an air-conditioner for the
health SIZ office). On the other hand, when it came to proposals
for financing the commune's annual health care program
involving millions of dinars, there tended to be very little
discussion, let alone opposition.

In sum, the results of Yugoslav efforts to decentralize, de-
étaticize, and democratize the health sector have been mixed. On
the one hand, they have achieved a remarkable (some would say
excessive) degree of decentralization of health care delivery
facilities and of health insurance associations. They have also
succeeded in setting up various decision-making bodies composed of lay and professional members who have the opportunity to participate in decision-making which was previously
the exclusive prerogative of the central state bureaucratic
apparatus. On the other hand, government and other political
bodies, especially at the local and republic/provincial levels, can
and do intervene. And, to the extent that one can still speak of
democracy in the health sector, it is a democracy in which health
professionals have a greater voice than laypeople, and a

democracy which is constantly at odds with the bureaucratic authority of health insurance administrative staffs.

Decentralization and the redress of health inequalities

One of the ongoing promises and problems of the post-Second-World-War Communist regime has been the redress of inherited inequalities in socio-economic development in general, and in health resources and health status in particular. While accepting inequalities based on the socialist principle "to each according to his or her work," the Yugoslavs have declared their intentions to transcend differences stemming from economic underdevelopment and other unequal conditions of life and work (SFRY 1976: 21). By implication, health inequalities are among those social differences which the Yugoslavs seek to prevent and eliminate since they are not (or should not be) based on application of the principle of distribution according to work performed. While no society has yet created a truly equal health system, this issue is especially critical in a country which has made a collective commitment to provide for the health needs of its people. Thus, even if full equality is an elusive goal (Anderson 1972), it would seem important for the regime's legitimacy that its health inequalities are at least diminishing.

In the light of Yugoslavia's decentralization of responsibility for organizing and financing health care to the republics and communes, begun in the early 1950s and essentially completed by the mid-1960s, both *inter*regional and *intra*regional inequalities merit consideration. Of the two sets of inequalities, *inter*regional disparities among the different republics and provinces have been especially politically problematic, since regional boundaries correspond roughly to the homelands of the several Yugoslav national groups, which historically and to the present day have held divergent views on the appropriate distribution of power and privileges. With most funding for health care since the mid-1960s coming from contributions to local insurance associations or republic-level solidarity funds, the redress of interregional health inequalities has not been as divisive an issue as, say, the redress of economic inequalities. Yet, since decisions over the past two decades on supplemental federal grants for social services to the less developed regions, as for development funds more generally, have required consensual agreement among the eight regions, interregional health disparities are not without political significance.

While a complete evaluation of the Yugoslavs' efforts to redress interregional health disparities over the post-war period is beyond the scope of this paper, data on a few selected indicators can be presented which illustrate that there is both good news and bad news.[12] On the one hand, in terms of relative physician distribution measured by indexes of physician/population ratios (Yugoslavia = 100), regional inequalities declined until the mid-1960s and thereafter remained relatively stable until the 1980s when a trend towards further declines can be noted (see Table 6.1). Significantly this positive development in physician density also applies at the extremes, where the relative position of the least developed region (Kosovo) has improved in recent years. Likewise, there have been gains in the regional distribution of general hospital beds (Table 6.2). Kosovo remains at a disadvantage, although it is encouraging that the decline in its relative position from 1960 to 1980 appears to have stopped. Interregional disparities in life expectancy have also decreased (Table 6.3). On the other hand, significant gaps in infant mortality rates persist, with two of the less developed regions (Kosovo and Macedonia) lagging far behind the rest of

Table 6.1   *Physicians[1] per 100,000 population, by region: 1952–84*

Region	Physicians/100,000 (Yugoslavia = 100)					Physicians/ 100,000 1984
	1952	1961	1971	1981	1984	
Less developed regions	45	59	65	72	75	152.3
Bosnia–Hercegovina	41	57	63	73	75	153.1
Kosovo	30	35	38	40	46	94.5
Macedonia	59	72	87	95	97	197.5
Montenegro	57	75	76	81	80	162.8
More developed regions	125	120	119	116	115	234.4
Croatia	132	124	114	115	112	227.5
Serbia Proper	122	120	121	119	122	247.6
Slovenia	151	141	129	123	117	238.8
Vojvodina	96	97	114	106	102	208.6
Yugoslavia	100	100	100	100	100	203.7

Sources: Federal Statistical Office (various years); Federal Institute for Public Health (various years)
Note: [1] Including stomatologists.

Table 6.2   *General hospital beds per 10,000 population, by region: 1952–83*

Region	General hospital beds/10,000 (Yugoslavia = 100)					General hospital beds/10,000
	1952	1960	1970	1980	1983	1983
Less developed regions	66	71	80	83	83	33.2
Bosnia-Hercegovina	57	59	75	85	86	34.1
Kosovo	49	73	63	57	59	23.6
Macedonia	90	86	98	91	93	36.9
Montenegro	89	109	96	108	104	41.5
More developed regions	115	114	111	110	110	43.7
Croatia	137	117	113	114	115	45.8
Serbia Proper	102	109	99	101	102	40.4
Slovenia	145	155	164	147	141	56.1
Vojvodina	77	83	91	91	92	36.1
Yugoslavia	100	100	100	100	100	39.8

Source: Federal Statistical Office (various years)

Table 6.3   *Life expectancy at birth, by sex: 1952–4, 1981–2*

Region	1952–4		1981–2	
	Male	Female	Male	Female
Less developed regions				
Bosnia-Hercegovina	53	55	68	73
Kosovo	49	45	67	71
Macedonia	55	55	69	72
Montenegro	58	60	72	76
More developed regions				
Croatia	59	63	67	74
Serbia Proper	59	61	69	74
Slovenia	63	68	67	75
Vojvodina	58	62	67	74
Yugoslavia	57	59	68	73

Source: Federal Statistical Office (1986b: 42)

the country (Table 6.4). Indeed, at the extremes, the relative position of Kosovo is worse in 1985 than it was in 1952!

Thus, even with decentralization of administration and financing of health services, there do seem to be definite trends towards lessening interregional inequalities. These trends are

Table 6.4   *Infant mortality rates,[1] by region: 1952–85*

Region	1952	1961	1971	1981	1985
Less developed regions					
Bosnia-Hercegovina	113.9	98.7	54.7	30.1	24.2
Kosovo	145.9	125.9	89.6	62.9	59.2
Macedonia	129.8	112.1	82.2	51.1	48.3
Montenegro	80.4	61.4	27.8	22.8	20.9
More developed regions					
Croatia	102.3	62.9	29.5	18.9	15.7
Serbia Proper	87.0	66.3	37.3	23.8	24.9
Slovenia	64.3	29.4	25.5	13.1	14.0
Vojvodina	113.2	71.6	34.5	17.5	11.6
Yugoslavia	105.1	82.0	49.5	30.8	28.8

Sources: Federal Statistical Office (various years, 1986b)
Note: [1] Infant mortality rate = number of infant deaths per 1000 live births.

particularly heartening given higher birth-rates in the less developed regions (especially in Kosovo) and given the increasing interregional gap in per capita health care expenditures and even greater disparities in per capita income (see Tables 6.5 and 6.6 respectively). Accordingly it would appear that federal policies to establish medical faculties in the less developed regions (in Bosnia-Hercegovina in 1946, in Macedonia in 1947, and in Kosovo in 1969) and to provide supplemental grants for social services in these regions have had ameliorative effects.[13] On the other hand, the inability of federal policies to mitigate broader disparities in standard of living, significant cultural differences as well as differences in the quality of health services among the regions would seem to account for persisting interregional variations in infant mortality rates.

*Intra*regionally, two overlapping sets of health inequalities can be distinguished: disparities among the different categories of insurees (workers vs. farmers, in particular) and intercommunal disparities. Perhaps reflecting the Communists' ambivalence towards private enterprise, private peasant-farmers have at least until recently occupied a second-class status in Yugoslavia's health care system. For despite its important role in the national liberation struggle during the Second World War, the peasantry was initially excluded from compulsory health insurance coverage. As part of the regime's goal to industrialize the country and to entice the rural population to the cities, social insurance

Success and Crisis in National Health Systems

Table 6.5 Workers' insurance expenditures per capita,[1] by region: 1963–84

| Region | Yugoslavia = 100 | | | | Per capita expenditures (in dinars)[2] |
	1963	1971	1981	1984	1984
Less developed regions	74	74	59	61	6,896
Bosnia-Hercegovina	80	80	59	70	7,979
Kosovo	60	67	56	44	4,995
Macedonia	68	67	60	52	5,914
Montenegro	80	74	68	63	7,105
More developed regions	113	112	122	122	13,868
Croatia	114	116	122	122	13,875
Serbia Proper	99	98	112	116	13,086
Slovenia	148	143	171	160	18,097
Vojvodina	94	99	93	95	10,726
Yugoslavia	100	100	100	100	11,329

Source: Federal Statistical Office (various years)
Notes: [1] Excluded are cash benefits under workers' health insurance (e.g. sick and maternity leave pay, funeral benefits, etc.) and insurance administration costs.
[2] Dinars per US$, average of daily figures for June 1984 = 143.2 (OECD 1984).

Table 6.6 Income per capita, by region: 1954–80

| Region | Gross material product per capita (Yugoslavia = 100)[1] | | | | | Gross national product per capita[2] (US $) |
	1954	1965	1970	1975	1980	1980
Less developed regions	71	65	61	62	60	1,580
Bosnia-Hercegovina	82	69	67	69	66	1,737
Kosovo	48	37	34	33	31	812
Macedonia	69	73	64	69	66	1,721
Montenegro	53	72	78	70	80	2,086
More developed regions	110	118	121	121	123	3,233
Croatia	119	119	125	124	127	3,314
Serbia Proper	84	95	97	92	97	2,534
Slovenia	188	187	193	201	198	5,193
Vojvodina	88	116	110	121	122	3,189
Yugoslavia	100	100	100	100	100	2,620

Source: World Bank 1983: 237
Notes: [1] Based on current prices.
[2] GNP per capita computed according to World Bank Atlas methodology.

benefits were extended in 1946 only to blue- and white-collar workers employed in the socialized sector and their dependents (then numbering about 12 per cent of the entire population). By the time that compulsory health insurance for farmers was introduced through federal law in 1969 and republic implementing legislation in 1970, almost half of the population was insured under compulsory workers' insurance. Even then, the range of benefits insured for farmers was less comprehensive than that for workers, in effect leading to continued higher out-of-pocket costs and/or lower utilization rates for peasant-farmers (Hrabač 1968; Berg *et al.* 1976). These disparities may at last be diminishing in the wake of continued migration from rural to urban employment and moves in the 1970s and 1980s towards unification of the workers' and farmers' insurance programs (e.g. by 1981, over 80 per cent of the population was covered by workers' insurance).

Intercommunal variations in access to health care are another form of what I have defined here as intraregional inequalities. Although in part due to disparities inherited from the past, they have been perpetuated by the decentralized nature of financing health services via communal insurance associations and, to a lesser degree, by the reluctance of physicians to work in the "provinces". Much like public education in the United States, wealthier communes have been able to develop their health delivery facilities and expand their insurance coverage beyond that possible in poorer communes. And, like their counterparts elsewhere, physicians have tended to be disproportionately located in urban areas, particularly in the capital cities of the different regions. On balance, republic-level solidarity funds do mitigate some of these disparities by assuring coverage of a basic level of health service as noted earlier. And, of course, a certain measure of concentration of expensive technology and specialist services is clearly desirable, provided that the services are geographically and financially accessible to those beyond a given communal boundary. While difficult to measure, one hears enough reports of higher prices being charged for services rendered in one commune to patients from other communes, or of efforts to keep health insurance funds within the commune (e.g. by limiting access to care elsewhere or by developing the commune's own capacity despite unused capacity in a neighboring commune), to realize that the problem of intercommunal inequalities has not completely been resolved.

Balancing user and provider demands and rising costs with the country's economic possibilities

Like all countries, Yugoslavia is confronting the dilemmas of an explosion in costs in the wake of seemingly endless demands from users for health services and from providers for new technology and facilities as well as increasing incomes. These dilemmas are especially problematic in a country such as Yugoslavia, where decentralization has tended to spark communal particularism and, in turn, unnecessary and expensive duplication of services, facilities, and health insurance administrative staffs among neighboring localities. It is also problematic in a country whose current regime's legitimacy has at least partially been based on the promise to insure an ambitious package of health benefits at the same time as it has been moving out of the Third into the Second World. Even Yugoslavia's renowned leader, Josip Broz Tito, was to acknowledge in a 1965 article in *Borba* that more had been promised than could effectively be delivered:

> Immediately after the war, we introduced a series of measures beyond our material possibilities, for instance, with respect to social insurance and other social benefits, which are now causing difficulties. But we cannot go back on this so that we could start afresh in a more realistic way. We were wrong not to begin at a level in line with our material possibilities; because of that mistake we suffer now, but we have to persist. All our citizens know that. All sorts of social benefits which nobody dreamt before are now considered by people to be their natural due. People think that our standard of living must constantly rise and I agree with them.
>
> (quoted in Sirc 1979: 141)

Throughout the post-war period, the Yugoslavs have used various methods to contain health expenditures while simultaneously extending compulsory health insurance coverage to virtually the entire population and expanding the supply of health personnel and facilities. As already mentioned, the federal government has repeatedly intervened to freeze wages and prices or to put a cap on the rate of contribution for health and other social services. In the country's current economic crisis marked by a $20 billion foreign debt, an inflation rate approaching 100 per cent and a 15 per cent unemployment rate, limits have also been placed on the rate of growth of health SIZ expenditures. Such limits can indeed be quite effective in containing rising expenditures, as evidenced by the declining share of the social product allocated for health (from 5.5 per cent in 1979 to 4.5 per cent in 1983) (Djurković 1984; Meštrović 1984).

In the context of the current as well as earlier economic crises, the responses of health delivery facilities and/or health insurance associations can be summarized under the rubric of three main strategies: marketization, rationalization, and externalization (Svetlik 1986). Marketization entails the identification of potential patients with funds and the attempt to sell them services directly without the involvement of the health insurance associations (or SIZs). This strategy is illustrated by the sale of preventive examinations of workers directly to an enterprise, a type of contractual relationship which was foreseen at least as early as the 1974 Constitution, if not actively pursued until more recently. Other examples of marketization include the advertising of the highly developed Ljubljana Clinical Hospital Center to people in Third World countries or of health tourism in the country's hotels and spas to people in the First World. Marketization is still a rather limited strategy for coping with economic crises, at least to the extent that it resembles a reprivatization of the health sector. This latter point was brought home to me in the late 1970s when a socially owned and self-managed health facility proposed to develop a "private" diagnostic center at the Zagreb Hotel Intercontinental. The proposal met with considerable resistance since the center was intended to serve not only foreign patients but also Yugoslavs who were willing to pay extra for the privilege of a faster diagnostic workup than the socially owned facility could provide. And, although a very modest amount of individual private medical or dental practice has been permitted in a few republics, the idea for such a diagnostic facility went beyond the boundaries of tolerable private enterprise and it was not permitted.

Rationalization, or the attempt to use available labor and capital more efficiently, has been a more common response to economic crises, and one which has had the full support of the state. From the 1950s on, one sees frequent calls in the health service literature to make better use of "internal reserves" in health facilities. Initially this took the form of efforts to minimize duplication of diagnostic tests, to reduce unnecessary overtime, or to merge all in-patient and out-patient facilities in a given commune into a "medical center" with a common professional administration which paralleled the self-management bodies discussed earlier. More recently rationalization can be seen in moves to substitute less expensive services for more expensive ones. For example, as in other countries, since the late 1970s the Yugoslavs have placed greater emphasis on primary health care as a way to reduce more costly secondary and tertiary care. In addition, health insurance associations have produced detailed time normatives as standards against which to assess the quantity and quality of service delivery (cf. Letica 1984). While the latter represents an attempt to increase the efficiency of provider institutions, efforts to rationalize the operations of communal health insurance associations are also underway (e.g. through the creation of common administrative staffs for neighboring communes).

Finally, externalization, according to Svetlik (1986), involves a shifting of responsibility for either provision of services from health institutions or payment of services via the health insurance associations to individuals or enterprises. On the one hand, a shift in responsibility for health care can be seen in attempts to organize home care for the sick as an alternative to hospitalization as well as in calls for greater individual responsibility for preventing disease and maintaining health through self-care activities. On the other hand, shifts in responsibility for payment for health benefits *from* the insurance funds to individual or collective users have occurred at least since the 1960s. For example, coverage for certain services has been restricted (e.g. for treatment in health spas or drugs not on a list prepared by the health insurance associations). In addition, small users' fees (known in Yugoslavia as *participacija*, or participation payments) have increasingly been introduced for prescription drugs, house calls, some specialist exams, in-patient room and board charges, and other services. A shift in responsibility to specific collective users can be seen in enterprises' greater liability for payment of sick leave benefits before the health insurance funds take over. Namely, before 1966, enterprises covered only the first seven days of sick leave compensation; since then, they have paid for the first thirty days (with even some talk more recently to extend this to forty-five days). Or, should a health facility desiring to purchase a piece of equipment be unable to secure funding from the health insurance association, it is not uncommon for funds to be secured from a local enterprise.

Not surprisingly, these various efforts to balance user and provider demands and rising costs with available economic means have not yielded a "perfect" solution, if such a solution is indeed even possible. As elsewhere, deteriorating economic conditions and the resultant attempts at cost containment in Yugoslavia have not been without untoward effects on the population's health status (e.g. recent increases in infant mortality rates) and on the ability of health care providers to keep abreast of world developments in medicine (e.g. in the early 1980s, imports of professional journals were temporarily curtailed due to shortages of foreign exchange). And, like their counterparts elsewhere, Yugoslav physicians are confronting the ethical dilemma of having the knowledge and skills to treat patients but insufficient resources to do so (e.g. as in the care of patients with end-stage renal disease) (Nikolić 1986). With prospects for an easy or early solution of the country's current economic problems rather gloomy, it appears that, financially speaking, the Yugoslav health care system will remain on the "critical list" for some time to come.

Prognosis for the future of health care under Yugoslav self-managing socialism: some closing remarks

Not uncommonly, Yugoslav authors make no pretense to end their books or articles with conclusions. Instead, they call the last chapter or section *umjesto zaključka*, "instead of a conclusion." Given the evolving, dynamic character of their society, this is perhaps the most appropriate way to call attention to the fact that self-managing socialism is indeed a process, or set of processes. My closing remarks on the prospects for health care under Yugoslav self-managing socialism should likewise be viewed as a "process" report.

First, while the Yugoslavs have achieved a fair, even excessive measure of decentralization of their health sector, they have been less successful in their efforts towards de-étatization and democratization. To the extent that they continue to proclaim the latter objectives, they will have to grapple with the knee-jerk reaction of the state(s) to intervene and the difficulties of lay participation in very complex decision-making processes where lack of professional or administrative expertise puts laypeople at an immediate disadvantage. Second, while some progress has been made in reducing health inequalities, continued redistribution from the wealthier regions and communes to the less wealthy will be necessary given the substantial development differences which remain. Lastly, in the health sector as in the rest of the economy, the Yugoslavs are currently paying the price for having lived beyond their means. Yet, if the past can be used to predict the future, then the Yugoslavs' capacity to overcome seemingly insurmountable odds should give reason for optimism that they will eventually find a way out of their current economic dilemmas.

Notes

1 "De-étaticize" and "de-étatization" are admittedly awkward renderings of the Marxist "withering away of the state." The Yugoslavs have borrowed from the French (*état*) to create the Serbo-Croatian word, *de-etatizacija*.

2 Material in this section is based on Parmelee (1983; 1985a).

3 Private medical practice was made illegal though federal legislation in 1958, although older practitioners were still allowed to practice. In the wake of a fiscal crisis in the late 1960s and growing unemployment among physicians and dentists, Croatia and Slovenia reintroduced private practice on a very limited scale. In the 1970s Slovenia again dropped private practice, and through a new health law passed in 1980 in Croatia, it appeared that private practice would be gradually phased out there, too. However, plans to abandon it in Croatia have been put on hold and Serbia is in the process of re-introducing private dental practice, again in the context of an economic crisis and a surplus of health workers.

4 Ever since the disastrous attempt to collectivize agriculture in the later 1940s and early 1950s, the majority of Yugoslav farmland has been privately owned (*c.* 83 per cent in the 1980s). Over the course of the post-war period, the share of the population whose main source of livelihood is agriculture declined sharply (from 67.2 per cent in 1948 to 19.9 per cent in 1981) (Federal Statistical Office 1986b).

5 At a minimum, health insurance associations were required to insure prevention, control, and treatment of tuberculosis, venereal, and other infectious diseases subject to compulsory notification, care and treatment of patients with mental disorders, malignancies, rheumatic fever, and muscular distrophy; total health care for women during pregnancy and post-natal care for one year, for children up to age 15, for young people in school up to age 26, and for persons over 60; and various health education and environmental sanitation activities (Federal Committee of Labor, Health and Social Welfare 1979: 7).

6 The Socialist Alliance is a mass political organization. Its membership is considerably larger than that of the League of Communists (as the Communist Party has been called since 1952). In 1981, the League's membership was over 2 million (or 9.1 per cent of the population) while the Socialist Alliance had over 14.1 million members (or 63.1 per cent of the population) (Federal Statistical Office 1985).

7 The remaining 3.5 per cent were listed as "others."

8 Since 1970, data on the composition of health facility self-management bodies have no longer been published in the *Statistical Yearbook of Yugoslavia*. Although community representatives in health facility management are still mandated by republic/provincial legislation, I have not found further information on their exact numbers or actual influence apart from occasional anecdotal remarks implying that it is pro forma.

9 These data for health SIZs in 1975 exclude Slovenia. In that republic, separate delegates are not elected to different social service SIZ assemblies, but instead are rotated among SIZ assemblies according to the issues under consideration.

10 Although perhaps not typical, it is interesting to note that the executive secretary of the health SIZ in one of the communes studied was actually a physician who had previously been the director of the commune's medical center.

11 According to the minutes for ten meetings of one Zagreb SIZ for a sixteen-month period in 1983–4, only 3 out of a total of 109 agenda items were rejected by the assembly (e.g. a proposal to conclude a contract for provision of health services in another commune, a patient request for reimbursement of costs for treatment at a spa).

12 I would point out that I reported mostly "bad" news regarding the Yugoslavs' efforts to reduce interregional health inequalities in my earlier studies (Parmelee 1983; 1985a; 1985b). However, in light of more recent data from the 1980s, I must tentatively revise my previous assessments.

13 Data on the actual amounts redistributed to individual less developed regions as federal grants for health care are not readily available. Total supplemental financing of social services, in general, for the 1966–84 period amounted to around 150 billion dinars (current prices). For the 1976–80 period, this represented 0.93 per cent of the social product of the socialized sector of the economy (Federal Statistical Office 1986a: 194–5; World Bank 1983: 243).

References

Anderson, O. (1972) *Health Care: Can There Be Equity?* New York: Wiley.
Berg, R.L., Brooks, Jr., M.R., and Savičević, M. (1976) *Health Care in Yugoslavia and the United States*, Fogarty International Center Proceedings no. 34, Washington, DC: US Government Printing Office.

Danielson, R. (1979) *Cuban Medicine*, New Brunswick, NJ: Transaction Books.
Djurković, B. (1984) "Stabilizaciona politika u oblasti zajedničkih potreba i društvenih delatnosti u periodu u 1981–1984. godinama." [Stabilization policy in the field of collective needs and social activities in the period 1981–1984]. *Socijalna Politika* 34, 3: 3–8.
Federal Committee of Labor, Health and Social Welfare (1979) *The System of Health Development Planning in Yugoslavia*, Belgrade.
Federal Institute for Public Health (various years) *Statistički Godišnjak o Narodnom Zdravlju i Zdravstvenoj Zaštiti u SFR Jugoslaviji* [Statistical Yearbook of Public Health and Health Care in SFR Yugoslavia], Belgrade.
Federal Statistical Office (various years) *Statistički Godišnjak Jugoslavije* [Statistical Yearbook of Yugoslavia], Belgrade.
—— (1986a) *Jugoslavija 1945–1985*, Belgrade.
—— (1986b) *Statistički Kalendar Jugoslavije–1986* [Statistical Calendar of Yugoslavia–1986], Belgrade: Savremena Administracija.
Field, M.G. (1967) *Soviet Socialized Medicine: An Introduction*, New York: Free Press.
Georgievski, N. (1972) "Samoupravljanja u zdravstvo" [Self-management in the Health Service], in J. Djordjević, N. Pasić, and S. Grozdanić (eds) *Teorija i Praksa Samoupravljanja u Jugoslaviji* [The Theory and Practice of Self-management in Yugoslavia], Belgrade: Radnička Štampa.
Horn, J.S. (1969) *Away with All Pests: An English Surgeon in People's China, 1954–1969*, New York: Monthly Review Press.
Hrabač, T. (1968) "Osnovna zdravstvena zaštita u Bosni i Hercegovini" [Basic health care in Bosnia–Hercegovina], *Socijalna Politika* 23, 2–3: 36–40; 23, 5: 29–31.
Juzbašić, I. (1963) "Prva desetogodišnjica društvenog upravljanja u zdravstvenim ustanovama u SR Hrvatskoj" [The first 10-year anniversary of social management in health institutions in SR Croatia], *Zdravstvo* 5: 2–21.
Letica, S. (1984) *Kriza i Zdravstvo* [Crisis and the Health Service], Zagreb: Stvarnost.
Meštrović, V. (1984) "Povodom predloga o zaključivanju društvenog dogovora o osnovama zajedničke socijalne politike u Jugoslaviji" [On the occasion of the proposal on concluding the social compact on the elements of collective social policy in Yugoslavia], *Socijalna Politika* 34, 7: 13–15.
Navarro, V. (1974) "What does Chile mean? An analysis of events in the health sector before, during and after Allende's administration," *Milbank Memorial Fund Quarterly/Health and Society* 52, 2: 93–130.
—— (1976) *Medicine Under Capitalism*, New York: Prodist.
—— (1977) *Social Security and Medicine in the USSR: A Marxist Critique*, Lexington, Mass: D.C. Heath.
Nikolić, Z. (1986) "Eutanazija bez evidencije" [Euthanasia without records], *Danas* 7 October: 59–63.
OECD (1984) *OECD Economic Surveys: Yugoslavia*, Paris: Organization for Economic Co-operation and Development.

Parmelee, D.E. (1983) *Medicine Under Yugoslav Self-managing Socialism*, Ann Arbor, Mich: University Microfilms International.
—— (1985a) "Whither the state in Yugoslav health care?" *Social Science and Medicine* 21, 7: 719–32.
—— (1985b) "Medicine under Yugoslav self-managing socialism: does decentralization + democratization = equality?" Paper presented at the 113th annual meeting of the American Public Health Association, Washington, DC.
Parmelee, D.E., Burns, T.R., Krleža-Jerić, K., Sekulić, D., Skupnjak, B. and Svalander, P. (1979) *User Influence in Health Care – Some Observations on the Yugoslav Experience*, Lund: Scandinavian Institutes for Administrative Research.
Pejovich, S. (1979) *Social Security in Yugoslavia*, Washington, DC: American Enterprise Institute for Public Policy Research.
Sekulić, D. (1983) "Planning, self-management and crisis," Paper presented at the International Sociological Association Research Committee 10 Workshop on Future Prospectives of Industrial and Economic Democracy, Dubrovnik, Yugoslavia.
SFRY (1976) *The Constitution of the Socialist Federal Republic of Yugoslavia (1974)*, American edn., Merrick, NY: Cross-Cultural Communications.
Šiber, I. (1982) "Funkcioniranje i ostvarivanje delegatskog sistema u samoupravnim interesnim zajednicama zdravstva u gradu Zagrebu" [The functioning and realization of the delegate system in health self-managing communities of interest in the city of Zagreb], in P. Jurković, J. Stahan, and A. Puljić, *Ekonomski Aspekti Zdravstva i Zdravstvene Zaštite u Zagrebu* [Economic Aspects of the Health Service and Health Care in Zagreb], Zagreb: Ekonomski Institut.
Sidel, R. and Sidel, V.W. (1982) *The Health of China*, Boston, Mass: Beacon.
Sidel, V.W. and Sidel, R. (1973) *Serve the People*, Boston, Mass: Beacon.
Sigerist, H. (1937) *Socialized Medicine in the Soviet Union*, New York: W.W. Norton.
Sirc, L. (1979) *The Yugoslav Economy under Self-management*, New York: St Martin's.
Svetlik, I. (1986) "The social welfare system in Yugoslavia," Lecture, Ljubljana: 13 November.
Waitzkin, H. (1983) *The Second Sickness*, New York: Free Press.
World Bank (1983) *Yugoslavia: Adjustment Policies and Development Perspectives*, Washington, DC: World Bank.
Yugoslav Survey (1960) "Social Insurance" 1, 1: 65–72.
Zukin, S. (1984) "Yugoslavia: development and persistence of the state," in N. Harding (ed.) *The State in Socialist Society*, Albany: SUNY.

Part Three

National Health Service

Seven

A service within a service:
the National Health Service
in Scotland

T.D. Hunter

"Studies of British politics concentrate upon the politics of the largest single nation, England . . . The relationships between Westminster and its constituent parts are usually neglected."

(P.J. Madgwick and R. Rose (eds) (1982)
*Territorial Dimension in United
Kingdom Politics*, London)

Introduction

In recent years in Scotland, there has been an upsurge of interest in the nation's history and, above all, in the eighteenth-century Enlightenment, when Edinburgh was described by Smollett as "a hot-bed of genius." This upsurge of interest in past glories has been accompanied by a lively debate about the continuing existence of a distinctive "Scottish identity." Much has been made of Scotland's separate educational, legal, religious and banking systems; but the impact of Scottish values on health care has not been studied. This chapter proceeds on the assumption that even a tentative examination of the Scottish Health Service, in the light of "the Scottish social ethic" (Davie 1961), will be likely to shed fresh light, not only on the health service in Scotland, but also, cross-nationally, on other health services and, in particular, on the National Health Service in England and Wales.

Anglo-Scottish *pas de deux*

Geographically, politically, socially, culturally, and demographically, Scotland, with its own traditions and its own legal, educational, medical and religious institutions, is a very different country from England; and, not only at the level of structure, but also in terms of process and of individual behavior, the Scottish Health Service is a different service from its English counterpart. The ways in which the two health services differ is only now beginning to be subjected to serious study (D.J. Hunter 1982, D.J. Hunter and Wistow 1987). Are the differences merely variations on a theme? Or are the geographical, political, demographic, and, in particular, the socio-cultural differences, which still exist between England and Scotland, as meaningful today, and as influential in their impact on health, as they were in the sixteenth, seventeenth and eighteenth centuries?

The historian Maitland was well aware of the central paradox of Scottish history after the Reformation. Between the sixteenth and the eighteenth centuries, he said, "two kingdoms are drifting towards union, but two churches are drifting into discord and antagonism" (Maitland 1903).

In agreeing that "the attractions and repulsions involved in this process fill a large page in the annals of Britain," Davie (1961) has pointed out that, while it is right to bring into prominence the Heraclitean rhythm of a simultaneous drawing towards, and away from, England, it is misleading to identify the differentiating factors solely with religion. The Act of Union of 1707 is best regarded as combining a unity in politics (or, to be more accurate, in the political arrangements for the two countries) with a diversity in social ethics, that term being held to include medicine, education and law, as well as religion.

Over the last two centuries, a profound change in the nature of the relationship between the two countries has taken place. Carlyle's move, from "his wild moorland home" at Craigenputtock to London in 1834, to make his career as a writer in England, was one of the earliest manifestations of the fact that England's magnetic pull over Scotland had begun to extend to the cultural, as well as to the political, domain (Kaplan 1984).

This change was dictated by the primary importance, in the affairs of the joint kingdom, accorded in the nineteenth century to economics, technological advance, and, in short, to material, at the expense of personal or inner, growth. The successive phases of the Industrial Revolution have reinforced the concept of a "unified British way of life" which would be indistinguishable from the *English* way of life (Davie 1961).

The ambivalent "agreement to differ," which was the

hallmark of earlier centuries, has now been replaced by a process of anglicization, which is too easily assumed to be irresistible. What is actually in train may be a much more subtle process of cultural divergence, than that which obtained in earlier centuries (Ronen 1979). Are the Scots now diverging from a "unified British way of life," not so much in terms of externals, as in terms of their internal value system, with Scottish democratic humanism, imperceptibly as yet, but at a deeper level than ever before, cutting across the mechanistic and idealistic English world-view?

Carlyle's friend, David Masson, Professor of English at Edinburgh University in the middle years of the nineteenth century, seems to have realized that, beneath the superficial anglicizing trend, there was another trend based on a more profound and less obvious, less parochial, dimension of the Scottish identity. Masson's message to his countrymen was that there was no possibility of openly preserving the old distinctiveness. "For the future," he said, "it may be the *internal* Scotticism working on British, or on still more general objects, that may be in demand" (Masson 1859); and Robert Louis Stevenson made the same point when he spoke of writing English "with a Scottish accent of the mind."[1] Hume's careful removal of "Scotticisms" from his writings may have had less noble motives.[2] Current attempts to rid Scotland of its conventional, stereotyped image are undoubtedly aimed at uncovering the true essence of the Scottish dimension, and establishing it as a countervailing force to the anglicization, which has been in the ascendant for the last hundred years or so.

In so far as health care in Scotland is concerned, profound differences of principle were already evident, in the 1840s, at the time of Chadwick's sanitary reforms. Scottish doctors, while accepting the importance of dirt and squalor in the genesis of epidemics, were sceptical about the miasmatic theory of disease, which inspired the sanitary movement in England. Taking a deeper, and more *structural*,[3] view (which was also, however, as one would expect, a politically unpopular view) doctors like Professor W.P. Alison of Edinburgh attributed disease to the poverty and destitution of the new urban working classes (Brotherston 1952).

Flinn (1965) suggests that it was this difference of opinion which delayed a Health Act for Scotland until 1867, whereas in England the first Public Health Act was enacted in 1848.

"Theoretical correctness", he points out, "was the enemy of practical improvements in sanitation which were easier to effect than the elimination of poverty and destitution." It has also been suggested, however, that the Scottish legislation was delayed partly because of the need to establish the principle of *separate* health legislation for Scotland.

"At the same time," writes Brotherston (1952), "the problems in Scotland were more acute, for the country had been hustled with disastrous rapidity from a much more primitive social and economic state." And a former Secretary of State for Scotland had already made the same point:

> In the early forties, everything changed at once . . . . Power and machines were transforming Scotland overnight. England with its tradition of great houses, half-country, half-city, absorbed the new stream of energy and directed it along her ancient channels in which it has flowed, although not without some straining at the embankment, even to our own day. But in Scotland, its torrent burst its banks altogether and spread out in submerging flood.
>
> (Elliot 1932)

Housing was the worst environmental factor of all, the growth of factories in the great cities having been paralleled by the hasty erection of as many small houses as possible (with overcrowding being the general rule) on every available acre of ground (Ferguson 1958). Since the nineteenth century much has been done to remedy Scotland's housing problem. Nevertheless,

> the huge scale of this problem, at the present time, must be apparent to anyone who either lives in or visits the vast, poverty-stricken, damp-ridden, and culturally and socially impoverished proletarian ghettoes which ring too many of our towns and cities.
>
> (Wilson 1987)

The need for government intervention in health care, *provided that it was mediated through a Scottish agency*, "was appreciated in Scotland at least as early and as clearly as in England" (Brotherston 1952); and the most powerful voice in Britain, in the nineteenth century, calling for government intervention in "the condition of the people" problem, and, in the process, drawing attention to the ill-health, squalor, and destitution prevailing in Scotland's slums, was that of Thomas Carlyle. Nothing could have been more alien to the Scottish social ethic, based as it is on time-honored notions of "the community of the realm," than the distorted way in which *laissez-faire* economics developed in England in the early decades of the nineteenth century.

Consisting, at first, of responses on an *ad hoc* basis to epidemics as they occurred, intervention by the state gradually became institutionalized. In 1911 arrangements were made which ensured that working men could obtain general medical care without charge. In 1919 the Ministry of Health was set up in London; in 1948 the National Health Service was established, with *separate* health services in England, Wales, Scotland and Northern Ireland.

It is only in the light of this separateness, and of the complicated Anglo-Scottish *pas de deux* that continues to be its fascinating consequence, that the post-1948 evolution of the Scottish Health Service can be properly understood; and Maitland was never more perceptive than when he insisted (1903) that "the great continuities were not wholly on one side of the Border."

Now it is necessary to focus on the three elements of the NHS in Scotland, which are common to all organizational systems, namely, structure, process and behavior.

Structure rules OK?

Not always appreciated is the extent to which a poor country, thrust overnight as it were into the forefront of the Industrial Revolution, suffered from the ravages of a quantum-leap in British history; it overwhelmed Scotland, while only straining the fabric of society south of the border (Brotherston 1952; Elliot 1932). Moreover, in Scotland *rural* deprivation is also a problem, with its islands and remote Highland and other regions.

As a major instrument for tackling the health aspects of its "frightsome" social problems (Gibson 1985), the Scottish Health Service came into existence none too soon. If there were doubts in individualistic England about the need for such a service, there were few doubts in Scotland, where people were well aware of the great part played during the Second World War by the government-run Emergency Medical Service. In Scotland the NHS was, in general, warmly welcomed (Brotherston 1987).

The Scottish Health Service is broadly similar to that in England and Wales; but it is a separately administered service which was set up under a separate Act of Parliament. Although the United Kingdom has a unitary system of government, for certain internal services (for example, home affairs, health, education, personal social services) Scotland has, in the Scottish Office in Edinburgh, its own bureaucracy, linked to the bureaucracy in England through Dover House in Whitehall. The National Health Service in Scotland is administered from the Scottish Home and Health Department (SHHD), which is currently located in St Andrews House in Edinburgh. Through the Secretary of State for Scotland, the political control of SHHD and of the Social Work Services Group (SWSG) – which forms part of the Scottish Education Department (SED) – is retained in Scottish hands.

The Scottish Health Service has no regional tier and is administered directly by SHHD through fifteen health boards and local units of management, which have only recently been constituted. The health boards vary in size. The major ones are responsible for larger populations than the English district authorities, since being coterminous with local authorities was given precedence over smallness of size (D.J. Hunter 1982). New arrangements for unit management, i.e. management below health board level, were the subject of a recent report to SHHD by English-based management consultants (SHHD 1987). In an approach now regarded as inappropriate, even for industrial concerns, this applied "the general principles of management to management at unit level in the Scottish Health Service." These arrangements were put into effect in 1986.

Given SHHD's size and decentralized position, it can perform some of the functions of a regional health authority in England in addition to its civil service functions. There is, therefore, a different type of central-local relationship in Scotland, with the central department more directly involved in a managerial capacity. To aid SHHD in these functions a number of departmental and quasi-autonomous agencies operate at national level. These arrangements were introduced following the first major reorganization of the NHS in 1974.

A multi-professional Planning Unit within SHHD is charged with the development of planning for the NHS. The Scottish Health Service Planning Council (SHSPC), positioned between SHHD and the health boards, is a source of advice to the Secretary of State and acts as a bridging mechanism between the government and the health service in Scotland. A number of national consultative committees (NCCs) of the health care professions provide a source of specialized advice to SHSPC.

The Common Services Agency (CSA) provides a range of all-Scotland services (for example, information, supplies, blood transfusion, the ambulance service) under joint NHS/SHHD management. The CSA is a loose federation of agencies each providing a different service. Like SHSPC (which, with the NCCs, is unique to Scotland) it is testimony to a trend on the part of the Scottish Office (not always successful) to withdraw from involvement in the day-to-day running of services and share its managerial responsibilities with those working in the field.

Prior to 1974, one important difference between the Scottish and English Health Services was the fact that in Scotland the teaching hospitals associated with Scotland's four medical schools were not separately administered, as in England, but were part of mainstream provision. The idea of specialized (and possibly over-specialized) teaching hospitals, set apart from day-to-day provision, was wholly alien to Scottish medical traditions. That there were clear advantages in the Scottish system may account for the fact that, in 1974, the teaching hospitals south of the border ceased to be separately administered.[4]

Other differences between the Scottish and English Health Services are the relative lack of private medicine in Scotland, the close integration of general practitioners with the rest of the personal health services (there is no separately administered Family Practitioner Service in Scotland), the more rapid development of group and health center practice in Scotland (Hogarth 1987), and the greater amount of health services and of public sector, institutional provision in Scotland (Appendix 1).

At the heart of those differences lies the symbiotic relationship that exists between the humanistic traditions of Scottish democracy and the grim social problems of Scotland, where Glasgow and Edinburgh at one time boasted of slums among the worst in the civilized world, and where parts of the West of Scotland were still, until quite recently, reckoned to be among the most deprived areas in Europe.[5]

Generally speaking, these differences have been regarded as marginal, being little more than modest concessions to those quirky people (the Scots) who inhabit the social wasteland lying north of Hadrian's Wall. This may sometimes be the case, but, because of the above-mentioned anglicizing trend, it is a view which has been too readily accepted, in Scotland, as well as in England. Saunders makes the point (1950) that differences of the kind in question may appear to be trivial only in so far as Scottish traditions are not taken seriously, or are dismissed as incomprehensible.

Against the view that English values are the only proper ones, Saunders sets up a counter-argument: if one looks at collective ideals and group-preferences in a more detached spirit than is fashionable in Britain (influenced largely by the parochial, south-east England) and if one even admits a certain validity to Continental and American viewpoints, then conflict between English and Scottish values will no longer seem "an uninteresting episode in which the bringers of modern civilization were resisted by the devotees of a moth-eaten regional routine." On the contrary, it appears as a profoundly important argument between those who regard the traditional English outlook (even when carried to its current Thatcherite, or "radical reactionary," lengths) as normal and natural and those who hold it to be, in important ways, "eccentric and disturbingly out of line with Western norms" (1950).

While it stresses, as Adam Smith stressed, the career open to individual talent, as opposed to the privilege and fixity of an *ancien régime*, the Scottish concept of democracy also stresses, as he did, the invisible hand of a collective, or communal, morality based on the belief that human society is inter-dependent or it is nothing.

This concept of democracy aims at a flexible, just and harmonious society that would be a society of friends and equals in which, with the spread of intimacy and co-operation, the agencies of coercion would "wither away as unnecessary or be regarded as perverting" (Saunders 1950). It is crucial to the understanding of the Scottish ethos. At the opposite pole from the *laissez-faire*, authoritarian, and property-centered, "liberal" view of democracy, as this was formulated for the English middle class by John Stuart Mill and savagely criticized by

Carlyle (Kaplan 1984), Scottish democratic humanism has produced a marked emphasis in the Scottish Health Service on collective, public-sector provision, as against individualistic, or private, provision. It has also led to a participatory-planning ethos, rather than a managerialist one. Above all, it has resulted in general, as against over-specialized, medical services, with front-line, or generic, primary care services being regarded (long before this became the policy of the World Health Organization) as the whole basis and foundation of effective health care (Brotherston 1967).

The dilemma of accountability

These differences have financial applications; but Godber's complaint (1975) about higher per capita expenditure in the Scottish Health Service (Appendix 1) than in England is misplaced. Equally misplaced is the question raised by some health economists as to the lack of impact on health status of this extra expenditure. So far as health status is concerned, health services are still, in the main, safety nets which prevent worse outcomes, rather than springboards which produce better outcomes. Higher per capita expenditure in Scotland is the direct consequence of a physical and social environment hostile to health, and of the persistent gravitational pull in the direction of "downward accountability," which such an environment, in a profoundly democratic country, inevitably exerts on the health care system.

What application do rigid financial calculations and rigid Treasury procedures have to a situation in which (to such an extent has deprivation become a way of life) the inhabitants of the Western Isles chew with their gums and use their false teeth only as items of apparel on special occasions (Williams *et al.* 1980)?

At heart, the differences in structure between the English and Scottish health services reflect different approaches to the dilemma of accountability. In Scotland, accountability downwards to the community rates more highly than accountability upwards. The opposite is true in England and Wales; and this is why, in general, the *informal* structure is noticeably more important than the formal one in the administration of the Scottish Health Service.

In this situation, SHHD is "pig in the middle." Outposted from Whitehall and exposed in a unique way to local pressures the department is simultaneously constrained by the bureaucratic imperatives emanating from Whitehall, particularly the Treasury.

The belief that Scottish civil servants arrange matters so that, in questions with Whitehall, accountability downwards is made to prevail, is counterbalanced, in the eyes of critics of the Scottish Office, by what they regard as ambivalence, or drift, on the part of Scottish civil servants, leading to "managerial government." On this view, the Scottish Office has no life of its own. It exists only when it is reacting in "knee jerk" fashion (D.J. Hunter and Wistow 1987) to cues provided by an alien government, which, after the 1987 General Election, had difficulty even in finding Ministers for the Scottish Office, since it was reduced to having only ten out of Scotland's seventy-two Members of Parliament.

In a still more cynical view, Scottish civil servants react to cues from the south only when they have to, taking the line of least resistance, since their main aim is to secure for themselves as quiet a life as possible, and as much power without responsibility as possible – a debased example of the condition described by Strauss (1961) as "bureaucratic degeneration."

No doubt a combination of these responses is always at work. No doubt some battles with Whitehall are won, some lost and some (whether for the right or the wrong reason) simply avoided. There is no denying the importance of the general willingness on the part of Scottish civil servants to bend or ignore the rules, since doing this, rather than getting too involved in the formidable task of changing them, is an important way of proceeding, for a small and relatively powerless border people. It is particularly important that rigid criteria should not be applied north of the border, since, in terms of health status, Scotland is reckoned to be one social class behind England.[6] Only in odd pockets of the Scottish population (for example, Kelvinside in Glasgow) does the health of the inhabitants equate to that generally prevailing in south-east England. It is crucial, therefore, in questions of health care, to keep Scotland's dire social history of abominable housing, dirt, poverty, and disease in the forefront of one's mind, when any question arises as to informal methods of working or as to the gravitational pull of accountability downwards.

From structure to process

At the level of process in the NHS, efficiency versus effectiveness did not become an issue as long as it was believed that, as the British people became healthier as a result of their new health service,[7] the costs incurred by the NHS would stabilize, or even be reduced.

The NHS, however, launched in a blaze of euphoria both in England and Scotland, soon ran into what is now more than ever its central problem, namely, that of meeting rising expectations without precipitating an unmanageable escalation of costs. In 1956 the Guillebaud Committee (1956) recommended that costs could best be contained through greater efficiency. There ensued an acute bout of managerialism, which soon dominated the NHS in England, with the Scottish Health Service taking its cue somewhat skeptically from the South.

In the 1960s, there appeared a quick succession of various managerial panaceas, and in every part of the country training programmes for NHS administration were directed toward "dynamic management."[8] More ominously, the need for a "Health Service Beeching" was also noised abroad. From one point of view the 1974 reorganization, with its emphasis on managerial unification, was simply the apotheosis of the 1960s bout of crisis management.

From another point of view, however, the reorganization was about an integrated system of health care. Accordingly, the emphasis on managerial unification was counter-balanced (in Scotland, more than counter-balanced) by an emphasis on integrated care and on health planning as the best and most cost-effective way of providing interrelated services to meet interrelated needs.[9] It was widely recognized that, between 1948 and 1974, muddling through had been the characteristic posture of the NHS.

Two approaches to health planning

Health planning having thus originated in the ambivalent context of the 1974 reorganization, two contrasting approaches emerged:

1 The rational-comprehensive, bureaucratic approach, which

calls for a detailed study of all the options before "the plan" is decided upon. Chiefly concerned with resource planning – i.e. with planning *for* the future instead of planning the future, this approach starts from "here" instead of "there", and, rather than adjusting means to ends, it chooses ends that are appropriate to available means. Rational planners concentrate on planning *health services*; and they want what they get: they do not try to get what they want. Their model of health care is the bureaucratic medical model, which puts social control at the center of the health care task.

2 The interactive, adaptive or "mixed scanning" approach whereby, after an initial "broad scan," there is a process of "zooming in" for detailed work on key problems. Interactive planners are not willing to settle for the current state of affairs, or the way they are going. Starting from "there" instead of "here," they want both to design a desirable future and to invent ways of bringing it about. Their model of health care eschews social control and is primarily a socio-therapeutic, or human–ecological model. They are not content to plan health services: they plan for health in the sense of basic well-being.

Mixed scanning is a dynamic synthesis of muddling through (or disjointed incrementalism) and rational planning. In effect, it is a methodology of guided, or jointed, incrementalism, which is not inhibited from crossing agency boundaries, and indeed, depends upon skilful networking.

The DHSS settled for an in-house, rational-comprehensive planning system, whereas Scotland, after an abortive flirtation with WHO's Project System Analysis, turned, with the help of the Tavistock Institute for Operational Research, to mixed scanning. This was, in any event, more in keeping with the Scottish Home and Health Department's participatory approach, and with the notion of planning as a process continuous and innovative.

In 1975, at a conference in Nottingham, Keith Barnard and the writer debated the state of the art in the two countries. In an article on the English planning system, Barnard (1974) had already said: "In the past planning has all too often been simplistic. The present danger is to attempt a sophistication beyond the grasp of those affected."

Invoking the fable of the tortoise and the hare, the writer suggested that the mixed scanning process would just be getting properly under way in Scotland, when the English planning system, by contrast, would just be starting to collapse; and, sure enough, a few years later, abandoning the "paper chase" into which the rational model had degenerated, the DHSS also turned to mixed scanning. Simultaneously, Scotland – drawing towards as well as away from England – had adopted some of the characteristics of the DHSS approach. For a brief moment, therefore, it looked as if both countries might be able to make use of an increasingly sophisticated mixed scanning approach to health care planning.

Unfortunately the value differences, inevitable between a modern nation-state bent on economic growth and military power, and a border people with a profoundly contrary, or cross-cutting, *Gemeinschaft* tradition, were not to be so easily reconciled. Just when the stage was set for a constructive synthesis of the two approaches to health care, the financial crisis of the mid 1970s and the recession of the early 1980s panicked the Government into a fresh upsurge of managerialism. This knocked innovative planning on the head and took the pundits back to crisis-management and to notions about rationing health services, which have always been repugnant to the Scottish belief in a public service ethos; and which are particularly repugnant, when, as now, rationing (with the consumer in mind) increasingly looks like taking the form of "marketable" packages of health care. So far as the health service in Scotland is concerned, what matters is the universal availability, accessibility, and acceptability of technically competent and cost-effective health care. For the time being, however, managerialism rides again in both countries, although its rigours have been modified in Scotland. Instead of Guillebaud, this time round it has been the Griffiths Report (DHSS 1983) with a classic, cost-cutting package which has been carefully wrapped up in some typically manipulative consumerist concepts.

This renewed emphasis on financially-orientated crisis-management (based on the management consultant's credo that what the NHS needs is the "driving force" of an army of industrial "bosses") has precipitated a return, in the guise of "strategic management," to incremental decision-making and its associated policy drift, with muddling through in the ascendant once again. This time, though, the new breed of "aggressive" managers could still find themselves in an extremely grim situation of "still muddling, not yet through."

The English "planning system" had failed to take account of street-level realities (Lee and Mill 1982) and of the resource implications of the rational-comprehensive approach to health planning. Hence, its difficulties.

In Scotland, national guide-lines in the form of a report issued by the Secretary of State under the title of "Scottish Health Authorities Priorities for the Eighties" (SHAPE) (SHHD 1980, and see Appendix 2) contrasted favorably with its English counterpart *Care in Action* (DHSS 1981) which actually raised questions as to what would be monitored in England (D.J. Hunter 1982). The implementation of the SHAPE priorities continues to be monitored by SHHD, but a report updating SHAPE and entitled "Scottish Health Authorities Priorities for the Eighties and Nineties" (SHARPEN) has not yet been published; and an ominously worded consultative paper on the future of SHSPC and the NCCs, which was issued by SHHD in October 1987, would appear to have sounded the death-knell of strategic planning in SHHD. There is some evidence that, in adopting this and other managerialistic initiatives, like competitive tendering for the cleaning, catering, and laundry services in the NHS, SHHD may be getting out of touch (especially as the Scottish Ministers have no mandate in Scotland), bearing in mind Scottish distrust of efficiency savings, and of managerial panaceas or "quick fixes." Macaulay said that there was no more absurd spectacle in the world than the English indulging in one of their periodic fits of morality. The same could be said of the periodic fits of managerialism which afflict the English from time to time, and which do not come anywhere near dealing with the real problems of the NHS. In the next section of this chapter we turn to these problems, and to ways of tackling them which are more in accord with the Scottish social ethic. Planning of health services has collapsed in the DHSS, but such planning is still only under threat in Scotland. It may yet be possible to resurrect it, in a larger context, as "planning for health."

A behavioral synthesis

Speaking as long ago as 1964 in Cambridge, Professor Alex Kennedy of Edinburgh University Medical School claimed that a Copernican revolution was under way "with medicine waiting for a single turn of thought, such as that the earth is not flat," before it could take the next leap forward (Kennedy 1964). Structural and managerial approaches to health care organization are blind to insights of this kind; and that is why in Scotland it is now being argued that the basic problems of the NHS have been left untouched, and have even been suppressed, south of the border, by current cost-cutting strategies and the *furor antitherapeuticus* which accompanies them.

Structural illness

In effect, Professor Kennedy's "single turn of thought" takes us back to Dr Alison's preoccupation with poverty and with what we would now call the structural determinants of illness. For we are now beginning to see, all over again, that illness is located, not in the individual, but in the social, economic and political structures of society. This approach, which emphasizes a health service rather than a disease service, has close links with Lalonde's concept of "the health field," and with Halbert Dunn's notion of the "health grid" (1979) shown in Figure 7.1.

Wildavsky's verdict (1977) is, according to the *Great Equation*, medical care equals health. The best estimate is that the medical system (doctors, drugs, hospitals) affects about 10 per cent of the usual indices for measuring health:

* Whether you live at all (infant mortality).
* How well you live (days lost due to sickness).
* How long you live (adult mortality).

The remaining 90 per cent are determined by factors over which doctors have little or no control . . . *most of the bad things that happen to people are beyond the reach of medicine.*
Bierer's health care scenario (1960) is:

* The particularistic phase – concentrating on one part of the body or mind.
* The holistic phase – concentrating on the whole person.
* The universal phase – concentrating on the whole person in his/her whole environment.

Figure 7.1   *The health "grid"*

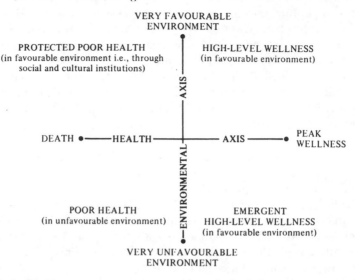

The health grid, its axes and quadrants. (Source: U.S. Department of Health, Education, and Welfare, Public Health Service, National Office of Vital Statistics)

The development of the treatment of illness in accordance with this scenario has been well summed up by Brotherston (1967): "It is not that acute disease or acute infection has left us forever, but it is no longer the primary challenge." The primary problem today, Brotherston goes on to say, is "degenerative disease, for which medical science has no final answer" and which is so demanding in terms of care that the emphasis has now switched from treatment to prevention and health promotion. Wildavsky's point that "the things which make people ill are beyond the reach of medicine" is heavily reinforced by the recent change in Britain from a predominantly young to a predominantly old population. Current attempts to solve this problem through salvage medicine – rescuing drowning people from the river and bringing them back to life – leads only to escalating costs and diminishing returns.

Demedicalization

It becomes necessary to demedicalize the NHS[10] and to turn it through 180 degrees, first, by going upstream a little in order to rescue people, through strategies of prevention and health promotion, before they have begun to drown, and second, by going still further upstream in order to stop people being thrown into the river in the first place.

This would result in a health service which was indeed a health service; but it is a strategy which can be successful only if society, too, turns itself through 180 degrees and shares in the health care task. There is no health for all, unless all are for health. This means accepting the view of Carlyle, Ruskin, and of Adam Smith too (*pace* the egregious Adam Smith Institute) that the purpose of society is "not to make money, or even to make goods, but to make people."[11]

In England (as evidenced by the Griffiths Report on general managers) the NHS is regarded as an agency which, with its emphasis on hospital, or salvage, medicine, provides a maintenance service for the enterprise culture and, as "the health industry," is an inherent part of that culture.

In Scotland, health, haleness, or wholeness is a value in its own right; indeed, as the ability to function spontaneously and to realize one's full potential, it may now be said to have replaced holiness as the value which principally binds society together and holds it to a common purpose. This means integrating the enterprise culture into the health and welfare culture, through processes of co-operative planning (Denman 1973) based on Mary Parker Follett's concept of freedom, not as freedom from relation, but as freedom through organized relation – organization being precisely what Adam Smith meant by his "invisible hand."

Towards co-operative planning

As a wholly shared endeavor, co-operative planning for health has to be based, not on "power over," but on "power with." Accordingly, the Bierer scenario is accompanied, as in Figures 7.2, 7.3 and 7.4 as matching organizational developments which take full account of behavioral considerations.

Jack the Giantkiller had nothing to fear. According to the biologist, D'Arcy Thompson, men cannot become giants without their legs breaking. Similarly, as organizations grow in size and complexity, they cease to be hierarchies; and they need a

Figure 7.2 *Managerialism*

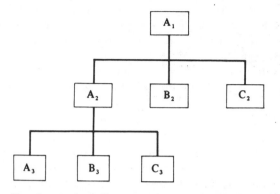

For the particularistic (or factory) phase: Hierarchical (or scalar) model (emphasizing "disease-centered medicine").

Figure 7.3 *Planning health services*

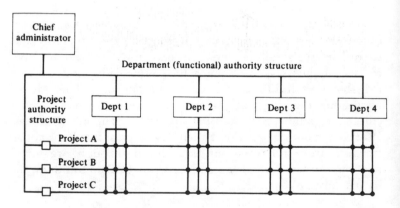

For the holistic phase: Matrix model (emphasizing cross-cutting, multi-disciplinary teams to meet needs of whole person).

new model of leadership. Discernible, therefore, in health care system and other large organizations today, like a new skin forming beneath the old, the social technology of the arena is an outwardly connective mass of self-transforming networks, ordering themselves round a central supportive hub which can function properly only within agreed but flexible strategic frameworks. The arena, a concept in good currency in Scotland since 1967, functions holistically, that is, in terms of people and organizations "as parts of larger wholes rather than" – and this is

Figure 7.4   *Planning for health*

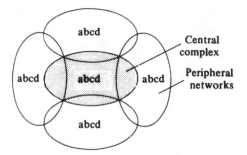

(a) (emphasizing *intra-organizational* networks and linkages and needs of whole person in his/her whole environment).

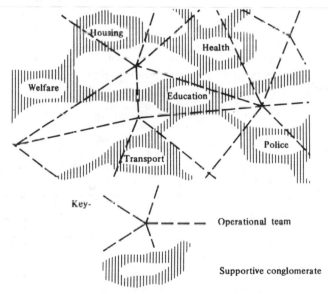

(b) (emphasizing *inter-organizational* networks and linkages and needs of whole person in his/her whole environment).

the essence of scientific management – "as wholes to be taken apart." Accordingly, arena structures (in effect, "congealed behavior") are characterized by collateral relationships; and they gain their identities, not at the expense of, but through other structures, so that, with interdependence replacing independence as the linchpin of the social system, it is no longer a question of "a society held together by its divisions."

In this situation, the traditional "hands on" manager is a giant with broken legs. Accordingly, he has to change: he has to become a resource for the organization: a developer of self-managed networks, who is set free by these networks to act as a strategic planner and "reticulist," spending most of his or her time interfacing with other organizations, both upwards and laterally, in order to build cross-agency coalitions and thereby formulate new possibilities in regard to the core processes of innovation and change, which are now crucial to survival (Schulz and Johnson 1983).

It is necessary, therefore, to graduate from all the different management packages which, over the last twenty years or so, have been made available within the fairly narrow parameters of Blake and Mouton's "managerial grid" (1964). Instead of Blake and Mouton's parameters, namely, "concern for production (authority)" and "concern for people (participation)" we have to begin functioning (although this continues to be disputed by authorities south of the border) within the parameters of a new "strategic planning grid," or negotiative arena, shown in Figure 7.5.

Figure 7.5 *The Strategic Planning Grid*

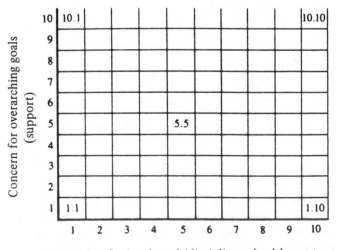

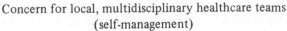
Concern for local, multidisciplinary healthcare teams
(self-management)

Planning for health?

Paradoxically, SHHD (1987) recognizes the problem of escalating costs, finds current managerial strategies inadequate but at the same time (possibly because the Scottish Office is now, as never before, an extension of Whitehall) rejects strategic planning just at that moment in time when the Ibbs Report (Jenkins *et al.* 1988) has stressed the overwhelming need for such an approach.

In this situation, it is important to remember that the bout of managerialism which resulted from the Guillebaud Report, soon turned (particularly in Scotland) into its opposite, namely, the joint planning of interrelated services to meet interrelated needs. In spite of dire predictions that the current situation of bureaucratic degeneration in government is here to stay, the hope must persist that, on the basis of *reculer pour mieux sauter*, current regressive trends in the NHS will also, before too much damage has been done, turn into their opposite. Certainly in Scotland, which does not suffer from the managerial ethos, or the incumbus of a fairly sizeable private health sector,[12] this process cannot get under way too soon, with "planning for health" going to the top of the agenda, and with the "managerial grid" being replaced, at every level of the Scottish Health Service, by a strategic planning grid.

Concluding postscript

Significant contributions have been made by the Scottish people at important turning points in the history of the modern world.

It was the Scotland of John Knox which, in the sixteenth century, gave Europe its first taste of democracy, and also its first taste of social justice (Smout 1969). Here is how Carlyle (1875) described this paradigm change in world history:

> Scottish Puritanism, well considered, seems to me distinctly the noblest and completest form that the grand 16th century Reformation anywhere assumed. We may also say that it has been by far the most widely fruitful form; for, in the next century, it had produced English Cromwellian Puritanism with open Bible in one hand, drawn Sword in the other . . . irrevocably refusing to believe what is not a Fact of God's

Universe but a mighty mass of self-delusions and mendacities in the region of Chimera. So that now we look for its effects, not in Scotland only, or in our small British Islands only, but over wide seas, huge American continents, and growing British Nations in every zone of the earth.

With the eighteenth century Enlightenment, when Hume revolutionized philosophy and Adam Smith founded the new science of political economy, there was born the concept of an *educated* democracy, and the way was cleared for the growth of bureaucracy and of the modern professions, in particular, perhaps, the healing professions. This is so if we believe that Rudolf Virchow (1973) that "politics is merely medicine on a large scale," or if we agree with Goethe (1973) that, in the end, humanity will win through from an "educated", or representative, to a "caring", or participatory, democracy.

The Edinburgh Medical School (in the eighteenth and nineteenth centuries, one of the great medical schools of the world) played a notable part in developing classical, or particularistic, medicine; names to conjure with, in this connection, being those of Cullen, Simpson, Syme, and Lister.

From a more holistic point of view, and in terms of the organization of specific services, or of general services on a regional basis, developments of world-wide significance in the field of tuberculosis were pioneered by Sir Robert Phillip at the turn of the century; and the Highlands and Islands Health Service, set up in 1913, was a model of a regional service for many other parts of the world. More recently, Sir Dugald Baird's development of the maternity services in Aberdeen on a "collective basis" (Gill 1980) has inspired similar initiatives, not only in Britain but also in a large number of other countries.

The future is still seen, by some specialists in the South, to lie in the development of high technology, or "salvage," medicine. While the importance of technological advance is not underestimated in Scotland, it is recognized that highly specialized, highly expensive (and highly seductive) technologies, in addition to being subject to the law of diminishing returns, may benefit only a very small number of patients. Given, therefore, the Scottish preference for a generalist approach, as this was neatly expressed by Geddes in his maxim to the effect that administrators must "not sacrifice resources enough for general well-being to the elaboration of single improvement," technological advance has been kept on a tight rein. Between 1974 and 1978, the careful planning of cardiac surgery north of the Tweed was *de rigeur* and planning and organizing medical physics on a regional basis was a Scottish invention; it had a significant influence on the recommendations of the United Kingdom Hospital Scientific and Technical Services Committee (the Zuckerman Committee). The report of this committee (1968) led to the cautious establishment of regional departments of medical physics in the English provinces during the 1970s and early 1980s. Evidence now accumulating suggests that a similar change is called for if the blood transfusion service in England is to become as effective as the more highly organized Scottish service.

The pioneering development of medical ultrasonic imaging (in the teeth of initial skepticism) by Professor Ian Donald at Glasgow University between 1958 and 1985, by which date four companies had been established in Scotland that were the only manufacturers of all-British equipment for medical ultrasonic imaging, has recently been described by Lenihan; but the author concludes his paper by relating technological advance to the central problems of the NHS, as these are regularly encountered by health care professionals, voluntary workers, and, above all, by the community itself:

> Much more remains to be done in harnessing technology (often in relatively simple ways) to the service of the increasing number of patients who are not sufficiently ill or disabled to be in hospital, yet not sufficiently fit to enjoy the quality of life that they expect the health service to provide.
>
> (Dow and Lenihan 1987)

Important here is Lenihan's emphasis on a philosophy which chimes in with the Scottish trend towards demedicalization. Also important to note, apropos of demedicalization, is a marked increase in the readiness of the health professions in Scotland to lay aside their fears about dilution. This is on the basis that health care needs are now so complex and are multiplying at such a rate, that, far from more auxiliary workers being a threat to the status and numbers of professionally trained staff, their deployment, properly carried out, should both enhance the status of professional staff and create the need for still more professionals, acting in a consultative capacity. One caveat has been entered by Brotherston (1967):

The guiding aphorism is that nobody should be doing tasks which could be done by a lesser level of skill . . . I do not think that the sub-doctor is "on" for our service; but I do think that we need categories of auxiliary people, who, although clearly identifiable and not to be confused with doctors, nevertheless do some tasks which our hospital doctors and general practitioners do now.

Community care – the ultimate in demedicalization – is proceeding steadily but organically in Scotland since it is increasingly being regarded, not so much as an extension of traditional patterns of care for certain groups into a different location in the community (House of Commons 1985), but more as a different quality of care for all groups, irrespective of where it happens to be located. In short, it is a health-directed alternative to inherited, social control patterns of care, which are inherently divisive and which militate, therefore, against the integration into society of stigmatized (but "priority") groups like the elderly, the mentally ill, and the mentally handicapped.

Challenge and response

These are all indications that professionals and voluntary workers in Scotland have taken the measure of the health care problem, as this problem increasingly becomes a problem of the whole person in his or her whole environment; and the recent unrivalled growth of self-help groups within the wider Scottish community, has a similar message to convey.

Could Scotland, therefore, once again have a central role to play at a turning point in the history of Western society? Could a small nation, which was part of the dough that was left on the griddle when the nation states were formed, and which has not succumbed to the social sclerosis that now paralyses these states, play a major part in yet another paradigm change of world-significance, namely the change to a genuinely caring, or "fulfil-ment", society (Ritchie-Calder 1979)? Could Scotland, in short, be the first country to demonstrate that health services can be *health* services, and that the basic problem of health care systems, namely, their potential to consume the entire national product, can be resolved only if, instead of planning health *services*, we involve the whole society in the enterprise and *plan for health*?

Such a reversal of perspectives would mean exchanging

attempts to run the health care system like a second-rate industry for attempts to run the industrial world like a first-rate health service, with the enterprise culture being progressively integrated, through techniques of co-operative planning, into the health and welfare culture.

Since the ever-increasing complexities of health care call not for *less* but for *more* policy analysis, more policy development and more strategic planning, setting guide-lines within which the different agencies involved can move forward, is now the requisite social technology. The crisis in the NHS involves the whole society. Accordingly, *health service* planning is dead – long live planning for health!

Officials in St Andrews House are well aware that there is a time-bomb ticking away beneath traditional, "great doctor" models of health care and, above all, beneath current managerialist concepts (SHHD 1987).

> The first paragraphs in Chapter 1 gave some details of the workload undertaken by hospitals of waiting lists and of expenditure upon the National Health Service. These are a reminder of the major problem which is manifesting itself in all health care systems – namely, to limit the apparently limitless possibilities for diagnosis and treatment of disease with the finite resources available to support them. A response in management terms . . . and a medical response concerned only with clinical freedom are both inadequate . . .
>
> (SHHD 1987)

Unfortunately SHHD is fairly pessimistic about finding a solution:

> There are indications, albeit partial and disjointed of recognition of the problems and of attempts to find solutions. It would be rash to predict success. The divergence between what is possible and what can be afforded may widen more rapidly than an acceptable solution can be developed but the National Health Service offers a unique base from which to attempt to develop an understanding of the problem and to find ways in which to bridge this gap.
>
> (SHHD 1987)

Although unclear as to the way ahead, this is a striking

advance on the narrowly-based approach to the problems of the NHS which characterizes the review at present being carried out, in secret, by the Cabinet. And clearly, the Scottish people are developing self-help approaches as their own way of sharing the health care problem. Our life styles, however, are chosen for us not by us; and health care is a problem for the whole society, since it can be resolved only through a "total push" against the structural determinants of illness (T.D. Hunter 1988).

Although SHHD has chosen this moment to launch a serious assault on its professional advisory system, some SHHD officials are nevertheless claiming that they have begun to detect signs that the Scottish Office is, once again, acquiring that "life of its own" which is the *sine qua non* of good government in Scotland. That the basic problem of the NHS has been identified is certainly the essential preliminary to its solution.

Today, as a small border people on the edge of Europe, Scotland is charged with the duty of fulfilling, yet again, its historic, innovatory role, by establishing within the UK "system" the first outlines in the world of a genuinely caring, or fulfilment, society. The hope must be that SHHD will match the growth of self-help in the community with a whole new dimension of commitment and leadership. As the price paid for two hundred years of staggering material progress there is a huge burden of structural illness in society; but this is a burden which it is no longer necessary to labor under.

In McLachlan's view (1987):

> The special characteristics and traditions of Scotland's institutions and people give it a unique base, with a potentiality for development more promising than exists in any of the English regions and, indeed, in most other countries.

Today, the struggle is not between nations or classes. Rather it is a Jekyll-and-Hyde[13] struggle between values. So the task now for the Scottish people is to turn society the right way up, first, by subordinating the state to the aspirations of its citizens for self-determination and, secondly, by organizing society on a genuinely collective and interdependent basis so that it is at last able to meet the needs of its members both for basic well-being and for fullness of life. Man-against-himself is the last great barrier. Scotland – a nation within a nation – through its health service – a service within a service – is uniquely well-equipped, given its religious and literary heritage, to overcome this barrier.

Notes

1 Writing to his mother in 1873, Stevenson made it clear that nothing was further from his mind than "going English."

> I cannot get over my astonishment – indeed, it increases every day – at the hopeless gulf there is between England and Scotland, and English and the Scotch. Nothing is the same; and I feel as strange and outlandish here as I do in France or Germany.
>
> (Daiches 1981)

Stevenson also felt ill at ease with England's imperialist leanings and its class structure. Associated with the latter, of course, is the rich/poor divide between south and north England, which is now making it more difficult to re-allocate NHS resources in England than is proving to be the case in Scotland.

2 Hume had a friend who eliminated his "Scotticisms" so that his books would sell in England.

3 Indirect or structural violence is violence which is built into society's social, political and economic structures (Hicks 1985). It is time that this concept was applied to illness. In this connection, the Health Education Council in England was converted, at the beginning of 1987, into the Health Education Authority in order to rid the government of a "turbulent priest" in the shape of the council's director, Dr David Player, a Scottish community medicine specialist, who fell foul of vested interests in the food, alcohol, and tobacco industries because his approach to health care problems was, in the best Scottish tradition, structural and, in consequence, *political*.

4 The setting up of the Mental Health Act Commission in 1984 was another instance of England taking its cue from Scotland, which has had a Mental Welfare Commission (recently given a broader remit) since 1960.

5 In 1895 Patrick Geddes showed Israel Zangwill slums in Edinburgh that were worse than the worst slums in London. "Do you wonder that Edinburgh is renowned for its medical schools?" asked Geddes (cited in Boardman 1978).

6 In Scotland, twenty years before, on the strength of the Griffiths Report the new "general manager" system was adopted by DHSS and exported overnight to SHHD. The Farquharson-Lang Committee, reporting in 1966, pre-empted (or tried to pre-empt) the whole debate about the management of the NHS by proposing a "chief executive" system based on eliciting, rather than on imposing, consensus. Emphasizing political, diplomatic and "reticulist," or networking, skills as against traditional managerial ones, Farquharson-Lang struck a sensible balance between professional autonomy and organizational

imperatives. It may yet prove to have been prescient in a way that is
well beyond the contemplation of those who are responsible for the
current bout of managerialism.

7 Speaking in 1948, Tom Driberg MP claimed that the British
people "would now get healthier and healthier."

8 Lord Beeching was notorious for the extensive cuts which he
effected, in the early 60s, in the British railway network.

9 Brotherston (1987) writes:

> Unlike the situation in England, where the equivalent 1973 Act was
> made the vehicle for schemes designed to improve management, the
> simplification of health service administration was not the main
> objective of the Scottish Act. In Scotland, the prime motivation
> behind the Act was the improvement of patient care by means of a
> fully integrated service. The National Health Service (Scotland) Act
> of 1972 instructed the Secretary of State for Scotland to "secure *the
> effective provision of an integrated health service in Scotland*" (emphasis
> added).

10 Demedicalization (Appendix 3) implies a recognition of the fact
that many problems call for what Erving Goffman described as "people
work," rather than for highly specialized medical, nursing, or social
work services, and that, in many cases, better use is made of specialists
if they can be employed in a consultative role. Debureaucratization and
deprofessionalization of what are essentially social problems is deeply
rooted in Scotland's culture. Indeed, it is an article of faith, which can be
traced back in a philosophical sense to Dr Alison at the beginning of the
nineteenth century and in more practical form, early in the present
century, to the MacAlister Report entitled "A scheme of medical service
for Scotland." At a time when the trend in Britain and elsewhere was
towards specialism, the MacAlister Report (1920) declared that:

> we regard it as of primary importance that the organization of the
> Health Service of the Nation should be based on the *family* as the
> normal unit and on the *family doctor* as the normal medical attendant
> and guardian. It is not for disease or diseases in the abstract that
> provision has to be made; but for persons liable to or suffering from
> disease.

11 It is not generally appreciated in England that Adam Smith was
essentially a welfare theorist as well as a wealth theorist. Indeed, like
Ruskin, "the desire for better men rather than larger national incomes"
was what chiefly motivated him.

12 The Scottish attitude to the private sector is well expressed in the
following excerpt:

> English Ministers will not repair the damage their party has suffered
> in Scotland if they continue to charge the Scots with lack of
> enterprise. That will be seen to be as patronizing as it is foolish.
> What they have to perceive is that their policies express a philosophy

and standards which are fundamentally at odds with the Scottish character. Scots are well acquainted with the consequences of the unbridled enterprise culture, whether in terms of housing or public health, and are not prepared to accept that private prosperity should be elevated to being the main object of public policy. They have always been more egalitarian than their English cousins and tend to measure a society's worth not by how easy it makes the accumulation of private wealth but by how well it provides for its less fortunate.

(*Scotsman* 24 November 1987)

13 For "the divided self" in Scottish literature, see, apart from Stevenson, James Hogg (1824) *The Private Memoirs and Confessions of a Justified Sinner*, London: Oxford University Press (1969), and more recently, R. D. Laing (1959) *The Divided Self*, London: Tavistock.

Appendix 1

Resources in the Scottish Health Service

1 In 1980–1 Scottish health boards' per capita expenditure was approximately 25 per cent higher than their English equivalents. Most of this "additional" expenditure was in the hospital sector where Scotland spent roughly one-third more per capita than was spent in England in 1980–1, and it appears to have grown over time. Scotland has a much higher volume of resources in terms of medical staff and beds. There were 46 per cent more beds per 1,000 population and 41 per cent more medical staff per 100,000 population in Scotland than in England (Scotland had an average list size for general practitioners of 1,704 in 1984). The manpower figures revealed that in 1980–1 the Scottish Health Service employed 33 per cent more staff per 100,000 population than did England. In the hospital sector there are 40 per cent more medical and nursing staff per 100,000 population. Scotland has over 40 per cent more consultants on a per capita basis, and expenditure on distinction awards is 8 per cent higher than in England. Scotland had higher levels of staffed beds and discharges per 1,000 population and a higher level of out-patient attendances. Throughput, however, was not greater and length of stay was longer. Discharges per available staffed beds were 13.1 in Scotland compared with 15.9 in England. The lower cost per in-patient week probably reflected the lower throughput per bed in Scotland. Given the relatively larger teaching sector in Scotland, expenditure and resources are concentrated in the four health boards with medical schools and supra-regional commitment (McGuire 1985).

2 This Scotland versus England situation has focused attention on the relationship between the higher level of Scottish spending and its relatively poor health record. The health service in Scotland has to provide for a population with a greater volume of ill-health, as evidenced by mortality rates, than most other parts of the United

Kingdom or western Europe. Death rates from coronary heart disease, cancer, and strokes, the three main causes of death, are among the highest in western Europe, while expectation of life at birth for both male and female Scots is among the lowest (Brotherston 1987).

3 Existing data make it difficult to isolate the effect of health care upon outcome; but in any event, higher expenditure in Scotland simply reflects the hostile-to-health environment which is Scotland's legacy from the past, and is not aimed at achieving a better health record than obtains in England. In suggesting that the government is failing in its duty by not achieving equality between England and Scotland, Sir George Godber (1975) makes the elementary mistake of confusing equality with equity; a mistake which the World Health Organisation is now careful to avoid.

4 Total gross expenditure on the NHS in Scotland in 1986–7 was expected (SHHD 1987) to amount to £2,119 million. In that year it was anticipated that 88 per cent of NHS spending would be raised by general taxation, just over 9 per cent from national insurance contributions and a little over 2 per cent from charges to patients for items such as prescriptions or dental care. The broad allocation between Family Practitioner Services and the Hospital and Community Services is summarized in Figure 7.6.

Figure 7.6   *NHS gross expenditure in Scotland 1986–7 by category*

1   Hospital and community health services **£1,555m**
2   Capital building and maintenance **£104m**
3   Family practitioner services **£431m**
4   Centrally financed services **£133m**

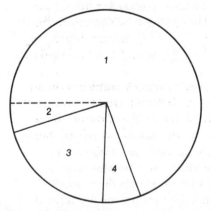

Figures taken from provisional accounts

Source: SHHD 1987

Appendix 2

Scottish Health Authorities' priorities for the 1980s

1 In 1980 the Secretary of State for Scotland published the report *Scottish Health Authorities' Priorities for the Eighties* (SHHD 1980) in which national priorities for the health services in Scotland were identified in three broad categories:

Category A
Prevention
Services for the multiply deprived
Care of the elderly
Community nursing services
Elderly with mental disability
Mentally ill
Mentally handicapped
Physically handicapped

Category B
Primary dental services (general dental services and community dental services)
Maternity services
General medical services
General ophthalmic services

Category C
Child Health
Acute hospital services
General pharmaceutical services

2 Review and Monitoring Process
Review meetings between SHHD and each board every two years
Broad strategy for ten years ahead
Operational plan (up to three years)

3 Growth assumptions (1986)
1986–7 – 1988–9 – 1% (plus or minus 0.5%)
1989–90 – — – 0.5% (plus or minus 0.5%)
1% efficiency savings

4 Joint plans
In 1985 health boards were asked to prepare – jointly with local authorities and voluntary organizations – plans for the development of community care.

5 Guide lines for the 1990s
As policy guidance beyond the 1980s is now required, SHAPE is itself under review at present. As mentioned in the text, a new report SHARPEN (*Scottish Health Authorities Review of Priorities for the Eighties and Nineties*) has been completed, but has not yet been published by the government, pending further consultation.

Appendix 3

Demedicalization

1 The Prime Minister of Britain has recently proclaimed that there is no such thing as society, only individuals. As the nation which, in the eighteenth century, gave expression to the new sciences of sociology, social anthropology and economics in their most mature and sophisticated form, and which was already discussing the problem of "asylum-made lunatics" in the 1890s, Scotland has taken the opposite view. Having had little difficulty in seeing problems in their social context, the Scottish people have moved much more quickly than their English neighbours to remove children and young people from the criminal justice system, with its traditional social control philosophies of punishment or treatment, by setting up a system of Children's Hearings which make it possible for the social control model to be replaced by a decriminalized and demedicalized, sociotherapeutic regime.

2 Similarly, the Special Unit set up in Barlinnie Prison on the outskirts of Glasgow (a unit established to "manage" Scotland's most violent criminals by demedicalized social therapy principles) is still a striking innovation (in spite of some recent backpedalling on the part of the Scottish Office) which stands in sharp contrast to an English experiment (now abandoned) with "control units."

3 Highly relevant to the Scottish scene was the research carried out in Edinburgh in the 1970s by Dr John Hamilton (now physician superintendent at Broadmoor Hospital) and others, which demonstrated that substantially better results could be achieved with habitual drunkards if they were managed by psychiatrists, nurses, and social workers in a sociotherapeutic setting than if they were dealt with through the criminal justice system and the medical and other social control techniques employed in that system.

4 Looking at demedicalization from a different angle, attempts to *medicalize* social problems by misapplying drug therapy came under critical scrutiny in Scotland long before they became the national scandal that is now leading to litigation (Howie and Bigg 1980); and there is increasing criticism of "that strain of demoralization in the Scottish character" which has resulted in a serious drug problem, and in far too many Scottish men and women (and young people) "smoking cigarettes, consuming alcohol to excess, eating unbalanced diets containing too much fat and not enough fibre and taking little or no exercise" (Wilson 1987).

5 In a notable exception to the general rule, a deliberate policy of *medicalization of birth* was embarked upon in Scotland twenty-five years ago, because of poor social conditions, particularly in the West. This is claimed to have led to a dramatic fall in perinatal and infant mortality rates over the last ten years or so (SHHD 1985). At the opposite end of the spectrum, it is worth noting that the Scottish Health Education Group (SHEG) now has an ongoing in-service training program for a

variety of professionals and para-professionals, with the aim of demedicalizing the care of the elderly and encouraging independence.

6 The fact that demedicalization has made significant advances in Scotland while private health care based on "the medical model" is only of marginal importance (Donnelly 1986) does not mean that bureaucratic medicine (which exists in a state of tension between managerial imperatives and traditional medical autonomy) has been driven out of circulation by the holistic or universal approach to health care now called for. There is still a long way to go. As Mooney and Stuart (1987) have shown, it is still the case in Scotland that, because of medical influence on decision-making, the acute services continue to be given priority over the government's official "priority groups."

References

Barnard, K. (1974) "Planning in the National Health Service," *Observer*, 1 September.

Bierer, J. (1960) "Past, present and future," *International Journal of Social Psychiatry* 6: 165.

Blake, R.R. and Mouton, J.S. (1964) *The Managerial Grid*, Houston, Texas: Gulf.

Boardman, P. (1978) *The World of Patrick Geddes*, London: Routledge & Kegan Paul.

Brotherston, J.H.F. (1952) *Observations on the Early Public Health Movement in Scotland*, London: H.K. Lewis.

—— (1967) "Government Viewpoint: Current State of the National Health Service," in *21st Fellows Seminar on the British National Health Service*, Chicago: American College of Hospital Administrators.

—— (1987) "The National Health Service in Scotland," in G. McLaughlan (ed.) *Improving the Common Weal: Aspects of the Scottish Health Services 1900–1984*, Edinburgh: Edinburgh University Press for the Nuffield Provincial Hospitals Trust.

Carlyle, T. (1875) *The Portraits of John Knox*, London: Chapman and Hall.

Daiches, C. (1981) "Stevenson and Scotland," in J. Calder (ed.) *Stevenson in Victorian Scotland*, Edinburgh: Edinburgh University Press.

Davie, G.E. (1961) *The Democratic Intellect*, Edinburgh: Edinburgh University Press.

Denman, D.R. (1973) *Co-operative Planning*, Warburton Lecture, Manchester: Manchester University Press.

DHSS (1981) *Care in Action*, London: HMSO.

—— (1983) *NHS Management Inquiry Report*, London: DHSS.

Donnelly, C. (1986) "Private Health Care in Scotland," in D. McCrone (ed.) *Scottish Government Yearbook*, Edinburgh: Unit for the Study of Scottish Government, Department of Politics, Edinburgh University.

Dow, D. and Lenihan, J. (1987) "The Impact of Technology," in G.

McLachlan (ed.) *Improving the Common Weal: Aspects of the Scottish Health Services 1900–1984*, Edinburgh: Edinburgh University Press for Nuffield Provincial Hospitals Trust.
Dunn, H.L. (1979) "High-level wellness for man and society," in J.F. Folta and E. Deck (eds) *A Sociological Framework for Patient Care*, 2nd edn, New York: Wiley.
Elliot, W. (1932) "The Scottish Heritage in Politics," in J.G. Stewart-Murray, 8th Duke of Atholl (ed.) *A Scotsman's Heritage*, London: Maclehose.
Ferguson, T. (1958) *Scottish Social Welfare*, Edinburgh, London: E. & S. Livingstone.
Flinn, M.W. (ed.) (1965) *Edwin Chadwick's Report on the Sanitary Conditions of the Labouring Population of Great Britain*, Edinburgh: Edinburgh University Press.
Gibson, J.G. (1985) *The Thistle and the Crown*, Edinburgh: HMSO.
Gill, D. (1980) *The British National Health Service: A Sociological View*, Washington, DC: US Department of Health and Human Services.
Godber, G. (1975) *The Health Service Past, Present and Future*, London: Athlone Press.
Goethe, J.W. von (1973) quoted from *Italienische Reise* in Philip Rieff: *The Triumph of the Therapeutic*, London: Penguin.
Guillebaud Committee (1956) *Report of the Committee of Enquiry into the Cost of the National Health Service*, Cmnd 9633; London: HMSO.
Hamilton, J.R., Griffiths, A., Ritson, E.B. and Aitken, R.C.B. (1978) *Detoxification of Habitual Drunken Offenders*, Scottish Health Service Studies No 39: SHHD.
Hicks, D.W. (1985) *Education for Peace: Issues, Dilemmas and Alternatives*, Lancaster: St Martin's College.
Hogarth, J. (1987) "General Practice," in G. McLachlan (ed.) *Improving the Common Weal: Aspects of the Scottish Health Services 1900–1984*, Edinburgh: Edinburgh University Press for Nuffield Provincial Hospitals Trust.
House of Commons Select Committee on the Social Services (1985) *Report on Community care with special reference to adult mentally ill and mentally handicapped people*, London: HMSO.
Howie, J. and Bigg, A.R. (1980) "Family trends in psychotropic and antibiotic prescribing in general practice," *British Medical Journal* 830:8.
Hunter, D.J. (1982) "Organizing for health in the UK," *Journal of Public Policy 2*: 263–30.
Hunter, D.J. and Wistow, G. (1987) *Community Care in Britain: Variations on a theme?*, London: King's Fund.
Hunter, T.D. (1987) "Mental health and mental handicap services," in G. McLachlan (ed.) *Improving the Common Weal: Aspects of the Scottish Health Services 1900–1984*, Edinburgh: Edinburgh University Press for Nuffield Provincial Hospitals Trust.
—— (1988) "Re-thinking health care," in *Hospital and Health Services Review*, February: 23–7.
Jenkins, K., Caines, K., and Jackson, A. (1988) *Improving Management in Government: the Next Steps* (the Ibbs Report), London: HMSO.

Kaplan, F. (1984) *Thomas Carlyle: A Biography*, Cambridge: Cambridge University Press.

Kennedy, A. (1964) Cited in E. Davis (ed.) *Depression*, Cambridge: Cambridge University Press.

Lee, K. and Mill, A. (1982) *Policymaking and Planning in the Health Sector*, London: Croom Helm.

MacAlister Committee (1920) *Report on A Scheme of Medical Services for Scotland*, Edinburgh: Scottish Board of Health.

McLachlan, G. (1987) "A 'Complaint of the Common Weill of Scotland'?" in G. McLachlan (ed.) *Improving the Common Weal: Aspects of the Scottish Health Services 1900–1984*, Edinburgh: Edinburgh University Press for Nuffield Provincial Hospitals Trust.

McGuire, A. (1985) "Scotland v. England," *THS Health Summary* 2: 11 November.

Maitland, F.W. (1903) "The Anglican Settlement and the Scottish Reformation," in H.C. Cam (ed.) (1957) *Selected Historical Essays of F.W. Maitland*, Cambridge: Cambridge University Press.

Masson, D. (1859) *British Novelists*, Cambridge: Cambridge University Press.

Mooney, G. and Stuart, P. (1987) "Economic Aspects of Health Care in the Twentieth Century," in G. McLachlan (ed.) *Improving the Common Weal. Aspects of the Scottish Health Services 1900–1984*, Edinburgh: Edinburgh University Press for Nuffield Provincial Hospitals Trust.

Ritchie-Calder, Lord (1979) "The case for non-work," *Nevis Journal* 2: 70–8.

Ronen, D. (1979) *The Quest for Self-Determination*, New Haven, Conn. and London: Yale University Press.

Saunders, L.J. (1950) *Scottish Democracy 1815–1840*, Edinburgh: Oliver & Boyd.

Schulz, R. and Johnson, A.C. (1983) *The Management of Hospitals*, New York: McGraw-Hill.

SHHD (1966) *Report of the Committee on the Administrative Practice of Hospital Boards* (Farquharson-Lang Committee), Edinburgh: HMSO.

—— (1980) *Scottish Health Authorities: Priorities for the Eighties* (SHAPE), Edinburgh: HMSO.

—— (1985) Health in Scotland 1984, Edinburgh: HMSO.

—— (1987) Health in Scotland 1986, Edinburgh: HMSO.

Smout, T.C. (1969) *A History of the Scottish People 1560–1830*, London: Collins.

Strauss, E. (1961) *The Ruling Servants*, London: Allen & Unwin.

Virchow, R. (1973) cited in Henry Miller: *Medicine and Society*, Oxford: Oxford University Press.

Wildavsky, A. (1977) "Doing better and feeling worse," in J.M. Knowles (ed.) *Doing Better and Feeling Worse*, New York: Norton.

Williams, R., Bloor, M., Horobin, G., and Taylor, R. (1980) "Remoteness and disadvantage: findings from a survey of access to health services in the Western Isles," *Scottish Journal of Sociology*, 4, 2: 105–24.

Wilson, S. (1987) "The public health services," in G. McLachlan (ed.) *Improving the Common Weal: Aspects of the Scottish Health Services 1900–1984*, Edinburgh: Edinburgh University Press for Nuffield Provincial Hospitals Trust.
Zuckerman Committee (1968) Report on *Hospital Scientific and Technical Services*, London: HMSO.

Part Four
Socialized medicine

Eight

The Soviet health system: a national health service in a socialist society

Christopher M. Davis

Introduction

The health system in the Soviet Union occupies an important place in a cross-national comparison of medical care provision in industrialized countries because it is the world's largest health system, is the oldest example of a national health service (that is, a publicly owned network of medical institutions which provide services to patients without direct charge), and operates in a socialist society with a communist party political system and a centrally planned economy. The Soviet health system has numerous unique features that are the result of the nation's history, contemporary political, social, and economic environment, and principles of medical care organization. In a comparative analysis it is of course appropriate to study these particular aspects. On the other hand, the health service in the USSR has characteristics in common with those of other countries as a result of the impact of universal influences (the scientific approach to disease and medicine, the acceleration of technological progress, and the growing specialization in the medical field), the similar functional roles of medical systems in the broader health production process, and the need to confront many of the same challenges as other nations (such as how to cope with a virtually insatiable demand for medical care with limited resources).

The objectives of this chapter are threefold: to identify both the common and particular features of the Soviet health service; to assess the performance and problems of the medical system in the USSR; and to evaluate whether there has been a convergence over time of the characteristics of the Soviet health system and those of other industrialized countries. Due to space constraints only cursory coverage is given in the second section (pp. 234–42) to background topics such as the health production process, the political system, economy, and society in the USSR, and the organization of the contemporary Soviet health service. Instead, attention is focussed in the third section (pp. 242–60) on several important issues and problems of the health system in the USSR: the growing demand for medical care, cost containment, rationing, shortages, second economy activities, medical technology, and the effectiveness of the health system in reducing mortality. Finally, conclusions are drawn about the success of the Soviet model of medical care and the validity of the hypothesis concerning the convergent development of health systems.

The environment and organization of the Soviet health system

All industrial societies attempt to improve the health of their populations for reasons which may range from an idealistic desire to better individual welfare to pragmatic concern about raising national labor productivity. Many features of health promotion programs, institutions, and techniques are similar across countries due to the universal nature of the health production process, discussed on pp. 234–7 as well as of modern scientific medicine and medical technology. However, the health systems of nations also have unique characteristics that are determined by political, economic, social, ideological, and organizational factors. The rest of this section briefly examines the influences on the health system in the USSR that have produced its particular features.

The health production process in the USSR

Changes in the population's health are produced by a complex process involving the interaction of demographic, consumption, environmental, medical, political, and economic variables, and the activities of a variety of institutions. Although the subject of this study, the health system, plays an important role in the health production process it does not completely determine outcomes, such as morbidity, invalidity, and mortality. These also are strongly influenced by factors such as the population's consumption habits, pollution, societal stress, and the effectiveness of the nation's pharmaceutical and medical equipment industries.

This author has developed a model of the Soviet health production process that is presented elsewhere (Davis 1987). It shows the interconnections between the institutions in the economy that are closely involved in the production of the primary output, the population's health. These are the consumers, health system, pharmacy network, medical industry, biomedical research and development (R & D), medical foreign trade, and the central health bureaucracy. Each of these institutions generates measurable outputs, uses inputs of labor, capital and intermediate goods, and obtains finance from various sources. They also interact with each other and function in a co-ordinated manner as components of the health production process shown in Figure 8.1.

The Soviet medical system has acquired certain universal features due to the invariant nature of its functions within this health production process. First, it attempts to prevent or cure the population's illness, which changes in pattern and magnitude in response to developments in demographic, consumption, and environmental forces. Second, medical services are only intermediate outputs in the health production process; the final output is improvement in the population's health. Third, the quantity and quality of medical service outputs are determined by the efficiency of production of medical establishments and the scale and quality of their inputs. Fourth, the health system receives inputs of labor, capital (buildings and equipment), and intermediate goods (medicines, medical supplies, food) from a variety of other institutions; each of these inputs makes a vital contribution to medical service production. Fifth, the technological state of the health system is a function of both its demands and the supply from domestic medical industry or foreign trade organizations. Sixth, there are close relationships between developments in inputs; for example the growing

Figure 8.1 *The health production process in the USSR*

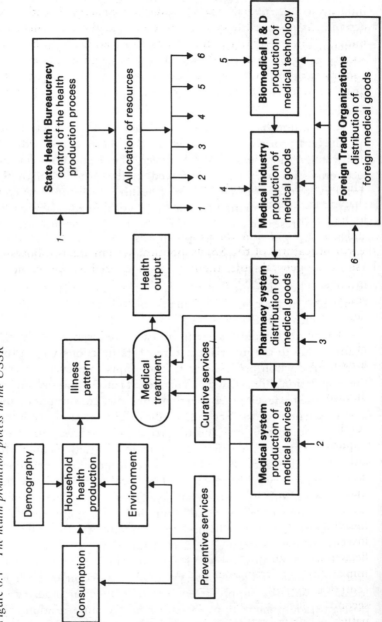

sophistication of medical techniques and technology generates increased specialization among medical personnel. Seventh, health system managers (e.g. hospital chiefs) have limited influence on the overall health production process. Eighth, the activities of the health system are constrained by its financial budget. The sources of finance vary across nations but no society allocates unlimited means to the medical system. In consequence difficult choices have to be made about how to distribute relatively scarce resources between health system establishments, programs, and patients.

The Soviet political system

The political system in the USSR has played a decisive role in shaping the health system and exerts a continuing influence on its functioning in the contemporary period (Lane 1978; Hough and Fainsod 1979). For the purposes of this chapter on health, the salient features of the Soviet political system are as follows. First, as a general rule there is a dictatorial social choice mechanism in the USSR. This means that the preferences of a small group in the society, the self-selecting party elite, determine most choices between alternative policies, instead of the will of the population expressed through free elections. However, it should be kept in mind that although the Soviet Union has had an authoritarian political system, the CPSU (Communist Party of the Soviet Union) elite often has been divided into factions, tendencies, or groupings with differing policy agendas. In consequence there usually has been greater conflict over social choices and more high-level representation of popular preferences than the totalitarian model implies. Second, although the central authorities have tried to gain complete control of the economy and society, this has proved impossible due to the complexity of the USSR and lack of necessary information. Third, the imperfect nature of central control means that there is some room for independent maneuver by lower-level individuals, groups, and institutions. This is reflected in phenomena such as institutional conflict over policy, ministerial empire-building, party bureaucracy resistance to central directives, regionalism, nationalism, corruption, and second economy activity. Fourth, despite the authoritarian nature of the political system, there is some scope for popular participation in decision-making and management at the local level. Although the electoral system does not provide a channel through which citizens can communicate their preferences, they can make suggestions and complaints through letters to newspapers or state organs, through personal representations to their local soviet or trade union, or, if they are party members, through the party apparatus. Under General Secretary Gorbachev this type of low-level participation is being encouraged (Gorbachev 1987).

The Soviet economy

Developments in the Soviet health production process are also strongly influenced by the characteristics and dynamics of the economy. The basic features of the contemporary Soviet economy emerged by the early 1930s and reflected the objectives and values of the Stalinist political elite (Ellman 1973; Gregory and Stuart 1981). The state owns all land as well as industrial enterprises and service sector institutions. This means that all medical facilities, pharmacies, pharmaceutical factories, and biomedical R & D institutes are government property. The state also has a monopoly of foreign trade and carefully controls the flow of the goods, services, and currencies across its borders. So all imports and exports of medicines and medical equipment are governed by state plans.

The activities of the producing units of the Soviet economy are governed primarily by state plans, and not markets. The general shape of state plans is determined by the objectives and priorities of the party leadership. Throughout Soviet history the primary objectives have been to ensure survival of the communist system, to stimulate rapid industrialization, and to achieve economic self-sufficiency. The regime also has wanted to improve the well-being of the population through advances in private consumption and public welfare programs such as the health system. However, resources never have been sufficient to achieve all objectives simultaneously. Furthermore, internal and external pressures have given urgency to the attainment of the most important objectives. In consequence, the leadership has established clear priorities governing the allocation of resources. With respect to end-use of national income, investment and defense are favored over private and public consumption. Among the sectors of the economy, highest priority has been given to defense industry, heavy industry, and transportation. The traditional low priority sectors have been agriculture, light industry (including the pharmaceutical industry), and public services (including the health system).

In the economy, the Ministry of Health USSR has the primary responsibility for preparation and implementation of health system plans (Malov and Churakov 1983; Popov 1976). The Planning-Finance Main Administration of the Ministry, in conjunction with the Health and Medical Industry Department of Gosplan USSR, provides subordinate units with methodological assistance and information about plan objectives. Each of the fifteen republican ministries of health also has a Planning Finance Administration which has responsibility for health planning in the republic. Under the ministry are regional, city, and rural district health department planning sections. These health authorities produce plans that usually call for modest, steady growth of inputs and the production of medical services. As a general rule, Soviet health planning is more concerned with the quantitative development of inputs, such as doctors and hospital beds, than with health outputs, the quality of medical services or the efficiency of production.

Although the planning organs produce detailed plans that are supposed to govern economic transactions and developments, the planning process suffers from many problems. One major difficulty is that the modern Soviet economy is simply too big for its operations to be planned accurately. Gosplan has limited staff, technology, and time, so it cannot possibly control every aspect of the economy. For example until 1978 there was no national plan for pharmaceutical production (Davis 1987). The inevitable consequence of this situation is that Soviet economic plans are inconsistent even at the time of formulation, so many demand–supply relationships are initially out of balance. As the plans are implemented, shortages of labor and commodities and bottlenecks in production arise. In order to cope with the economic disequilibrium Communist Party leaders and planning officials at national and regional levels have to intervene continuously to revise plans and redirect resources. In altering allocations, reference is again made to national priorities. The most important sectors, such as defense, suffer least from shortages. But as a result, the constraints in other low priority areas, such as health, grow tighter and their original plans become more difficult to fulfil.

A final economic issue to consider is distributional policy. In the period since the revolution resources devoted to consumption in the Soviet Union always have been scarce relative to need because of the general low priority of welfare and the chronic shortage environment. The communist leadership soon realized that the maintenance of inequalities and development of rationing schemes were necessary in order to attain high priority objectives. As a result the political elite introduced distributional policies which favored citizens working on or affiliated with important political and economic organizations. Those who fell into a privileged category received higher wages and benefited from closed distribution systems for housing, consumer goods, and health services (Davis 1983b; 1986; 1988). But given the general low priority of consumption and the limited resources allocated to support welfare programs the non-egalitarian policies resulted in greater shortages and lower service standards in the public consumption sphere. Over recent decades the substantial growth of the Soviet economy has resulted in living standard improvements for all segments of the population. Nevertheless, distributional policy has remained non-egalitarian and has influenced development in areas such as health.

Soviet society

The behavior of patients and medical staff in the Soviet health system is affected not only by universal, functional forces that act on people in a given situation, but also by social and cultural patterns and habits of Soviet society. Although there are hazards associated with generalizing about the population in a large multinational country such as the USSR, the following social characteristics of relevance to health appear to exist. First, the average Soviet citizen probably has a greater bond to the collectives which influence his/her life (family, friends, colleagues), less individual egotism than a western counterpart, and a greater tolerance of society's power to constrain the right of the individual to obtain maximum satisfaction of needs, including that for medical care. Second, Soviet citizens have learned to be more deferential, or at least to avoid open conflict, when confronted by authority. This trait is changing over time as memories of the Stalinist period fade, but it is probably true that Soviet people are more accepting of orders, instructions, and decisions than are citizens of several western nations, such as the United States. Third, the difficult experiences of Soviet history, combined with the challenging weather in much of the country, have instilled in Soviet people a stoicism in the face of suffering. Fourth, the Soviet people are aware of the backward state of their country at the time of the revolution, the numerous obstacles to development, and the recent substantial progress in living standards. They therefore tend to evaluate their current welfare relative to previous levels within the country rather than to the highest standards achieved elsewhere. Fifth, the Soviet ideological environment, fostered by the CPSU, encourages citizens to approve of and appreciate the status quo in their developing socialist society and to look critically on the capitalist west. This tendency is reinforced by the state censorship system which restricts the flow of information into the USSR about positive features of western nations. As a result, few citizens are able to compare knowledgeably standards in the health system with those achieved in the more developed west.

The organization of the Soviet health system

The organization of the contemporary health system in the USSR has developed over the past several decades in response to changes in the health production process, advances in medical sciences, and particular political and economic forces within Soviet society. One important particularistic influence has been the prevailing Marxist-Leninist ideological environment and its related principles (Field 1967). In the current period there appear to be six main principles of health organization and strategy in the USSR:

1 The health service has a state socialist character.
2 Qualified medical care is provided free-of-charge to all who need it.
3 The medical system is unified and develops according to a central plan.
4 The health service has a preventive orientation.
5 Biomedical science and clinical practice develop in a unified manner.

6 Health service activities involve public participation.

(Lisitsyn 1972)

Empirical evidence suggests that several of these principles are more aspirations than descriptions of reality (Davis 1988). For example the Soviet health system should have a unified organization and be planned and managed by a central authority, the Ministry of Health USSR. In reality, the organization is different from the ideal model (Field 1967; Ryan 1978). First of all, several different authorities besides the Ministry of Health control medical facilities in departmental subsystems. Second, within the Ministry of Health there are two different types of closed subsystems (elite and industrial) and three open ones (capital city, provincial city, and rural). Each of these has somewhat different characteristics and provides medical care of varying quality to the population group it serves (Davis 1988).

The organization of the delivery of medical care exhibits considerable diversity, reflecting differences between subsystems and client groups. For example first contact care of patients in large city, medium city, and rural district subsystems is organized on a territorial basis, according to place of residence, whereas access to services in elite, departmental and industrial subsystems depends upon place of work. Despite this complexity, there are some common features of first-contact care and patient referral in the USSR. In most cases the initial consultation between a patient and a general doctor occurs in an out-patient facility called a polyclinic (Serenko et al. 1976). If the complaint cannot be easily dealt with a referral is made to either the polyclinic diagnostic department or a specialist doctor within the polyclinic. In the event that the patient requires hospitalization, the polyclinic will refer the patient to a linked general hospital. This facility will deal with most cases. But a small percentage of patients needing more sophisticated treatment will be referred to specialized hospitals with large catchment areas (Safonov and Loginova 1976).

Soviet health system issues and problems

The contemporary Soviet health service must cope with many challenges similar to those faced by the other national medical systems under study in this volume. These include growing demand for medical services, pressures for cost containment, the effects of technological progress, the need for flexible responses to contingencies, and determination of the appropriate balance between popular and central control. This situation is understandable in light of the universal pressures acting on the health systems that were discussed in the second section. On the other hand, the particular features of the Soviet environment described above have generated differing responses to common problems. Furthermore, a number of medical system problems exist in more pronounced form in the Soviet Union than in western countries, such as shortages, rationing, second economy activity, low-quality medical care, and rising mortality rates. The objective of this section is to identify and analyze these various issues and problems in order to facilitate the comparison of Soviet health system performance with that of other countries.

The concentration on problems in this section does give a negative bias to the portrayal of the Soviet health system. It therefore should be noted that in the USSR there are many skilled and caring medical personnel, numerous good hospitals and polyclinics, and some excellent biomedical research scientists. Furthermore, the health system provides free medical care to all citizens and its production of services has been expanding (Davis 1987). These positive features should be considered as well as the problems discussed below in order to obtain a balanced appreciation of the health system in the USSR.

Growing demands for medical care

Over the past two decades the need for medical care in the USSR has grown substantially due to developments in demography (population growth of 48 million, aging, higher share of males), consumption (growth in alcoholism, smoking, and cholesterol intake), and the environment (increased pollution, worsening of sanitary conditions) (Davis 1988). These negative influences have not been offset by effective preventive medical programs. In consequence, many illness rates have increased in the USSR.

As a general rule, one would expect that as a nation becomes more urban and industrialized, living standards will improve and there will be a shift in its illness pattern. Usually this involves a decrease in nutritional and infectious diseases and an increase in degenerative illness. In the Soviet case, however, the government's unbalanced development policy, especially its neglect of consumption, has impeded the normal transition. As a result, the illness pattern has some of the features of both developed and under-developed countries.

The incidence of infectious diseases is higher in the USSR than in other industrialized nations and in recent years there have been unfavorable upward trends in the prevalence of typhoid and paratyphoid, diphtheria, whooping cough, measles, mumps, hepatitis, and salmonellosis (Feshbach 1983; 1986). Accidents and poisonings have also risen due to the rapid mechanization of Soviet society and growing consumption of alcohol. The most significant development has been the increase in degenerative diseases caused by the aging of the population, urbanization, stress, smoking, alcoholism, poor diet, and pollution. During the past two decades the Soviet Union has experienced a coronary illness epidemic of growing severity (Cooper and Schatzkin 1982). This is reflected in the death-rate from all cardiovascular disease, which rose from 247 deaths per 100,000 in 1960 to 459 in 1975 to 535 in 1983 (Davis 1977; Feshbach 1986). Similar upward trends can be detected in cancer statistics. Furthermore, the Soviet population still suffers from a high incidence of nutritional disease, such as rickets, and respiratory illness, such as influenza and pneumonia.

Another problem confronting the Soviet health system is that of large-scale untreated illness. Studies by Soviet specialists in the 1970s indicated that about one-third of all cases of illness in cities were not treated by doctors and about two-thirds in rural areas (Davis 1988).

The demand for medical services is a function of not only the population's needs but also income, education, prices, and supplies. In recent decades trends in virtually all of these variables in the USSR were conducive to the growth in demand: real per capita income rose by 59 per cent from 1970 to 1984; educational standards increased markedly; no money prices were introduced for medical services (although time prices remained substantial); and the capabilities of the health system were enhanced, which contributed to the upward pressure because in the medical services market some of the demand is supplier-induced.

As a result of these developments, the Soviet population's demand for medical care rose substantially during the past fifteen years. This is reflected in the growth in the quantity of medical services consumed in the USSR. From 1970 to 1985 the number of annual hospitalizations per 100 people increased from 21.5 to 25.1 and the number of out-patient visits to doctors (including home visits) per capita went up from 8.0 to 11.4 (*Narodnoe Khozyaistvo SSSR v 1985 g.*, 1986). This experience of growing demand is similar to those of most other industrialized nations.

Health cost containment

In their book *The Painful Prescription* Aaron and Schwartz (1984) show that the British national service has been much more successful in containing the costs of medical care than the United States. As a result, the health share of the United States' GNP rose from 6.1 per cent in 1965 to 10.8 per cent in 1983 whereas in Britain it merely increased from 4.2 per cent to 5.2 per cent (*Statistical Abstract of the United States* 1985). However, this restraint has forced British planners, medical staff, and patients to confront difficult choices about how to allocate scarce resources.

The reviews of the Soviet Union's politics, economy, society, and health system in the second section suggest that the USSR is closer to the UK model than the US one, but that conditions facilitating medical cost containment are even more favorable. In the Soviet Union the CPSU is the permanently ruling and only party. Its strong internal discipline ensures a high degree of support by the party and state bureaucracies and the parliament for most policies. State ownership and control of the health system is even more complete than in Britain, where general practitioners and hospital consultants have some autonomy. For example the Soviet state owns and manages the other components of the health production process such as pharmacies, medical industry, biomedical research institutes, and foreign trade organizations. Within the medical system a sequential referral process exists. Since all medical staff in the USSR are salaried state employees and used to working within plan-imposed constraints it is even easier to screen patients and enforce central government budget limits. Finally, the average population member tends to accept decisions of authorities, has a modest individualistic drive, and has a relatively passive acceptance of illness-related suffering.

One component of an effective cost containment policy not

discussed explicitly by Aaron and Schwartz is a government's setting of a relatively low priority for health in the resource allocation process. Without this the other conditions listed above would be insufficient to restrain expenditure. In the second section it was argued that the political leadership in the USSR has given the health sector a low priority. Ample evidence exists to support this conclusion, such as low wages of medical personnel, stingy financial norms governing the calculation of medical institutions' budgets, and unresponsiveness of health spending to growth in consumer demand for medical services. Furthermore, health system expenditure plans for purchase of medical commodities and capital investment are underfulfilled by a greater degree than is normal for the economy and shortage intensity is higher because central authorities protect high priority sectors at the expense of the health system (Davis 1987).

The combination of factors outlined above has enabled the Soviet government to constrain the growth of national health spending. Health system wage and price increases have been held down to about 1–2 per cent a year and the growth rate of Ministry of Health expenditure has been lower than that of the total state budget. As a result, the health share of the budget declined from 6.5 per cent in 1965 to 4.6 per cent in 1985. Expenditures on health from other sources have grown slightly more rapidly, so from 1970 to 1985 total health expenditure roughly doubled from 11.7 to 22.5 billion roubles. But this growth has been from a low base and its rate has been declining. In the period 1975–80 health spending rose by an average of 6 per cent per annum, whereas in 1980–85 it went up by 4 per cent a year. Success in the cost containment effort was also reflected in the low, stable health share of national income (or net material product utilized), which remained in the 3.9–4.0 per cent range. An authoritative western reconstruction of the GNP of the USSR indicates that the health share declined from 2.7 per cent in 1965 to 2.4 per cent in 1980 (US Congress Joint Economic Committee 1982).

This brief assessment of health expenditure in the Soviet Union indicates that the Soviet government has allocated a relatively low share of national income to the health system in accordance with national priorities. During the past two decades, a period of rapidly rising health spending in many countries, the USSR has been able to restrain growth to low rates. Naturally this has meant that the medical system has operated subject to tight resource constraints. The effects of this successful cost containment policy on the health system are examined below.

Shortages in the health system

Shortages in the health system arise when the demand for medical services or commodities exceed available supplies (Culyer 1976). They can be observed in any country, at least on a temporary basis. In normal circumstances equilibrium is returned to an excess demand market either by increasing the supply of the deficit commodity or raising prices to reduce demand.

The health system in the USSR operates in a chronic excess demand environment. It was argued on pp. 243–5 that the demand for medical services is high and rapidly growing. Money prices are not used as a regulatory instrument. Although time prices do discourage visits by patients, there are political constraints on their upward movement. On the supply side, production of medical services is constrained by the established plans and budgets of medical facilities governing the acquisition of inputs as well as by general shortages in the national labor market, distribution errors of the pharmacy network, production problems of the medical industry, and the insufficiency of imports. The low priority of the health sector means that the central authorities are prepared to tolerate a fairly high intensity of shortage in the health system before they will take decisive corrective measures.

In the USSR shortages are evident in the provision of medical services to patients by the health system. In many medical facilities there are crowded waiting rooms, cramped work spaces for staff, and location of diagnostic or treatment units in inappropriate areas. The amount of floor space per hospital bed is often below minimum sanitary levels because beds are crammed into insufficient ward areas or, not infrequently, placed in corridors. There are deficits of many types of personnel relative to established positions in polyclinics and hospitals. This results in the substitution of nurses for doctors, queues of patients, and the reduction in average doctor consultation time. In certain medical specialities there are enough doctors but inadequate numbers of nurses and technicians, which disrupts the work of teams. Throughout the Soviet health system there are shortages of medical equipment, machinery, and instruments; virtually no disposable instruments and supplies are available. This contributes to bottlenecks in the diagnosis and treatment of patients. The supply of medicines to patients within hospitals is normally not enough to satisfy demands. For example, an April 1986 article revealed that in the Erevan republican hospital, which as a capital city hospital should be well supplied, 126 medicaments out of the authorized list of 825 were in deficit (Zagaskii 1986). The stocks of many other critical drugs were at minimal levels, for example this 1,100-bed hospital had only 10 ampules of antistaphylococcic gamma-globulin.

The inadequate supplies of medical services and medicines obtained by patients within the health system are primarily caused by shortages of inputs of labor, capital stock, medicines, and other commodities. These can occur for several reasons. First, the state plan may allocate the medical system insufficient quantities of an input, so even if everything is delivered there will be a shortage. Second, the planned quantity of a commodity may be sufficient but the health service may receive a below-plan amount. Third, in the case of labor the wages on offer may be too low to attract or retain the planned number of staff.

In the case of medicaments deficits are caused by inadequate health facility budgets as well as the substandard work of other institutions in the health production process. For example, the pharmacy network often makes errors in forecasting demand and determining orders for medical industry, so supplies are out of balance to begin with (Gorenkov 1984). Even if the aggregate supply of goods is sufficient, medicaments frequently are distributed inappropriately between regions and facilities. Another problem is that pharmacies have substandard storage facilities due to under-investment. As a result losses are greater than planned, which contributes to supply deficiencies.

The Soviet pharmaceutical industry is even more responsible than pharmacies for shortages of medicines in the health system. In 1979 the Ministry of Health did not receive planned amounts of 226 preparations and its orders for various medicines were only 58–60 per cent satisfied ("Industriya zdorovye" 1980). Although the medical industry's output rose by 40 per cent over the next five years it remained insufficient. For example, in 1986 the Ministry of Health claimed that the industry satisfied only 75 per cent of its undoubtedly understated demands for medicines ("Utverzhdat delom" 1986).

The Soviet health system

Figure 8.1 indicates that deficiencies in commodity supplies could be remedied through imports. However, foreign trade is a state monopoly in the USSR and is conducted in accordance with national economic plans. Import decisions therefore are only indirectly responsive to consumer demands. Despite a recent expansion in trade, the volume of supplies acquired abroad has not been enough to eliminate the chronic shortages of modern medicines in the USSR (Davis 1987).

From the material presented above it should be clear that shortages are an important feature of the Soviet health system. They affect the provision of medical services to patients, the efficiency of health facilities, and supplies to the medical system. Although shortages arise in all countries they usually are not as pervasive and chronic as in the Soviet case. This relatively unique phenomenon is a function of a national health service operating with a low priority in an imperfectly planned socialist shortage economy (Davis forthcoming).

Rationing of medical care

Rationing of medical care usually arises in any nation which is confronted by a growing demand for medical services but sets fairly stringent limits on health spending. The excess demand in the medical care market results in shortages which potentially could affect the treatment of all patients. However, most societies have value systems that rank certain illness conditions (e.g. cancer) and population groups (e.g. infants) more highly than others (e.g. arthritic and elderly people). Thus efforts are made to ration medical care in an attempt to ensure that the most important patients receive care irrespective of general circumstances. Analyses of rationing in the British national health service can be found in several books (Cooper 1975; Culyer 1976; Aaron and Schwartz 1984).

The Soviet Union has chronic excess demand in the market for medical services because of the factors discussed on pp. 247–9. In theory, the leadership in the USSR could respond to this situation with egalitarian rationing. However, it was argued on p. 240 that in the Soviet shortage economy a non-egalitarian approach to distribution has been adopted. This has had a significant effect on rationing medical care and has influenced both the organization and functioning of the health system.

One of the clearest expressions of this rationing has been the division of the health service into the six subsystems described in Davis (1983a; 1988) and mentioned above. All of the closed facilities are relatively well funded and supplied, so they offer their patients a higher standard of care than could the open ones. In addition, there is very little referral between the three public subsystems (capital city, medium city, and rural district). This means that a differential approach to resource allocation can ensure that the important urban population groups, especially those in capital cities, receive better care than residents of small towns and villages. Rationing also partly explains the organization of specialized facilities for two important population groups, pregnant women and children.

Queuing is another instrument of rationing in the health system. Queues act as a rationing device because they impose time prices on patients and therefore allocate medical services to those who can afford or are prepared to wait. Their advantage is that they restrict the demands of patients to a manageable scale through an apparently neutral mechanism, and thereby save medical staff from having to make unpopular decisions about whether or not each potential patient can be treated.

Although queuing exists in all health systems, in the USSR it has a pervasive, systemic character. In polyclinics the most frequent queue found is of patients waiting to see the doctor of first contact. The therapist attempts to regulate the number of patients referred for specialized diagnosis or treatment in order to keep demand in balance with supply. Despite this screening, many are still sent forward. Diagnostic departments in polyclinics often operate at below capacity due to equipment failure or staffing problems so bottlenecks arise in the treatment process. As a result patients have to wait long periods in the polyclinic before they receive X-rays or other diagnostic services. The same situation obtains with respect to seeing specialist doctors for treatment within the polyclinic.

In hospitals queues exist as well, but they involve waiting in bed rather than in corridors outside offices. Again, this is caused by production bottlenecks in diagnostic and treatment departments due to relative shortages of technology or skilled personnel. This bed-queuing forces patients to wait for attention and helps to explain why residence in hospitals is considerably longer in the Soviet Union than in the west.

Waiting lists are used by the Soviet health system to ration scarce medical care. In the case of polyclinics, a patient who cannot obtain scarce diagnostic or specialist services during an initial visit can be either given a future appointment or put on a waiting list. Those on waiting lists are contacted at an unspecified future date when an appointment becomes available. Admission to Soviet hospitals is governed by waiting lists for many non-urgent cases. The length of wait depends upon the general level of hospital provision and availability of specialized services in a region.

The existence of wide-spread rationing in the Soviet health system is a predictable consequence of the chronic excess demand in the medical care market. Although western countries are also forced to ration scarce services using the instruments of queuing and waiting lists, this is not allowed to become too severe by governments because of greater popular expectations and fear of adverse feedback through the open western electoral systems. For reasons discussed in the society section above, rationing is tolerated more in the USSR. Furthermore, the Soviet Union is unusual in its practice of rationing medical care through closed subsytems within a state-financed national health service. Most western societies have closed facilities, particularly for the military, but provide above-average medical care to elite groups through privately financed medical facilities or programs. It appears that Soviet arrangements are made possible by the one-party political system, lack of requirements for public accountability, and censorship.

The second economy in medical care

In any country that has a national health service with shortages and rationing a universal response by a proportion of patients is to try to obtain adequate medical care through manipulation of the bureaucracy or use of the legal or illegal private sector. In the Soviet Union, particular conditions have existed in recent years which generated substantial second economy activity by patients and staff: chronic, acute shortages; severe rationing; low salaries of medical personnel; negligible opportunities for staff to earn extra money through legal channels; and the general decline in moral standards during the Brezhnev period that spawned extensive corruption (Gorbachev 1987; "Trudnye shagi perestroika" 1987).

The result of this situation was that during 1970–85 second

economy activity flourished throughout the health and pharmacy systems (Knaus 1982). In medical facilities doctors often expected "gifts" of a modest nature for providing routine treatment. More substantial payments frequently were made to secure rapid admission to better public hospitals, treatment by top specialists, better dental work, and discreet cure of socially embarrassing medical conditions. Nurses and ward attendants in hospitals were usually paid small sums on a regular basis to provide normal services such as changing bed pans and sheets or supplying edible food. Evidence also existed of substantial corruption in the education system. In several republics medical school admission officers regularly received substantial bribes in return for admitting students with substandard records.

In the pharmacy network as well the chronic deficits of medicines and low wages of personnel stimulated the emergence of a widespread second economy. Medicines often were illegally acquired by black marketeers through thefts from factories, warehouses, importing agencies, and pharmacies. These goods were then sold through informal networks to hospital and polyclinic patients. In other cases speculators or pharmacy personnel legally purchased at full retail price, large quantities of desirable goods and thereby contributed to shortages. After a suitable period these medicines were re-sold to consumers. A third practice was for pharmacy personnel to keep medicines in high demand "under the counter" for sale to acquaintances at official prices or to others who paid a premium.

Although these unethical and illegal practices have been severely criticized and punished when uncovered by state authorities since Gorbachev assumed power, it is unlikely that these second economy phenomena will be eradicated as long as serious shortages exist in the markets for medical services and pharmaceutical goods. For example, in October 1986 the Collegium of the Ministry of Health stated that "In pharmacies and medical equipment organizations inadequacies are only slowly being removed, cases of embezzlement of and speculation in medicaments have not been eliminated" ("Utverzhdat delom" 1986).

Medical technology in the health system

Over the past several decades the organization, effectiveness, and costs of health systems in the west have been significantly influenced by the substantial advances made in biomedical sciences, medical technology, and clinical techniques. On the whole, the scientific-technological revolution in medicine has been beneficial and has raised the effectiveness of health systems in coping with illness. But it also has had negative side effects, such as the promotion of narrow specialization of medical personnel, creation of a more alienating technocratic environment for patients, and rapid growth in the cost of medical care.

The health system in the USSR has been affected by these universal developments in biomedical science and technology, but to a lesser degree and in a more uneven manner than have most health services in western countries. Relative to international standards the Soviet Union has low levels of technology and slow rates of technological progress in the health sector. This backwardness has been caused by particular features of the political and economic systems that adversely affect both the demand for and the supply of technology.

On the demand side, the impact of consumers on medical technology acquisition is minimal due to several factors: lack of knowledge about available technologies, especially those in the west; satisfaction at receiving medical care based on relatively outdated technologies given the shortage environment; willingness to accept the explanations and decisions of medical authorities in the areas of diagnosis and treatment; and inability to influence production decisions through the market for medical care. The health system itself has a weak influence on technological progress. In the USSR medical facility managers are primarily concerned about raising the quantity of services provided in order to reduce excess demand rather than, as in the west, constantly increasing quality on the basis of new technologies. In addition there is no pressure for doctors to engage in resource-intensive "defensive medicine." Staff are not worried about consumer complaints and concentrate on working competently with existing technology, even if it is outdated. Among other factors inhibiting the demand of the medical system are tight constraints on capital acquisition budgets, the low priority status of health, and ineffectiveness of price signals in a shortage environment.

Since the Soviet economy is a supply-constrained system, it follows that many of the technological problems of the health service are the result of deficiencies in distribution and production. The agency which manages wholesale trade in medical equipment and instruments, Soyuzmedtekhnika, is plagued by many of the same shortcomings as pharmacies: inaccurate projections of demand, inadequate storage facilities, inappropriate distribution of products between regions and institutions, and poor after-sales repair service and spare parts supply ("Utverzhdat delom" 1986).

Other institutions of the health production process contribute to problems in technology supply as well. Medical industry, for example, has chronically under-fulfilled its plans for technology deliveries to the health system ("Industriya zdorovye" 1980). Although the output of medical technology has risen in recent years, industrial performance has continued to be relatively substandard throughout the 1980s. A January 1987 report stated that health system requirements for medical equipment were only 75–80 per cent satisfied and that

> Domestic industry did not produce a whole series of contemporary apparatuses, such as angiographic complexes, mobile photo-flurographic stations, artificial blood circulation machines, biochemical analyzers, and many other types of equipment.
>
> ("Trudnye" 1987)

A major cause of the deficiencies in the supply of equipment and machinery by the medical industry is the sluggishness of technological progress. In the USSR technological innovation proceeds at a slow pace in the medical industry due to numerous obstacles: absence of effective incentives to innovate in industrial enterprises; lack of effective domestic or foreign competition; operation in a shortage environment so consumers will take all their output; and judgment of success by plan fulfilment rather than consumer satisfaction. In consequence, managers prefer to stick to old methods and products rather than engage in the troublesome process of introduction (*vnedrenie*) of new technology. A related obstacle is that prices of new products are determined by the bureaucracy, not the market, and often are not set high enough to compensate enterprises for the trouble of innovation.

Scientific R & D institutions in the biomedical field also are partially responsible for sluggish technological innovation ("Rezervy nauki" 1985). They often engage in irrelevant projects, maximize their expenditures instead of scientific outputs, and have little interest in ensuring that discoveries are put into mass production ("Po puti uskoreniya" 1986).

Given the factors influencing both demand and supply in the USSR, it is not surprising that, in general, the level and rate of introduction of technology in its health system have been low by western standards. Outside of the various well-provided closed subsystems, medical establishments are short of machinery and equipment of all kinds. Public health facilities in the USSR are poorly provided with sophisticated technologies for diagnosis, such as computer-aided tomography and other advanced X-ray equipment, and for treatments such as organ transplantation, kidney dialysis, hip surgery, coronary artery surgery, and intensive care of premature babies. There are shortages of more basic technologies as well, such as stethoscopes, thermometers, and syringes. Few disposable medical products of glass, plastic, or paper are available either, due to shortcomings of Soviet industry. Existing equipment often is utilized in rooms that were designed for other functions and do not meet modern hygienic standards. Much of the machinery is obsolete due to low replacement rates, which are a function of the stingy budget norms mentioned above. In addition, maintenance of existing medical technology is made difficult by shortages of engineering staff and spare parts.

The relative backwardness of the technological environment in the Soviet health system naturally enough has impacts on the behavior of patients and staff and on the effectiveness of diagnosis and treatment. The consequences for the patient are both positive and negative. On the one hand the low level of technology contributes to a more relaxed patient–doctor relationship because there are lower expectations about the technical effectiveness of treatment and a less alienating technocratic environment. On the other hand, shortages of machinery and equipment contribute to medical service production bottlenecks, unpleasant queuing by patients, and a lower quality of medical care. In the case of staff, the lack of medical technology hinders the development or implementation of new diagnostic and curative techniques. There also is less pressure for subspecialization, since the technological support for many new western specialities does not exist. The general deficit of equipment of all kinds, including typewriters and computers, means that the Soviet health system is less mechanized and automated than a western one. Since middle medical personnel are in short supply too, doctors must devote substantial amounts of time to low-level medical and administrative work.

The conclusion from this assessment appears to be that technological progress is not an irresistible force determining developments in all health systems. No doubt there is a universal tendency for advances in scientific knowledge and medical technology to influence medical organization and techniques. However, the Soviet case indicates that a combination of particular political, economic, and cultural factors can hold back the pace of technological change and lessen its impact on the health system. The analysis in this section suggests that all the institutions in the Soviet health production process have some responsibility for the existence of technological backwardness. It therefore is evident that an acceleration of technological innovation in the health sector cannot be stimulated by a few simple policy changes. Instead, wide-ranging systemic reforms will be needed to bring the level of medical technology in the health system up to international standards. In sum, study of the Soviet health system shows clearly that there are limits to the autonomous force of technology in a modern industrialized society.

The health system and mortality trends

The primary objective of the health production process shown in Figure 8.1 is to improve the various indicators of final health output, such as recovery, invalidity, and mortality rates. The health system plays a crucial role in this process and is the institution with primary responsibility for ensuring that death-rates decline and life expectancy rises. It can accomplish this either by reducing illness rates through programs designed to improve consumption or environmental health conditions or by upgrading the effectiveness of curative medical services to cope with the new challenges posed by developments in the illness pattern. In virtually all industrialized countries mortality rates have been reduced over the past two decades, which suggests that health systems have been effective in fulfilling their responsibilities. The Soviet Union, however, has had a very different experience with respect to mortality and life expectancy trends and therefore should be carefully examined in an international comparison of medical care.

Throughout most of the period 1945–64, mortality and life expectancy indicators improved in the USSR, in conformance with international trends. All age-specific death-rates, including infant mortality, declined and the crude death-rate fell to 7.1 deaths per 1,000 by 1964/5 (Davis 1977; Davis and Feshbach 1980; Dutton 1979). These improvements were taken by many in the Soviet Union to be proof of the effectiveness of the socialist health service.

During the next two decades, however, there was a striking reversal of previous mortality trends. From 1965 to 1984 the crude mortality rate in the USSR rose dramatically, from 7.1 to 10.8 deaths per 1,000, or by 52 per cent. Since the US rate declined from 9.4 to 8.6 deaths per 1,000 over the same period, the Soviet experience does not represent an immutable process caused by the aging of the population. Instead, the upward trend implies that there were increases in age-specific death-rates.

The infant mortality rate, which measures deaths during the first year of life, fell from 27.2 deaths per 1,000 live births to 22.9 between 1965 and 1971, but increased in following years (Davis and Feshbach 1980; Field 1986). By 1976 its estimated value was 31.1 deaths per 1,000 or 36 per cent above the rate in 1971. After that it apparently was reduced to 27.3 in 1980 to 25.3 in 1983 ("Naselenie SSSR" 1986). The infant mortality rate went up in each of the next two years, reaching 26.0 deaths per 1,000 live births in 1985. This upward trend is in striking contrast with the experience of most industrialized countries. In the case of the United States infant mortality decreased uninterruptedly from 20 deaths per 1,000 live births in 1970 to 10.6 in 1984 (*Statistical Abstract of the United States* 1985).

Most other age-specific death-rates exhibited similar upward trends in the 1970s. The rate for the 0–4 age group went up from 6.9 deaths per 1,000 in 1969/70 to 8.1 in 1980/81 ("Statisticheskie materialy" 1986). In the next three quintiles, covering ages 5–19, minimum post-war rates were maintained up to 1980/81. But all older age groups exhibited increases from the minimum, which were in the range of 2 to 33 per cent. For example the rates (deaths per 1,000) rose from 6.0 to 8.0 in the age group 45–49 years and from 18.0 to 20.6 in the age group 60–64 years.

During the 1980s the trends in age-specific death-rates have become more varied (Davis 1987). Of the fifteen age groups for which official statistics are available, nine had declining rates from 1980/81 to 1984/85, one remained stable, and five rose. Those exhibiting increases were the age groups 40–44, 50–54, 55–59, 65–69, and over 70 years.

It is evident from these official statistics that in the USSR during the past two decades mortality has risen, which is a trend contrary to the experience of other nations. This raises serious questions about the effectiveness of the medical system with respect to final output. Although the production of medical services and inputs to the health system increased, it appears that the improvements in the health service were insufficient to cope with the new challenges confronting it.

Conclusions

In this chapter an attempt was made to carry out three general tasks. The first was to identify the universal and particular features of the Soviet medical system and to assess the balance between them. A second was to evaluate the performance of the Soviet medical system relative to prevailing international standards. Third, an effort was made to assess the dynamics of Soviet health system development over time to determine whether universal forces, such as technological progress, stimulated a convergence toward other existing models or whether particular factors within the USSR maintained unique national features.

The analysis of the Soviet health service in this chapter indicates that it does have some universal features because Soviet biomedical scientists make use of modern scientific theories of disease and medicine, clinicians attempt to employ internationally recognized preventive and curative medical techniques, and the health system in the USSR functions within a universal health production process. Furthermore, the Soviet health system is influenced by real developments that occur in most countries, such as growth in the population's demand for medical services and pressures for containment of health costs.

Despite this, the evidence presented in the chapter indicates that there are very strong forces within the USSR which modulate internationalizing influences and maintain the national characteristics of the Soviet health service. The second section argued that the communist political system, the imperfectly planned socialist economy, and various social circumstances and cultural traits combine to produce a unique country environment. This, together with Soviet medical care principles based on Marxist-Leninist ideology, produce a health system with a distinctive organizational form: a national health service in a socialist society. It represents one of the end points of the range of medical care organization in industrialized countries.

The third section argued that the unique health system in the Soviet Union has performance characteristics and problems different from those in other industrialized nations. First, the Soviet illness pattern reveals a high incidence of both infectious and degenerative disease. Second, cost containment has been effective in the USSR and the health system is subject to tight resource constraints. Third, pervasive and chronic shortages of medical services and health system inputs exist in the Soviet Union. A fourth feature is that rationing is extensively used to distribute scarce medical services between population groups; an unusual aspect of Soviet practice is rationing through closed medical subsystems within a publicly financed national health service. Fifth, technological progress has had a limited impact on the Soviet health system; in the USSR the average level of medical technology is low by international standards and the indigenous technological innovation process is sluggish. Finally, during the past two decades the medical system in the USSR, unlike most others in industrialized countries, has been ineffective in coping with developments in the national illness pattern and has allowed mortality rates to rise.

The evidence presented in this chapter suggests that recent trends in the development of the Soviet health system are inconsistent with the convergence hypothesis. It appears likely that medical care organization and practice in the USSR in the mid-1980s is as different from that in western industrialized nations as it was in the 1960s. One reason for this is that the impact of medical technology has been severely restrained by barriers to international diffusion through scientific exchange and foreign trade, the slow pace of indigenous technological innovation, problems in the domestic production of machinery and equipment for the health service, and tight budgetary constraints on technological acquisition. In consequence, the force of industrialism on medical production in the USSR has been relatively weak. Other universalistic influences also are muted in the Soviet environment due to the countervailing effects of political, economic, cultural and bureaucratic variables. As a result, the Soviet health system has evolved slowly and incrementally over the past two decades. Since this has been a period of rapid change in other industrialized societies, the possibility should be considered that there has been a relative divergence, not a convergence, of the features of the Soviet and other national health systems. If these past tendencies within the Soviet Union are maintained in the late 1980s then there is little chance that the Soviet health service will lose its distinctive features and either move toward western systems or provide an attractive alternative model.

References

Aaron, H.J. and Schwartz, W.B. (1984), *The Painful Prescription: Rationing Hospital Care*, Washington, DC: Brookings Institution.

Cooper, M.H. (1975) *Rationing Health Care*, London: Croom Helm.

Cooper, R. and Schatzkin, A. (1982) "Recent trends in coronary risk factors in the USSR," *American Journal of Public Health* 72: 431–40.

Culyer, A.J. (1976) *Need and the National Health Service*, Oxford: Martin Robertson.

Davis, C. (1977) "An analysis of mortality and life expectancy trends in the USSR: 1959–1975," Cambridge (England), discussion paper.

—— (1983a) "The economics of the Soviet health system," in US Congress Joint Economic Committee, *Soviet Economy in the 1980s: Problems and Prospects*, Washington, DC: USGPO.

—— (1983b) "Economic problems of the Soviet health service: 1917–1930," *Soviet Studies* 35: 343–61.

—— (1986) "The development of the Soviet medical system during the First Five-Year Plan: 1928–32," Toronto, paper presented at the Conference on the History of Russian and Soviet Public Health.

—— (1987) "Developments in the health sector of the Soviet economy, 1970–90" in US Congress Joint Economic Committee, *Gorbachev's Economic Plans*, Washington, DC: USGPO.

—— (1988) "The organization and performance of the contemporary Soviet health service," in G. Lapidus and G. Swanson (eds) *State and Welfare, USA/USSR*, Berkeley, Calif: Institute of International Studies.

—— (Forthcoming) "Priority and the shortage model: the medical system in the socialist economy," in C. Davis and W. Charemza (eds) *Models of Disequilibrium and Shortage in Centrally Planned Economies*, London: Chapman & Hall.

Davis, C. and Feshbach, M. (1980) *Rising Infant Mortality in the USSR in the 1970's*, Washington, DC: Bureau of the Census Report, Series P-95 no. 74.

Dutton, J. (1979) "Changes in Soviet mortality patterns, 1959–77," *Population and Development Review* 5: 267–91.

Ellman, M. (1973) *Planning Problems in the USSR*, Cambridge: Cambridge University Press.

Feshbach, M. (1983) "Issues in health problems," in US Congress Joint Economic Committee, *Soviet Economy in the 1980s: Problems and Prospects*, Washington, DC: USGPO.

—— (1986) "Recent research on Soviet health conditions," Cambridge, paper presented at the NASEES Annual Conference.

Field, M. (1967) *Soviet Socialized Medicine: An Introduction*, New York: Free Press.

—— (1986) "Soviet infant mortality: a mystery story," in D.B. Jelliffe and E.F.P. Jelliffe (eds) *Advances in International Maternal and Child Health*, Oxford: Clarendon.

Gorbachev, M.S. (1987) "O perestroike i kadrovoi politike partii," speech delivered at the January 27, 1987 CPSU Central Committee Plenum, *Sovetskaya Rossiya*: January 28.

Gorenkov, V.F. (1984) *Organizatsiya i Ekonomika Sovetskoi Farmatsiya*, Minsk: Vysheishaya Shkola.

Gregory, P.R. and Stuart, R.C. (1981) *Soviet Economic Structure and Performance*, New York: Harper & Row.

Hough, J.F. and Fainsod, M. (1979) *How the Soviet Union is Governed*, Cambridge, Mass: Harvard University Press.

"Industriya zdorovye" (1980) *Pravda*: February 9.

Kaser, M. (1976) *Health Care in the Soviet Union and Eastern Europe*, London: Croom Helm.

Knaus, W. (1982) *Inside Russian Medicine*, New York: Everest House.

Lane, D. (1978) *Politics and Society in the USSR*, London: Martin Robertson.

Lisitsyn, Yu (1972) *Health Protection in the USSR*, Moscow: Progress Publishers.

Malov, N.I. and Churakov, V.I. (1983) *Sovremennye Osnovy i Metodi Planirovaniya Razvitiya Zdravookhraneniya*, Moscow: Ekonomika.

Narodnoe Khozyaistvo SSSR v 1965 g . . . v 1985 g, (1966 . . . 1986) Moscow: Finansy i Statistika.

"Naselenie SSSR" (1986) *Ekonomicheskaya Gazeta* 43.

"Po puti uskoreniya" (1986) *Meditsinskaya Gazeta* July 23.

Popov, G.A. (1976) *Ekonomika i Planirovanie Zdravookhraneniya*, Moscow: Izdatelstvo Moskovskogo Universiteta.

"Rezervy nauki" (1985) *Meditsinskaya Gazeta* December 25.

Ryan, M. (1978) *The Organization of Soviet Medical Care*, London: Martin Robertson.

Safonov, A.G. and Loginova, E.A. (eds) (1976) *Osnovy Organizatsii Statsionarnoi Pomoshchi v SSSR*, Moscow: Meditsina.

Serenko, F., Ermakov, V.V. and Petrakov, B.D. (1976) *Osnovy Organizatsii Poliklinicheskoi Pomoshchi Naseleniya*, Moscow: Meditsina.

Statistical Abstract of the United States (1985) Washington, DC: US Bureau of the Census.

"Statisticheskie materialy" (1986) *Vestnik Statistiki* 12: 71.

Treml, V. (1982) "Death from alcohol poisoning in the USSR," *Soviet Studies* 4.

"Trudnye shagi perestroika" (1987) *Meditsinskaya Gazeta* January 23.

US Congress Joint Economic Committee (1982) *USSR: Measures of Economic Growth and Development, 1950–80*, Washington, DC: USGPO.

"Utverzhdat delom" (1986) *Meditsinskaya Gazeta* October 15.

"V Politburo TsK KPSS" (1986) *Meditsinskaya Gazeta* September 17.

Zagalskii, L. (1985) "Tabletki dlya Zolushki," *Meditsinskaya Gazeta* November 29.

—— (1986) "Tabletki pod podushkoi," *Meditsinskaya Gazeta* April 16.

Zhuk, A.P. (1968) *Planirovanie Zdravookhraneniya v SSSR*, Moscow: Meditsina.

Zhuravleva, K.I. (1981) *Statistika v Zdravookhranenie*, Moscow: Meditsina.

Nine

New ideas for health policy in France, Canada, and Britain

Victor G. Rodwin

There is a widely shared belief among American policy-makers that a national program providing for universal entitlement to health care, in the United States, would result in runaway costs.[1] In response to this presumptive wisdom, nations that entitle all of their residents to a high level of medical care and simultaneously spend less than the United States, are often held up as exemplars. Canada's system of national health insurance (NHI) is the most celebrated example.[2] French NHI, a prototype of western European continental health systems, is another case in point. Britain's National Health Service (NHS), although typically considered a "painful prescription" for the United States (Aaron and Schwartz 1984), assures first dollar coverage for basic health services to its entire population and spends the smallest share of its gross domestic product (GDP) on health care expenditures (Table 9.1).

All of these countries have produced some of the leading physicians and hospitals in the world. Judging by various measures of health status, they are in the same league or better than the United States. In Britain, life expectancy at 60 – when medical care may have an important impact – is lower than in the United States. But in the United States over 15 per cent of

Table 9.1   *Health care expenditures and health status*

| | Health expenditures (1984) as % of GDP | Life expectancy (1980) | | | | Infant mortality[2] (1983) |
| | | at birth | | at age 60 | | |
		males	females	males	females	
France	9.1	70.1	78.3	17.2	22.3	.89
Canada	8.4	71.0	79.0	18.0	23.0	.85
Britain[1]	5.9	70.2	75.9	15.9	20.5	1.02
United States	10.7	69.6	76.7	17.2	22.4	1.09

Sources: Data on health expenditures are from Schieber and Poullier 1986; data on life expectancy and infant mortality are from OECD 1985, Tables F.1 and F.2: 131.

Notes: [1] All data are for the United Kingdom.
[2] Infant mortality is expressed in death-rates of infants below 1 year per 100 live births.

the population remains uninsured for health care services while spending, as a per cent of GDP, surpasses that of all industrially advanced nations (OECD 1985).[3]

Virtually no one in Canada or in western Europe – not even the fiercest critic – would want to import or even emulate the American system of financing and organizing health care. But in spite of this prevailing view, a number of fashionable American ideas, most importantly the concept of a health maintenance organization (HMO), have drifted north to Canada and across the Atlantic to Europe. These ideas are hardly popular. They are simmering and they represent a potentially creative response to a number of present concerns in France, Canada and Britain. Although all three of these countries, especially Canada and Britain, have eliminated financial barriers to care, policymakers still face three festering problems.

Economists, for example, emphasize that cost containment should not be confused with allocative efficiency in the use of health care resources. They point to the possibilities of obtaining more value for the money spent on health care in France, Canada, and Britain, as well as in the United States.[4] This applies not only with regard to improving health status (Cochrane 1972) but also with respect to altering input mixes in the provision of health services – taking advantage of cost-effective treatment settings, e.g. ambulatory surgery, and personnel, e.g. nurse practitioners.

Public health and medical care analysts criticize the lack of continuity of care between primary, secondary, and tertiary levels. Although health planners in France, Canada, and Britain have called for redistributing resources away from hospitals to community-based ambulatory care services and public health programs, the allocation of resources within health regions has been notoriously biased in favor of the more costly technology-based medical care at the apex of the regional hierarchy (Rodwin 1984).[5] The consequence of this allocational pattern has been to weaken institutional capability for delivering primary care services. This has exacerbated the separation between primary, secondary, and tertiary levels of care thus making it difficult for providers to assure that the right patient receives the right kind of care, in the right place and for the right reason.

Consumers have noted the inflexibility of bureaucratic decision-making procedures and the absence of opportunities for exercising for what Hirschman calls "voice," in most health care organizations. Indeed, the problem of control and how it should be shared between consumers, providers, managers, and payers is at the center of all criticisms levelled against the current structure of health care delivery in France, Canada, and Britain (Rodwin 1987). In all of these systems, decisions about what medical services to provide, how and where they should be provided, by whom and how often, are separated from the responsibility for financing medical care.

In the context of these problems — inefficiency in the allocation of health care resources, lack of continuity between levels of care, and the absence of voice in most health care organizations — the concept of an HMO, in combination with elements of market competition, has a certain intellectual appeal. Since an HMO is, by definition, both an insurer and a provider of health services, it establishes a link between the financing and provision of health services. Since it is financed on the basis of prepaid capitation payments, its managers have an explicit budget as well as a clearly defined clientele (population at risk). Moreover, since an HMO is responsible — on a contractual basis — for providing a broad range of primary, secondary, and tertiary level services to its enrolled population, it has powerful incentives to provide these services in a cost-effective manner while simultaneously maintaining quality so as to minimize the risk of disenrollment.

There are currently so many models of HMOs in the United

States that it is unwise to generalize about them. Nevertheless, the evidence based on a large number of stable HMOs in the 1960s and 1970s is persuasive in demonstrating that this form of health care financing and organization can reduce hospital admissions by as much as 40 per cent when compared with conventional fee-for-service practice (Luft 1981).

The idea of introducing HMOs – or similar kinds of health care organizations – into national systems that provide universal entitlement to health care resembles, in many ways, the American experience of encouraging medicare beneficiaries to enroll in federally qualified HMOs or competing medical plans (CMPs). The idea usually involves two reforms. It spurs policy-makers to combine regulatory controls with competition on the supply side; and it encourages them to design market incentives for both providers and consumers of health care. In this chapter I examine some new ideas along these lines for France, Canada, and Britain, and conclude with an assessment of their viability.

France: les réseaux de soins coordonnés (RSC)

France is noted for combining NHI with fee-for-service private practice in the ambulatory care sector and a mixed hospital sector of which two-thirds of all acute beds are in the public sector, and one-third in the private sector (Rodwin 1981). Physicians in the ambulatory sector and in private hospitals (known as *cliniques*) are reimbursed on the basis of a negotiated fee schedule. Roughly 15 per cent of all physicians are allowed to set their own fees. And physicians based in public hospitals – the principal teaching and research institutions – are reimbursed on a part-time or full-time salaried basis. Private *cliniques* are reimbursed on the basis of a negotiated per diem fee. Public hospitals used to be reimbursed on a retrospective cost-based per diem fee but they have received prospectively set "global" budgets since 1984.

There are several problems in this system. From a public health point of view, there is inadequate communication between full-time salaried physicians in public hospitals and solo practice physicians working in the community. Although general practitioners in the fee-for-service sector have informal referral networks to specialists and public hospitals, there are no formal institutional relationships which assure continuity of medical care, disease prevention and health promotion services, post-hospital follow-up care, and more generally systematic linkages and referral patterns between primary, secondary, and tertiary level services.

From the point of view of economic efficiency criteria, there are additional problems in the French health care system. On the demand side, two factors encourage consumers to increase their use of medical care services: the uncertainty about the results of treatment and the presence of insurance coverage. To reduce the risk of misdiagnosis or improper therapy physicians are always tempted to order more diagnostic tests. Since NHI covers most of the cost, there is no incentive – neither for the physician nor for the patient – to balance marginal changes in risk with marginal increases in costs. This results in excessive medical care utilization.

On the supply side, fee-for-service reimbursement of physicians has provided incentives for them to increase their volume of services so as to raise their income. Likewise, per diem reimbursement of *cliniques* and hospitals created incentives to increase patient lengths of stay. The recent imposition of global budgets, in France, has eliminated this problem but they represent a blunt policy tool – one which tends to support the existing allocation of resources within the hospital sector and, possibly, to jeopardize the quality of hospital care. It is relatively easy for a hospital to receive an annual budget to maintain its ongoing activities but extremely difficult to receive additional compensation for higher service levels, institutional innovation or improvements in the quality of care. Even with prospective budgets, hospitals naturally seek to maximize the level of their annual allocations and to resist budget cutbacks.

In summary, providers under French NHI have no financial incentives to achieve savings while holding quality constant or even improving it. Consumers have few incentives, other than minimal co-payments, to be economical in their use of medical care. And, there are no incentives to move the French system away from hospital-centered services toward new organizational modalities.

Traditional solutions to these problems go in the direction of making patients pay higher co-payments. For example, a 3 dollar daily co-payment charge was recently imposed on all hospital in-patient stays. Reimbursement for drugs has become more restrictive, particularly for those with more questionable therapeutic effects. Also, the government is allowing more physicians to refuse assignment of their fees and engage in extra-billing. The problem with these proposals is that they focus only on the demand side. They do nothing to promote supply-side efficiency. It is in response to this challenge that a proposal was recently developed to introduce a system of HMOs under French NHI.

In French, the concept of an HMO was translated as a *réseau de soins coordonnés* (RSC) – a network of coordinated medical services. The proposal, published in the *French Review of Social Affairs* by two French economists, a French physician and the present author (Launois *et al.* 1985), is based on six principles:

Preservation of entitlements under NHI

All compulsory pay-roll taxes for NHI remain unchanged. All those covered under French NHI, i.e. 99 per cent of the population, remain covered. The current level of benefits becomes a minimum benefit package under the new plan.

Supply-side modernization through the creation of RSCs

Qualified RSCs – with minimum benefit packages – are required to allow open enrollment. RSCs could be organized by a variety of sponsors. They would promote vertical integration in the health sector and place hospitals, day surgery facilities, physicians, and other health-care professionals *at risk* for providing cost-effective medical services.

Promotion of integrated medical care

The RSC assumes a contractual responsibility for providing its enrolled population with all health services covered under French NHI. The patient chooses a primary care physician who is in charge of making proper referrals and managing patient care.

Prepayment on a capitation basis

The RSC receives a pre-paid capitated monthly fee directly from the beneficiary's NHI fund. This payment is equal to the actuarial cost based on the enrollee's age, sex, and health status. The RSC's annual budget is equal to its annual capitation payment multiplied by the number of its enrollees. Within that constraint, managers have an incentive to minimize costs and maximize patient satisfaction so as to avoid disenrollment.

Marginal shifts in health care financing

Most of the capitated fee is financed directly by the beneficiary's NHI fund. But since, in the aggregate, consumers pay roughly 15 per cent of all health expenditures through co-payments, to make the proposal financially viable there is an additional pre-paid contribution by the beneficiary at the time of enrollment. This would be equal to the difference between the capitation fee charged by the RSC and the actuarial cost calculated by the beneficiary's NHI fund. There is no payment at the time of service use, and all enrollees who cannot afford the additional contribution are eligible for a state subsidy.

Competition between RSCs

Enrollment in RSCs is voluntary. This results in three levels of competition. First, between RSCs and traditional NHI. Second, between RSCs themselves. Third, between health care providers to whom RSCs will send their enrollees presumably on the basis of their ability to keep quality high and costs low.

The six principles of this proposal were inspired by Alain Enthoven's (1980) Consumer Choice Health Plan for the United States. But whereas Enthoven's plan is designed to create a new form of NHI for the United States, the RSC proposal is largely a strategy to promote supply side efficiency within an already existing NHI system. As in the case of competing medical plans (CMPs) – HMOs for Medicare beneficiaries in the United States – if French beneficiaries choose to enroll in an RSC, they would lose their coverage under traditional NHI. Just as CMPs have to accept all Medicare beneficiaries who choose to enroll, all RSCs would have to accept all French NHI beneficiaries who choose to enroll, which could be 99 per cent of the population. Thus the problem of adverse selection is somewhat reduced, although by no means absent.

Canada: publicly financed competition

Under Canadian NHI, although coverage for drugs is far less than in France, there are no co-payments; there is first-dollar coverage for hospital and medical services. Physicians in ambulatory care are paid predominantly on a fee-for-service basis, according to fee schedules negotiated between physicians' associations and provincial governments. In contrast to France, physicians in hospitals are most often paid on a fee-for-service basis, as in the United States.

There are few private for-profit hospitals in Canada such as French *cliniques* and American proprietary or investor-owned institutions. Most acute care hospitals in Canada are private non-profit institutions. But their operating expenditures are financed through the NHI system. And most of their capital expenditures are financed by the provincial governments.

In the United States, Canada's health system is typically depicted as a model for NHI (Andreopoulos 1975). Its financing, through a complex shared federal and provincial tax revenue formula, is more progressive than the European NHI systems financed on the basis of payroll taxes. Canada's levels of health status are high by international standards. And it has achieved notable success in controlling the growth of health-care costs. What, then, are the problems in this system?

From the point of view of health-care providers, there is, above all, a crisis of underfinancing. Physicians complain about low fee levels. Hospital administrators complain about draconian control of their budgets. And other health care professionals note that the combination of a physician "surplus" and excessive reliance on physicians prevents an expansion of their roles. Although Robert Evans (1987) contends that Canadian cost-control policies cannot be shown to have jeopardized the quality of care, providers and administrators, alike, claim that there has been deterioration since the imposition of restrictive prospective budgets.

Leaving aside the issue of quality, the same issues discussed in the context of France are present in Canada, with respect to economic efficiency. Neither the hospital physician nor the patient have an incentive to be economical in their use of health care resources. On the demand side, since patients benefit from what is perceived as "free" tax-financed first-dollar coverage, they have no incentive to choose cost-effective forms of care. For example, in the case of a demand for urgent care, there is no incentive for a patient to use community health centers rather than rush directly to the emergency room.

On the supply side, physicians lack incentives to make efficient use of hospitals which are essentially a free good at their disposal. There are no incentives for altering input mixes to affect practice style (technical efficiency). Nor are there incentives for providers to evaluate service levels and the kinds of therapy performed in relation to improving health status (allocative efficiency). It could be argued that these problems are common to all health systems. But they are especially acute in a system characterized by a bilateral monopoly that tends to support the status quo. On the one hand, providers have strong monopoly power which they use to defend their legitimate interests; on the other, the monopsony power of sole source financing (under Canadian NHI) keeps provider interests in check at the cost of not intervening in the organizational practice of medicine.

Stoddard (1985) has characterized the problems of the Canadian health system as "financing without organization." In his view, Canadian provinces "adopted a 'pay the bills' philosophy, in which decisions about service provision – which services, in what amounts, produced how, by whom, and where – were viewed as the legitimate domain of physicians and hospital administrators" (Stoddard 1985: 3). The result of this policy is that provincial governments were concerned about maintaining a good relationship with providers. This concern has not avoided tough negotiations and occasional confrontations. But there has been no effort to devise new forms of medical-care practice, e.g. HMOs or new institutions to handle the growing burden of long-term care for the elderly. The side effect of Canadian NHI has been to support the separation of hospital and ambulatory care and to reinforce traditional organizational structures.

As in France, or the United States, there are, in essence, two strategies for managing the Canadian health system and making adjustments. The first involves greater regulation on the supply side – even stronger controls on hospital spending, more rationing of medical technology, more hospital closures and mergers and eventual prohibition of extra billing. The second involves increased reliance upon market forces on the demand side – various forms of user charges such as co-payments and deductibles now advocated as forms of privatization. Neither strategy is likely to succeed on its own. The former will control health-care expenditures in the short run but it fails to affect practice styles. Its effectiveness runs the risk of exacerbating confrontation between providers and the state and jeopardizing health care needs. The latter deals with only part of the problem – the demand side – and neglects the issue of supply side efficiency. It provides no mechanism by which consumer decisions can generate signals to providers to adopt efficient practice styles. Moreover, it is likely to raise the level of total (public and private) expenditures.

Due to the deficiencies which may occur if each strategy is followed independently, Stoddard (1983) has devised an innovative proposal for the province of Ontario, one that relies on the use of market forces while maintaining the full benefits of a compulsory and universal NHI program. His proposal, which he calls "publicly financed competition," rests on four principles:

Creation of three payment modalities on the supply side

Physicians would have the choice of practicing in solo or group practice in the *fee-for-service* modality, or accepting a *capitation* fee per person enrolled in their practices, or accepting *salary* payment in return for working in community health centers organized by the public sector. Fees in the fee-for-service modality would correspond to the current fee schedule and extra-billing would be allowed to continue. The capitation rate would be based on the average cost of insured services per patient across all three payment modalities. Salaries as well as staffing, programs, and service mix in the community health centers would be set by Ministry of Health planners.

Financing of NHI is unchanged

All citizens would pay for health care through the tax system as they currently do.

Choice of primary care provider

All citizens would continue to choose a primary care provider
but they would have to commit themselves to one modality of
selected primary care for a specified period of time. The NHI
program would no longer cover services not sought from or
approved by the primary care provider. All services used by
each patient over the course of the year would be charged to the
appropriate payment modality.

Calculation of premium for each payment modality

At the end of each enrollment period, the premium for each
modality would be adjusted, based on its total costs. The least
costly modality would then become the baseline which would
be fully covered under the Ontario Health Insurance Plan.
Patients enrolled in the two more costly modalities would have
to pay the difference between the baseline and the higher
premium.

Although these principles are not as elaborately developed as
the French RSC model, they are equally provocative and present
a serious challenge to the status quo. Since the relative premiums
of the three modalities are calculated on the basis of the average
per capita cost *including* utilization, there would be powerful
incentives to reduce such utilization. Assuming government
measures are taken to assure a minimum level of medical care
quality across payment modalities, these four principles create a
system in which the patient benefits from seeking an efficient
provider and the provider benefits by choosing cost-effective
styles of practice. The level of health benefits remains the same
across the three modalities; access to care would not be restrained
by user charges; and adverse selection between payment modalities would be carefully monitored by requiring open enrollment
and eventually introducing premium adjustments which would
take into account age, sex as well as health status.

Britain: internal markets and HMOs

Britain is the exemplar of a National Health Service. It is
financed almost entirely through general revenue taxation and

accountable directly to the Department of Health and Social Security (DHSS) and Parliament. Access to health services is free of charge to all British subjects and to all legal residents. But despite the universal entitlement, Britons spend only 5.9 per cent of their GDP on health care – one half of what Americans spend as a percentage of their GDP.

Although the NHS is cherished by most Britons, there are, nevertheless, some serious problems concerning both the equity and efficiency of resource allocation in the health sector. With regard to equity, in 1976 the Resource Allocation Working Party (RAWP) developed a formula for the allocation of NHS funds between regions (DHSS 1976). The formula represents one of the most far-reaching attempts to allocate health care funds because it incorporates regional differences in measures of health status. Slow progress is now being made in redistributing the aggregate NHS budget along the lines of RAWP, but substantial inequities still remain both from the point of view of spatial distribution as well as from the point of view of social class (Townsend and Davidson 1982).

With regard to efficiency, the problems are even more severe because NHS resources are extremely scarce by international standards. Since there is less slack, the marginal costs of inefficiency are higher than in western Europe or the United States. And since the NHS faces the same demands as other systems to make available new technology and to care for an increasingly aged population, British policy-makers recognize that they must pursue innovations that improve efficiency. But there are numerous institutional obstacles in the way.

The tri-partite structure of the NHS is, itself, a major source of inefficiency. Regional health authorities (RHAs) are responsible for allocating budgets to hospitals in their regions. Hospital-based "consultants" are paid on a salaried basis with distinguished clinicians receiving "merit awards" and all consultants have the right to see a limited number of private fee-paying patients in "pay beds." Outside the RHA budget are family practitioner committees (FPCs) responsible for remunerating general practitioners (GPs), ophthalmologists, dentists, and pharmacists. The GPs are reimbursed on a capitation basis with additional remuneration coming from special "practice allowances" and fee-for-service payment for specific services, e.g. night visits and immunizations. Separate from both the RHAs and the FPCs are the local authorities (LAs) that are responsible for the provision of social services, public health services, and certain community nursing services.

Such an institutional framework creates perverse incentives to shift borderline patients from GPs to hospital consultants, to the community, and back to the hospital. GPs, for example, have no incentive to minimize costs and can impose costs on RHAs by referring patients to hospital consultants or for diagnostic services. NHS managers can shift costs from the NHS to social security by sending elderly hospitalized patients to private nursing homes. And, consultants can shift costs back on to the patient by keeping long waiting lists thereby increasing demand for their private services. As in France and Canada, neither the patient nor the physician in Britain bear the costs of the decisions they make; it is the taxpayer who pays the bill.

Three recent strategies, all of them inadequate, have attempted to deal with this problem (Maynard 1986b). The first came promptly with the arrival of the Thatcher government. After cautious attempts to denationalize the NHS by promoting a shift toward NHI and privatization, the Conservative government backed off when they realized that such an approach would not merely provoke strong political opposition but also increase public expenditure and, therefore, conflict with their budgetary objectives (McLachlan and Maynard 1982). Instead, the strategy was narrowed in favor of encouraging competition and market incentives in limited areas. To begin with, the government allowed a slight increase of private beds in NHS hospitals. In addition, it introduced tax incentives to encourage the purchase of private health insurance and the growth of charitable contributions. Also the government encouraged local authorities to raise money through the sale of surplus property and to contract out to the private sector such services as laundry, cleaning, and catering.

The second response was the Griffiths Report, which resulted in yet another reorganization in the long history of administrative reform within the NHS. Mr Griffiths, the former director of a large British department store chain, introduced the concept of a general manager at the department (DHSS), regional, district, and unit levels. This individual is now presumably responsible for the efficient use of the budget of each level of the NHS. The problem, however, is that the tri-partite structure of the system remains unchanged; and the general managers have very little information about least-cost strategies (across the tripartite structure) for generating improvements in health status.

The third and most recent response to the problem of improving efficiency has been to reduce the drug bill. Since April 1985 the government has limited the list of reimbursable drugs and reduced the pharmaceutical industry's rate of return. These measures will help contain the costs of the only open-ended budget within the NHS. But there is no evidence that they will have any impact on the efficiency of health care expenditures.

The more innovative efficiency-improving ideas have been developed by Enthoven and Maynard. They concern the promotion of "internal markets" and HMOs within the existing system of entitlements provided under the NHS. The essence of these ideas is to create financial incentives for each district to provide its residents with the best medical care possible, even if it has to purchase services outside of its boundaries. The aim is to maximize the benefits of health service expenditures, as measured by some measure of health status, e.g. quality-adjusted life years (QALYs); or to minimize the costs of sustaining a given level of QALYs. It sounds entirely theoretical but cost-effectiveness studies can produce empirical results. Recent findings indicate that the cost of a QALY of hemodialysis in a hospital is fourteen times that of a coronary artery by-pass graft and more than fifteen times that of a hip replacement (Torrance 1984; Williams 1985).

Short of allocating the entire NHS budget so as to maximize QALYs, there are a number of efficiency-improving measures that could be taken in the short run. For example, to avoid long queues for elective surgery in some regions and excess capacity in others, incentives could be devised to reward those regions receiving what the British call "cross-boundary flows." Or to persuade GPs to prescribe economically, a system could be devised to allow GPs to share in the savings. Beyond these examples of internal markets, Enthoven and Maynard have proposed variations of an HMO Plan for the NHS.

In Enthoven's plan, which he considers a form of "market socialism," a district continues to receive a RAWP-based per capita revenue and capital allocation and remain responsible for providing health services to its resident population (Enthoven 1985). In contrast to the present system, however, it receives additional compensation for services provided to residents from other districts and it controls referrals to providers outside its district. In short, the district controls all budgets within the tripartite structure and purchases health services from the most cost-effective sources outside its borders. In effect, it operates as an HMO. Consultants and GPs enter into a variety of contractual arrangements with district authorities and district authorities are free to enroll consumers near the borders of a neighboring district.

In Maynard's plan the GP functions as a client budget holder (Maynard 1985). All Britons receive a voucher from the NHS which entitles them to sign up with a GP of their choice. The voucher generates a per capita payment to the GP in return for the provision of comprehensive health care for a year, after which the patient can choose another GP. The GP is responsible not merely for providing primary care but also for purchasing hospital services from public or private hospitals.

Both plans would provoke rapid reorganization of the health sector in Britain. The Enthoven plan would shift power to district managers – far more than they now exercise following the Griffiths reforms. The Maynard plan would shift power to GPs who would need to hire managers to assist with HMO formation. Needless to say, the details of these plans require a great deal more study. But even at such a level of generality, what is most interesting is the extent to which they resemble new ideas in France and Canada.

HMOs and universal entitlement: the promise and potential pitfalls

Ideas about introducing HMOs and elements of market competition into national health systems with universal entitlement hold promise because they point to the possibilities of combining some of the best features in the United States, Canada, and western Europe. The French plan for RSCs, the Canadian proposal for publicly financed competition, and the ideas about internal markets and HMOs in Britain focus on combining the supply-side efficiency embodied in a well-managed HMO with the financial security of a universal NHI system. To the extent that such ideas can be made to work in practice, they would probably provide more realistic models for the United States than the present structure of health care financing and organization in either France, Canada, or Britain.

But are these new ideas for health policy feasible in either the United States or France, in Canada or Britain? It would be naive to conclude without adding some cautionary observations.

The proposals we have examined rest on two important assumptions: first, that competition between health care organizations will increase efficiency in the allocation of resources; and second, that health care providers can be motivated to change their behavior in response to financial incentives. The first assumption fails to circumvent a fundamental characteristic of health care markets – "informational assymmetry." The prevailing uncertainty about the effectiveness of various forms of medical care and the inability of consumers to assess quality makes them likely to turn to physicians for advice. Economists have shown that in markets characterized by agent–principal relationships in which buyers and sellers are unequally informed, competition does not necessarily lead to efficiency (Arrow 1963). In traditional, fee-for-service medicine, financed by third-party payers, physicians are likely to err on the side of over-utilization. In HMO-type settings, due to prepayment, financial incentives are reversed and there is a risk of under-utilization. HMOs may increase competition between providers more than traditional indemnity coverage, but given the special characteristics of the health sector, it is impossible to draw inferences on the basis of economic theory about the impact of increased competition on welfare (Weisbrod 1983).

The second assumption fails to acknowledge that health care providers do not behave like profit-maximizing firms. Only a small fraction of hospitals in France, Canada, Britain as well as the United States, are proprietary institutions. In the main, they are public and non-profit organizations with powerful missions and community allegiances. As for physicians, although much of their behavior, particularly in France, Canada, and the United States, has an entrepreneurial character, they are, nevertheless, members of a highly reputed profession and have consequently internalized a powerful set of values and norms. The extent to which financial incentives will influence the behavior of health care providers is bounded by the psychological, cultural, and institutional context within which they work (Brown 1981).

If, in deference to realism, we relax these two assumptions, it is important to note that the combination of HMOs and universal entitlement betrays a number of potential pitfalls.

First, efforts to promote competition between RSCs in

France, the three payment modalities in Canada, and districts or GP client budget holders in Britain, may result in competition over attributes other than price and quality. The theory of monopolistic competition suggests that a system of competing health care organizations would lead to product differentiation. Competition may well be focussed on features other than delivering medical care, for example, amenities, marketing, and advertising. Also, there is a risk of collusion between competing health care organizations, which may result in providers demanding government regulation to maintain their market share.

Second, efforts to promote competition create incentives for providers to engage in risk selection. This would result in health risks or expected medical care costs being distributed unevenly among RSCs, payment modalities, or client budget holders. Of course, in elaborating the operational details of all these proposals, attempts would be made to identify the health risks of all beneficiaries based on criteria such as age, sex, residence, and perhaps even health status and certain socio-demographic characteristics. Nevertheless, even if health care organizations are compensated for beneficiaries with higher health risks, whatever system of risk rating is used, studies based on the experience of Medicare's competing medical plans (CMPs) suggest that the possibilities for risk selection are abundant (Eggers 1980).

Third, efforts to change physician behavior by confronting them with new financial incentives are likely to place physicians in the uncomfortable position of choosing between their ethical obligation to do the most for their patients, their natural inclination to pursue their own interests and organizational constraints, which encourage them to contain costs. Such a position is bound to erode doctor–patient relationships with no assurance of efficiency improvements in the allocation of health resources.

Fourth, all of the above potential pitfalls suggest that the new ideas for health policy, which we have examined, would create extraordinary possibilities for "gaming the system." For example, to skim healthy young patients and keep away frail elderly patients, a French RSC or the Canadian payment modality based in community health centers might decide to invest in exceptional amenities for a new birthing center and "under-service" geriatric cases. Or in Britain, GP client budget holders might make referrals with few limitations for young healthy patients but drastically restrict them for elderly people. Suppose the GP makes too few referrals and lowers the drug bill too much in order to appropriate a larger share of the savings. Would there be sanctions? Who would monitor the system?

That there are possibilities for gaming the system has led Alain Enthoven (1986) to recognize that consumers could not negotiate effectively on their own. They would need "sponsors" to "manage the demand side (and) to make the market achieve desirable results." But this fact should not detract from the promise held by the idea of combining HMOs and universal entitlement. It merely exposes the illusion that competing HMOs could somehow operate as an alternative to strong government regulation. Clearly in a system of competing HMOs under NHI or within an NHS, sponsors would demand vigilant government regulation.

The kinds of government rules and regulations under which any of the above proposals would most likely have to operate include the following:

1 Periodic open enrollment;
2 Standard benefit packages with minimum specified benefits;
3 Standardized information disclosure by all competing health care organizations of data on utilization trends, per capita costs (including premiums and out-of-pocket expenses), hospital mortality and patient characteristics (including health status);
4 Spot checks on the veracity of the disclosed information;
5 Monitoring of quality.

How would such a system of "regulated" or "managed" competition compare with existing forms of more centralized regulation and budget control in France, Canada, and Britain? Would it succeed in producing efficiency improvements, greater continuity of medical care, and more flexibility in decision-making procedures? The evidence, at this point, is too fragmentary to serve as any reliable guide for policy. Nor is it ever likely to persuade analysts who are predisposed to accept the competition/regulation dichotomy in health policy.[6] But the curious *mélange* of competition and regulation implied by these ideas for health policy in France, Canada, and Britain, do suggest one conclusive proposition. Whatever reforms are pursued in the health sector, there will always be a number of underlying tensions – between the patient's desire to take extra precautions and mobilize a maximum amount of attention, irrespective of costs, and a collective desire to contain costs; between a clinician's inclination to err on the side of overprovision, at the margin, and an HMO's or a government's rationale for making decisions on the basis of statistical averages; and between an HMO's or a government's persistent attempts to measure medical care activities and performance and the formidable difficulties of perceiving and measuring results.

Acknowledgements

I would like to thank James Knickman, who originally suggested that I write this paper and subsequently commented extensively on its content. I am also grateful for Lorraine Mead's diligent secretarial assistance.

Notes

1 An often cited empirical basis for this presumption is a study by J. Newhouse, C. Phelps and W. Schwartz, "Policy options and the impact of national health insurance," *New England Journal of Medicine* (1974) 290, 24: 1345–58.
2 See e.g. Andreopoulos (1975) and the more recent work of Robert Evans (1985).
3 Estimates of the uninsured range from 15 per cent to 20 per cent of the population. In 1984 the *Current Population Survey* estimated that 35.1 million people, 17.1 per cent of the population under 65, were without insurance. The percentage increases if one broadens the definition to include the underinsured and otherwise medically disadvantaged. See M.B. Sulvetta and K. Swartz (1986) *The Uninsured and Uncompensated Care: A Chartbook*, Washington, DC: National Health Policy Forum, George Washington University, June.
4 The literature in health economics is abundant with examples of efficiency-improving changes in patterns of health care organization. For classic statements on this theme, see Fuchs (1975) and Enthoven (1978). For examples in France, Giraud and Launois (1985); in Canada, Evans and Robinson (1980); in Britain, Abel-Smith (1976) and Maynard (1986b).
5 Daniel Fox (1986) traces the evolution of this pattern – what he calls "hierarchical regionalism" – in an historical study of health policy developments in Britain and the United States.

6 The misleading nature of this dichotomy has been well analyzed by Luft (1985) and Schramm (1986), among others.

References

Aaron, H. and Schwartz, W. (1984) *The Painful Prescription: Rationing Hospital Care*, Washington, DC: Brookings Institution.
Abel-Smith, B. (1976) *Value for Money in Health Services*, London: Heinemann.
Andreopoulos, S. (ed.) (1975) *National Health Insurance: Can We Learn from Canada?* New York: Wiley.
Arrow, K. (1963) "Uncertainty and the economics of medical care," *American Economic Review* 53, 5: 941–73.
Brown, L. (1981) "Competition and health cost containment," *Milbank Memorial Fund Quarterly* 59, 2.
Cochrane, A.L. (1972) *Effectiveness and Efficiency*, London: Nuffield Provincial Hospitals Trust.
DHSS (1976) *Sharing Resources for Health in England: Report of the Resource Allocation Working Party*, London: HMSO.
Eggers, P. (1980) "Risk differential between beneficiaries enrolled and not enrolled in an HMO," *Health Care Financing Review* 4: 55–73.
Enthoven, A.C. (1978) "Cutting costs without cutting quality of care," *New England Journal of Medicine* 298, 22: 1,224–38.
—— (1980) *Health Plan: The Only Practical Solution to the Soaring Cost of Medical Care*, Reading, Mass: Addison-Wesley.
—— (1985) "Reflections on improving efficiency in the National Health Service," occasional paper, London: Nuffield Provincial Hospitals Trust.
—— (1986) "Managed competition in health care and the unfinished agenda," *Health Care Financing Review*, annual supplement.
Evans, R.G. (1985). "Illusions of necessity: evading responsibility for choice in health care," *Journal of Health Policy, Politics and Law* 10, 3, Fall: 439–67.
—— (1987) "Holding the line: the Canadian experience with global budgeting," in M. Berthod-Wurmser, V. Rodwin, Y. Soutey and J.C. Henrard (eds) *Système de santé, pouvoirs publics et financeurs: qui contrôle quoi?* Paris: Documentation Française.
Evans, R.G. and Robinson, G. (1980) "Surgical day care: measurements of the economic payoff," *Canadian Medical Association Journal* 123: 873–80.
Fox, D.M. (1986) *Health Policies, Health Politics: The British and American Experience 1911–1965*, Princeton, NJ: Princeton University Press.
Fuchs, V. (1975) *Who Shall Live?* New York: Basic Books.
Giraud, P. and Launois, R. (1985) *Les Réseaux de soins, médecine de demain*, Paris: Economica.
Hirschman, A. (1970) *Exit, Voice and Loyalty*, Cambridge, Mass: Harvard University Press.
Launois, R., Majnoni-d'Intignano, B., Stéphan, J.C., and Rodwin, V.G. (1985). "Les réseaux de soins coordonnés (RSC): propositions

pour une réforme profonde du système de santé," *Revue Française des Affaires Sociales* 1 (January–March): 37–61.

Luft, H.S. (1981) *Health Maintenance Organizations: Dimensions of Performance*, New York: Wiley.

—— (1985) "Competition and regulation," *Medical Care* 23 (May): 383–400.

McLachlan, G. and Maynard, A. (eds) (1982) *The Public/Private Mix for Health: The Relevance and Effects of Change*, London: Nuffield Provincial Hospitals Trust.

Maynard, A. (1985) "HMOs in the NHS?" *Health Summary* 2, February: 5.

—— (1986a) *Annual Report on the National Health Service*, York: Centre for Health Economics.

—— (1986b) "Financing the UK National Health Services," *Health Policy* 16: 329–40.

OECD (Organization for Economic Cooperation and Development) (1985) *Measuring Health Care, 1960–1983*, Paris: OECD.

Rodwin, V.G. (1981) "The marriage of national health insurance and *La Médecine Libérale* in France: a costly union," *Milbank Memorial Fund Quarterly* 59: 16–43.

—— (1984) *The Health Planning Predicament: France, Quebec, England and the United States*, Berkeley, Calif.: University of California Press.

—— (1987) "Le contrôle des pouvoirs publics et des payeurs: comparaisons internationales," in *Système de Santé, pouvoirs publics et financeurs: qui contrôle quoi?* M. Berthod-Wurmser, V. Rodwin, Y. Soutey and J.C. Henrard (eds), Paris: Documentation Française.

Schieber, G. and Poullier, J.P. (1986) "International health care spending," *Health Affairs*, Fall.

Schramm, C. (1986) "Revisiting the competition/regulation debate in health care cost containment," *Inquiry* 23: 236–42.

Stoddard, G. (1983) "Publicly financed competition in Canadian health care delivery: a viable alternative to increased regulation?" in *Proceedings of the Conference on Health in the '80s and '90s and Its Impact on Health Sciences Education*, Toronto: Council of Ontario Universities.

—— (1985) "Rationalizing the health care system," in T. Courchene, D. Conklin and G. Cook (eds) *Ottawa and the Provinces: The Distribution of Money and Power*, Toronto: Ontario Economic Council Conference.

Torrance, G.W. (1984) "Health status measurement for economic appraisal," paper presented at the Aberdeen meeting on Health Economics.

Townsend, P. and Davidson, N. (eds) (1982) *Inequalities in Health: The Black Report*, Harmondsworth: Penguin.

Weisbrod, B. (1983) "Competition in Health Care: A Cautionary View," in J. Meyer (ed.) *Market Reforms in Health Care*, Washington, DC: American Enterprise Institute.

Williams, A. (1985) "Economics of coronary artery bypass grafting," *British Medical Journal* 291, August 3: 326–9.

Index

Index

density Canada 272; Scotland 223;
Spain 137–8, 151–2, 156–8;
Switzerland 41–2, 45; United
States 51, 59; USSR 239;
Yugoslavia 179, 183
payment, see fee-for-service
system; salary system; position of
7, 150, 153, 159, 280;
specialization 9, see also education,
medical
physiotherapists, concentration 152
plan, competing medical (CMP)
268, 271–2, 281
planning co-operative 211–14, 219;
Japan 106 7, 111; New Zealand
82–3; participatory 203; resource
206; Scotland 201, 203, 205–15,
218–19, 226; bureaucratic
approach 205–6, 207, 208;
mixed scanning approach 206–7
Spain 128, 134–5, 138, 152–3, 156,
159–62; Switzerland 26, 31–2, 33,
35, 43; United States 55, 58, 60,
66, 68; USSR 238–9, 241, 248;
Yugoslavia 168, 171, 173
Player, David 221n.
Plunket Society, New Zealand 82–3
policy
Japan 101–3, 105–14, 118–22
and 'creative conservatism'
113–14, 122–4
New Zealand 83, 98–9; Scotland
219; Spain 144; Switzerland 28–9,
31, 45; United States 50, 62, 265;
USSR 237
polity
role 4–5, 7, 8, 11, 17–18, 20, 282–3
Japan 101–3, 107–14, 122–4;
New Zealand 76–7, 83, 91;
Scotland 198–9, 220;
Switzerland 27–9; USSR 238–40,
245; Yugoslavia 168–9, 171–3,
176–7, 184, 187
polyclinic, USSR 242, 247, 250
poor, care 52–4, 57, 60–1, 65
prescriptions, charges 79, 80, 186
pressure groups Spain 162; United
States 60
preventive services 12, 210–11;
France 269; Japan 106, 108, 121;
New Zealand 83; Scotland 225;
Switzerland 38, 44; USSR 241,
243; Yugoslavia 185–6
price control United States 62, 68;
USSR 246

priorities Japan 112; Scotland 208,
225–6; USSR 239–40, 246–7, 249,
253
private sector Britain 276–7; Canada
272; France 268; Japan 103, 107,
113, 115, 124;
New Zealand 77, 80–2, 85, 86–7,
88, 96, 98; government
contribution to 80–1, 86, 88
non-profit organizations 32, 51–3,
272; Scotland 16, 201, 215; Spain
131, 144–6, 154–5; Switzerland
31, 32–3; United States 51–2,
56–7, 63, 65–6, 68; USSR 251–2;
Yugoslavia 166, 168, 185, 188n.
privatization 8, 69, 107, 115, 142,
146–8, 185, 228, 274, 277
problems, health expressive 12;
functional 11–12
product differentiation 281
promotion, health 160, 210–11, 234,
269
public health 82, 108, 111, 128,
158–9, 197, 267, 268, 277
Public Health Act, England, 1848
197
public/private sectors 11, 98, 122,
132, 136, 138, 144–5, 146–50, 154,
159–60, 268

QALYS (quality-adjusted life-years)
278
quality of life 94, 96
quality of services Canada 272, 275;
France 267, 269, 271; Japan 107,
113, 122, 124; monitoring 282;
New Zealand 99; Scotland 218;
Spain 146, 154, 159; United States
54–5, 62–3; USSR 235, 239–41,
242–3, 250, 253, 255; Yugoslavia
181, 186
queuing USSR 247, 250, 255, see also
rationing; waiting lists

radiologists, shortage 93–4
Raffel, Marshall W. 19
rationalization, Yugoslavia 85–6
rationing 9, 20; Britain 94, 249;
Canada 274; New Zealand 82, 97;
Scotland 207; Switzerland 35;
USSR 234, 240, 243, 249–51, 259,
see also distribution; queuing;
waiting lists
Red Cross hospitals 148, 150
referral system Britain 277, 279,